4/14

Katz. Mrs. April 15 Pue[illegible] S0-ASO-290 Hup 4/14

This woman has been to the commissioners for help she was said to be so homely that she stopped all the watches in the office she came to this society in the evening for a nights lodging she was very peculia[r] woman she said her husband was Colonel Hogan and drank himself to death that sh[e] is a daughter of Col. W. C Bane of Blooming[ton] Ill. And a graduate of Genoa Ill. she is a Bachelor of Art and become quite indigna[nt] because questions were asked she said th[at she] was not going to tell all her history for the past 40 years she said she was 44 years ol[d] and that she has \$40.000 coming to her if she w[ill] swear to being a pauper. she says she knows Mr. Sinton a lodging ticket was given her at the Cucharras House but she went to Mr. Benton ... Pueblo Hospital. He

Pike's Peak at Himself

DEEP ROOTS

AspenPointe and Colorado Springs

Together Since 1875

EILEEN WELSOME

ASPENPOINTE
COLORADO SPRINGS

For information, contact
AspenPointe
525 N. Cascade Avenue
Suite 100
Colorado Springs, CO 80903
www.AspenPointe.org

LCCN: 2013943430
ISBN-13: 978-0-9896185-0-2

Book Design by
Scott Johnson · Sputnik Design Works

Printed in Canada
First Printing

Deep Roots

(Colorado Room Information Files, Colorado College Special Collections)

For the people of Colorado Springs

who came before us

and carried the hope forward.

Waldo Canyon Fire, 2012. (R.J. Sangosti, *The Denver Post,* Getty Images)

Prologue

On June 26, 2012, a placid summer day was unfolding on the west side of Colorado Springs. Birdcages hung from patios, flowers bloomed in bark-filled beds, and gas grills glinted in the light. It was unseasonably hot and windy and the air had a curious, almost salty taste. Suddenly the wind shifted and the Waldo Canyon Fire crested a ridge and raced toward the quiet homes. Police and firefighters were at the doors banging, screaming, telling people who had not already been evacuated to get out. Yellow tape was hastily slapped onto the doors. Helicopters thumped across the sky, dropping fire retardant, and Hot Shot crews armed with axes fell upon the neighborhoods. Propane tanks exploded, decks caught fire, and the bark ignited.

The fire began to swallow up houses. Sensing her house was gone, a young girl wrote later that it was as if someone had "whipped away the whole unfinished story."

An oily black smoke rose high into the sky and drifted across the city. As the afternoon wore on, the clouds reddened and grew apocalyptic. In all, 32,000 residents were evacuated. The chaotic departures resembled the images that had flashed across television screens for the last decade – The Twin Towers, Iraq, Afghanistan.

The Waldo Canyon Fire turned out to be one of the most destructive wildfires in Colorado history, and one of the worst natural disasters to strike Colorado Springs. Two people were killed, 347 houses destroyed and 18,247 acres burned. Insurance claims topped $350 million and complications such as flooding could push that number higher.

Almost exactly a year later, on June 11, 2013, another fire broke out, this one in the Black Forest on the northeast side of Colorado Springs. Unbelievably, the destruction exceeded the Waldo Canyon Fire. Two people were killed, more than 500 homes destroyed, and tens of thousands of people evacuated.

AspenPointe deployed its employees during both crises. They worked quietly behind the scenes, bringing calm to the chaos, listening to the tearful residents as they described the indescribable: Losing everything. "The moment the fire went over that ridge and started coming down, that's when I stopped getting sleep," Gerald Albrent, AspenPointe's disaster response coordinator, said of the Waldo Canyon Fire.

When the fire danger passed, the dazed residents were allowed back in to their neighborhoods. The lines were a mile long. AspenPointe employees handed

"I've never been more proud of who we are as an organization, and our relevancy in our community, than when I saw our staff in action in my very own neighborhood."

MORRIS ROTH

out bottles of water, helped direct traffic, and listened to anyone who needed to talk. Some homes were eerily intact while others were completely destroyed. Suddenly, broken crockery, a singed map, a piggybank with the pennies melted inside, were freighted with significance. The residents walked through the rubble, kicking at twisted shapes, picking things up and then dropping them. Among them were Morris Roth, president and chief executive officer of AspenPointe, and his wife, Jan, who lived in Mountain Shadows, one of the most devastated neighborhoods. Roth had ordered his staff deployed even while he was waiting to hear the fate of his own home. The couple counted themselves among the lucky ones. They'd had enough time to think about what they needed and were able to gather up important papers and other valuables. The house next door burned to the ground, but their house was still standing and was relatively unscathed.

"It was a very humbling, frightening experience," he remembered. While the Roths were looking over their property, a couple of AspenPointe staffers knocked on the door and asked if they needed any help. For a brief moment, Roth was on the other side of the table and experienced what it was like to be a client. "They actually approached us while we were at our house. It was incredible," he said. "I've never been more proud of who we are as an organization, and our relevancy in our community, than when I saw our staff in action in my very own neighborhood."

For 138 years, AspenPointe has been helping Colorado Springs through crises. It was founded in 1875, four years after the city was established, and was called the Colorado Springs Relief Society. Like many of the city's histories, AspenPointe's begins with the town's founder, William Jackson Palmer, a Quaker, Civil War general, and railroad builder, who believed Colorado Springs could become a utopia where learning, leisure and healing could take place in a gorgeous natural setting.

The Springs' salubrious climate was advertised in newspaper articles and soon wealthy individuals who summered in Germany's Baden-Baden or wintered on the Riviera packed their valises and undertook the arduous westward journey. In their dark Victorian clothing, they picnicked among the rock formations of Garden of the Gods, went on flower-gathering expeditions into the foothills, and attended poetry readings and formal balls in rambling homes along Cascade and Wood avenues.

Almost immediately, it became clear that the young community would not be just for the well-to-do. Soon, the streets were filled with farmhands and factory workers, washerwomen and cooks. The poor made their ways to boarding homes, shanties, and tents. The rich took up residence in the mansions of friends or families or in luxurious hotels and sanatoriums.

Many desperately ill and impoverished residents sought help from the relief society, which was located in the early years in a building on Tejon Street opposite Acacia Park. Sometimes they were reeling from fever, cloaked in rags and wearing shoes in which their bare feet were visible. The relief society provided them with clothing, food and coal, and then tried to help them find work. When all else failed, the relief society wrote to clients' relatives and asked them to send money so a railroad ticket could be purchased for a trip home. The original relief society had a close relationship with local churches, schools, civic organizations, the city and county government, Colorado College and the YMCA. Those relationships continue to this day.

Following World War II, the charity transitioned into an organization that provided counseling services to families. Today, counseling and behavioral health services remain an integral part of the mission, but it does much more. It helps young people get their GEDs, assists veterans, links people up with volunteer opportunities, trains clients for new careers and helps them find jobs. Sometimes it does the hiring itself. To date, it has hired more than 200 former clients. They're indistinguishable

Victorians on a picnic, 1885-1895. (Pikes Peak Library District, Special Collections — hereafter noted as PPLD)

from the rest of the workforce and could be the employment counselor advising a client at the Ruskin Drive facility or the young chef grilling chicken at the AspenPointe Café.

Morris Roth has been with the organization for almost one-third of its lifetime and has played a huge role in its development. He joined the organization in 1971 and rose through the ranks to become president and CEO in 2000. He retired in August of 2013 after steering the organization through one of the most severe economic downturns since the Great Depression. Amazingly, the nonprofit thrived during this period of economic hardship. It implemented new programs to help returning veterans, stepped up its education and job-training programs, and was able to take advantage of the depressed real estate market to purchase two office buildings and a warehouse at reduced prices. "There are some advantages in a down economy, but no one wants a down economy," said Roth.

The Waldo Canyon Fire was officially declared over at 8 p.m. on July 10, 2012. Property owners began clearing off the rubble, contacting insurance companies, and replacing the innumerable things that they had lost, from Band-Aids to dog-food bowls. With the help of a Federal Emergency Management Agency grant, AspenPointe hired a diverse team to provide outreach support to affected communities. The team members continued their treks through the scarred neighborhoods, linking people up with resources. Called the Colorado Spirit Waldo Support Team, the members were redirected to the Black Forest Fire disaster zone when that blaze broke out. "One of the most important lessons I learned was how much we rely on one another during these trying times," said Roth. "From the first responders to my neighbors, friends and AspenPointe employees, the outpouring of assistance and genuine concern was truly overwhelming. In tragedies of these magnitudes, we learn how much we rely on the support systems in our communities and how human we all are."

Not long after the Waldo Canyon Fire was extinguished, the delicate green shoots of new aspen trees appeared on the charred hillsides. Aspen have roots that can be two and a half to three times as long as their height and rely upon disturbances like the Waldo Canyon Fire to regenerate, said Wayne Shepperd, a research forester in Fort Collins. Shepperd retired a few years ago from the U.S. Forest Service's Rocky Mountain Research Station and has devoted much of his life to studying aspen trees. Stimulated by hormones, the sudden sunlight, and the nutrient-rich ash, aspen trees grow extremely rapidly following a forest fire, he said. By September, the new trees in the area burned by the Waldo Canyon Fire could have well have been two to three feet tall, he added. "They are amazing trees."

Aspen are also resilient, a word heard often these days. A resilient person is said to be supple and strong and able to spring back from setbacks. As one of Colorado Springs' oldest organizations and oldest nonprofits, AspenPointe has shown itself to be remarkably resilient. It also strives to instill resiliency in its clients. In the process it has taken the idea of recovery to a new level. Counselors nowadays prefer to focus on the strengths of their clients rather than their weaknesses — the dreams and not the disabilities. In doing so, they hope to stick around a while longer. "We look to another 100 years of serving this community," said Roth.

1

A Great Migration

Gathering up her long dress, Mrs. D. Russ Wood hurried toward a room near the center of town. It was early evening and the grey shadows of the newly planted cottonwood trees stretched thin across the streets. In La Font's livery stable, the horses knocked against their stalls. Carpenters and brick masons had quit for the day, leaving their tools inside the half-finished cottages and large brick homes taking shape on Nevada and Cascade avenues. Mrs. Wood knocked lightly and then entered a room. In the gloom, she made out the shape of a young man sitting on a low box and surrounded by "all manner of rubbish." There was no table, no chair, no bed.

The man's eyes shone with fever and his emaciated body swayed on the low wooden box. He told her he was a schoolteacher and had come to Colorado Springs in hopes of regaining his health so he could resume his profession. When he got off the train at the depot, he was met by a man who knew of a place to rent. He had paid the man and this squalid place is where he had been left. Glancing around at the miserable surroundings, Mrs. Wood felt a wave of pity. "I saw the poor young man must be cared for immediately, as he showed unmistakably that his hours were few," she would later write.

Mrs. Wood called another member of the town's newly formed relief society. Together, they procured a carriage and transported the young man to more decent surroundings. A woman and her daughter were hired to watch over him. "He could scarcely believe that, stranger as he was, so much kindness and comfort could have fallen to

Facing page: Denver and Rio Grande Railroad Depot, 1890. (Colorado Springs Pioneers Museum – hereafter noted as CSPM)

At left: View of Pikes Peak Avenue from Tejon Street, c. 1873. (Denver Public Library)

"I have attended by the bedside of the dying in late evening hour to partake with them of the last supper, and have waited beside the dying till the last sigh was over."

MRS. D. RUSS WOOD

First building in Colorado Springs, 1871. (PPLD)

his lot," she remembered. Afterward Mrs. Wood returned to her own luxurious home, which was called "Woodside," and was one of the most beautiful residences in Colorado Springs. It had a flower-filled conservatory, a rolling green lawn, spacious rooms and every luxury available to a homeowner in the 1870s. Her husband, D. Russ Wood, was from Montreal, Canada. He was suffering from ill health and in 1873 the family had moved to the Springs. With the help of a carpenter named Winfield Scott Stratton, Wood had begun building villas on Weber Street for wealthy invalids such as himself. At the time, Mrs. Wood would have been about 55 years old. She had three children and in keeping with custom, she went by her husband's last name. As a member of "society," she could have spent her time fretting over servants or going to afternoon teas, but she was a serious and compassionate woman and was not about to fritter away her days.

The young schoolteacher lived through the night. The next day he died and was buried in a pauper's grave. His wallet was forwarded to Mrs. Wood. Inside, she found enough money to pay his caretakers and a sheaf of "testimonials" recommending him as a teacher. She put the letters back into the wallet and sighed. There would be more like him. Many more. One of the greatest migrations in history was underway. Between 1865 and 1900, more than 12 million people boarded ships to come to America. After they were processed through Ellis Island, millions continued their westward journey. Also traveling across the rutted girth of the continent were former soldiers of the Civil War; farmers fleeing droughts and low commodity prices; young men seeking their fortunes and invalids who sought to exchange the vitiated air of parlor rooms for the disinfecting sunshine and high altitude of the Rocky Mountains. The westward movement, writes General William Jackson Palmer, was the "natural law."

The Springs was one of the most favored destinations. The soil was said to be rich and productive. Nearby mines boasted extensive veins of gold and silver. A narrow-gauge railroad from Denver was making daily trips to the small town. There were sawmills, flour mills, pastures for cattle and sheep, coal, timber, mineral springs, wild and beautiful scenery, and best of all, a climate that was said to be mild as Italy's and capable of healing all sorts of ailments.

Stepping down from the Denver and Rio Grande Railroad, the newcomers inhaled the air and glanced up toward Pikes Peak. So pure was the air tumbling down from that granite peak, it smelled of snowmelt and sage and a wind uncontaminated by the vapors of tenement houses or sick rooms. Surely, this bracing substance could cure everything, including that great scourge of mankind – tuberculosis – which was often called consumption because of the way it seemed to consume the human body. "Consumption made an empire of this country and primarily all that Colorado is today she owes to the Consumptive invalid," wrote Dr. Boswell Preston Anderson, a former Confederate soldier who came to the Springs soon after it was founded and also suffered from consumption.

The founders of Colorado Springs had envisioned a fashionable European spa at the base of Pikes Peak that would be composed of wealthy invalids, thrifty settlers, and the great industrialists of the nineteenth century. They seemed surprised to discover poor people in their midst. Still, they were imbued with a strong sense of ethics and in 1874-1875 a relief society was organized. Mrs. Wood was a member of a "prudential" committee that decided what kind of aid the applicants should receive and a year or two later, was elected president, a post she would hold for the next two decades. She enlisted the help of wealthy matrons like herself to visit the poor and the sick and called upon local ministers to help her raise funds.

An early Colorado Springs street scene, 1875. (PPLD)

"Many young men between the ages of eighteen and twenty-five hearing of this 'El Dorado' and thinking nothing would be needed but light air and sunny skies reached here some way, but soon found themselves penniless," she would write. "There were often severe cases of frozen limbs among the freighters to the mountain districts. A very severe one, I remember, where the father was confined to his bed for weeks with a frightfully frozen arm and was only able to leave it when a dear little daughter was taken with diphtheria. To the sorrow of the family she only lived a week. They were perfect strangers without friends and my sympathies were enlisted in their behalf."

In the copper glow of a coal stove, Mrs. Wood often sat by herself in the winter dusk listening to the labored breathing. "I have attended by the bed-side of the dying in late evening hour to partake with them of the last supper," she would write, "and have waited beside the dying till the last sigh was over, and at one time, with no one to close the eyes and fold the hands upon the breast but myself." When the ragged gravediggers scraped open a hole in the pauper's cemetery and lowered the frail, withered shapes into the ground, it was often Mrs. Wood, wrapped in her long cloak, who was the sole witness to the end of their long migration.

2

The World's Sanatorium

In the beginning, there was just the flat, brown prairie, the brilliant blue air and Pikes Peak. From time to time, great herds of antelope passed through and grazed on the tough prairie grass and then drifted off. A few settlers had tried to do some farming and ranching, but the soil crumbled into dust and the cows and sheep didn't thrive. Toward the end of the 1860s, a coach rattled through the emptiness. Wrapped in blankets and sleeping atop the roof was William Jackson Palmer. The moon nudged him awake and he sat up and saw for the first time the dark outline of Pikes Peak. It may well have been from that moment that the idea began to form in him to build a resort at the base of the mountain for himself and his bride-to-be.

Thirty-two years old and longtime resident of Philadelphia, Palmer was one of those rare men who knew he was making history while he was living it. He was handsome, with brown hair, a mouth half-hidden by a ragged mustache, and mild eyes that masked aloofness and enormous ambition. He was a man of contradictions; a pacifist who excelled at war and a romantic who dreamed of an utopian society where owners and workers could live happily together while simultaneously building monopolies and fighting efforts by coal miners to increase their meager wages.

To the chagrin of his Quaker parents, he enlisted in the Union Army during the Civil War. As the leader of a cavalry unit composed of young Philadelphians like himself, he drove his troops mercilessly while hunting down Jefferson Davis, the president of the Confederacy. At war's end, he was hired by the Kansas Pacific to help extend its line west and find the best route through the Rocky Mountains to the Pacific Ocean. When the owners turned down his idea to build the railroad south through New Mexico's Sangre de Cristos, Palmer decided to build his own narrow-gauge railroad that would start in Denver and continue south to Mexico City. A branch of the railroad would connect with Colorado's southern coalfields that Palmer had discovered during his explorations. The railroad and the coalfields, writes University of Colorado historian Thomas G. Andrews, helped revive and industrialize the entire West.

Palmer saw no reason for Colorado Springs to suffer through the wretched lawlessness of Denver or nearby Colorado City. Instead, he and his colleagues would build a planned community, or what was referred to at the time as a "colony," which would spring from the earth full-blown and consist of churches, schools, li-

A photographer named Charles G. Gillingham took this stereoscopic picture of Pikes Peak Avenue from the Tejon Street intersection. The mountains have been retouched and the back of the picture notes it's 14 miles to the summit of Pikes Peak. c. 1882. (PPLD)

braries, bathhouses, an elected government and deputies to keep the peace. The sale of liquor would also be banned, which would do more than anything else to maintain the peace. "In the old times," Palmer would write, "a settler would have had to wait many years, perhaps a lifetime, to have gathered around him for himself and children the comforts and conveniences which are here at Colorado Springs."

With the help of Irving Howbert, Palmer and his investors purchased 10,000 acres from the federal government for a little over a dollar an acre. Howbert had arrived in the territory in 1860 as a teenager with his minister father and remembers looking back and glimpsing a train of wagons that extended over the horizon. "Next to General Palmer," wrote the *Gazette*, "Irving Howbert could be the man who made Colorado Springs." Howbert became El Paso County's first clerk and supported the relief society for many years.

On July 31, 1871, the first stake was driven into the ground at the southeast corner of Pikes Peak and Cascade avenues. Business lots were priced at $100, residential lots could be had for $50 and small farms were $250. Settlers began trickling in. The pace of settlement increased when Palmer's narrow gauge Denver and Rio Grande Railroad reached the Springs several months later.

Palmer knew that grass and trees would be needed to create a sense of healthful repose. With some of the hefty profits from the lot sales, two, 10-mile-long irrigation ditches were dug. Hundreds of cottonwood saplings were brought

"We would have been none too comfortable with three in a bed, but we soon discovered there were dozens of other occupants – bed bugs, great and small, and all hungry and intent on getting our last drop of blood."
ELIZABETH LENNOX

in from the Arkansas Valley and town officials offered to pay 50 cents for each tree planted. Residents were asked not to tie their horses to the new trees, not to let their swine run free, and not to throw debris into the irrigation ditches. In a few short months, Colorado Springs had become an Arcadia, writes historian Frank Hall. "The ditches meandered through the place like so many rivulets, their edges in summer embossed with flowers," he writes. "The water was carried in tubs to the houses of those who had no wells, for domestic purposes, and clear cold drinking water was peddled about the streets for twenty-five cents a barrel."

Palmer hired a young Englishman named J. Elsom Liller to edit *Out West*, the settlement's first newspaper. Liller was a tall rangy man with a receding hairline and a long sloping nose that coursed down through a brown, brambly beard. Liller arrived in the Springs on New Year's Eve of 1871 and set to work in a two-story building on Tejon Street. He was an ardent supporter of General Palmer's liquor ban and during one public meeting, Liller was hissed at and pelted with various missiles. He took the abuse calmly, saying, "Do not disturb yourselves, gentlemen, all the evening is before me; I am in no hurry, and will wait until you have quite finished." Though Liller lived only a couple of years in Colorado Springs – he would die in 1875 of an overdose of laudanum – he was a tireless town booster and his widely distributed newspaper articles contributed greatly to the city's reputation as one of the healthiest resorts in the world. "Colonists continue to arrive, almost daily, in Colorado Springs," he wrote in 1872 with characteristic ebullience. "Four families who have just come in from Kansas, made the journey over the Plains in the old-fashioned way, coming by wagon instead of by rail. The town grows rapidly, scarcely a day passing without some new building being commenced."

William Lennox

The Lennox family came from Iowa City, Iowa. After a long trip, the family was tired and looked forward to a quiet evening in the Colorado Springs Hotel, a rambling wooden affair with dormers and a large porch that had been erected at about the time the railroad reached the Springs. As they were being escorted toward their quarters, a man rushed out of a building firing his revolver at another man who fell wounded to the ground. It was their first introduction to the " wild and wolly West," wrote daughter Elizabeth Lennox. Things went downhill from there:

> When we reached the hotel, which was a very crude place, the only available place was one bed in a room with a married couple, and in order to reach that room we had to pass through a community room where about a dozen men were supposed to be sleeping on the floor. The partition between the rooms extended only about half way up, and as we started to undress, various and sundry heads began to appear over the partition, so we hastily doused the light and retired in darkness. We would have been none too comfortable with three in a bed, but we soon discovered there were dozens of other occupants – bed bugs, great and small, and all hungry and intent on getting our last drop of blood. We could not make a light so we got up and tried the floor, but they pursued us there, so there was no sleep for us.

The next day, the family moved to one of the portable cabins that had been brought in from Chicago and were located on the north side of Kiowa Street between Cascade Avenue and Tejon Street. So many people died there that it was dubbed "Dead Man's Row." Her brother, William, a 22-year-old asthmatic, took up the city fathers on their tree-digging offer. The following year, he gravitated into the feed and hay business, then coal and freight transfer, and finally took up mining in Cripple Creek where he became exceedingly wealthy. Four years after the family's arrival in the Springs, he returned to Iowa to marry a young girl with the melodious name of Anna Belle Cowgell. Anna Belle was a colleague of Mrs. Wood's and would become a dues-paying member of the relief society.

Within a year, Liller reported that the town builders had transformed the empty prairie into a thriving little town with "handsome Streets and Avenues, bordered by leafy trees and running water-courses, with Houses and Gardens rich in flourishing crops, with Hotels and Stores and Workshops, with Churches and Reading Room, with Newspaper and Telegraph Office; in fact, with almost every essential to the comfort and well being of an enlightened community." Some 277 lots had been sold and the population — based on five people per house — was estimated to be 795. "The growth has been a steady and a healthy one," he went on, "there has been no excitement, no great rush, such has frequently caused 'cities' to spring up like mushrooms, only to die down again like mushrooms."

Liller added that a large building for a school was to be erected, four areas for public parks set aside and "reservations made for academies, colleges, zoological gardens, and other public institutions, the intention of the founders of the colony being that Colorado Springs shall be, as far as possible, worthy of its beautiful location and surroundings – a beautiful, healthful city and the home of a prosperous, enlightened, and cultivated people."

Dr. William M. Strickler

The wealthy arrived at the depot with trunks stuffed with clothing and accessories. "Women were advised that a season's good wardrobe for a resort town should include four silk evening dresses and two carriage robes, two walking dresses, six morning dresses, four round hats, two dozen pair of gloves, two parasols, two pair of silk boots, two pair of slippers, a dozen fans to match the different dresses, coats, sashes, bows of ribbon, curls, puffs, and braids of hair, a large quantity of elegant clothing and two camels' hair shawls," writes author Amanda Ellis.

Ellis went on to say that one of the favored materials was "camel's hair batiste," which cost roughly $125 a yard. "For full dress," she wrote, "gentlemen wear instead of a watch chain, a fob ribbon, after the fashion of their grandfathers, with a seal attached, the older looking the better. This taste for old jewelry is in opposition to shoddyism, the object being to show that the wearer was not the first in the family who possessed any jewelry."

In keeping with Victorian style, the well-to-do decorated their homes with luxurious carpets, paintings, etchings, upholstered lounges, and knick-knacks to perform their "toilets with ease and elegance." Candles and coal oil lamps were used for lighting. On their shelves were books by Byron, Dickens, Shakespeare and an author named Ollendorf.

Liller published the names of the prosperous visitors in the newspaper along with reams of copy extolling the glorious sunshine, the mysterious healing powers of the altitude, and the regenerative powers of Manitou's foul-tasting soda waters. "One of the most potent aids to the renewal of health in Colorado is undoubtedly its bright and almost constant sunshine," he wrote. "Dyspeptics, and people with health broken down by over-work, sedentary occupations, anxiety, trouble and similar causes, may here recuperate their energies and take fresh hold of life."

In one issue, he exclaimed that Colorado was fast becoming the world's sanatorium. "It has been estimated that at least one-third of the present population of

Colorado consists of reconstructed invalids, and every day brings newcomers within its borders in search of health. Before many years are over, it will probably be recognized as the great Sanatorium, not only of the American Continent, but of the World, for invalids of certain types."

A great sanatorium would need great doctors and they came, too, some chasing the cure, others chasing the buck, a few chasing both. Dr. William M. Strickler, a Southerner with a bushy mustache, was the first physician to settle in El Paso County and the relief society called on him more frequently than any other doctor. Born in 1838 in the Shenandoah Valley, Strickler was educated at Dickinson College in Carlisle, Pennsylvania, and later the University of Virginia. When the Civil War began, he enlisted in the Confederacy as an assistant surgeon and was present for 35 battles. He met his future wife, Virginia Lipscomb, on the battlefield of Manassas where the Confederates routed the green recruits from the North. "Dr. Strickler's surgical skill, judgment, and originality ranked with the best of his time," writes local historian Manley Ormes. In addition to his medical practice, Dr. Strickler was very active in civic life and served in the 1870s as superintendent of the public schools; in the 1880s as county physician; from 1884 to 1885 as chairman of the city's finance committee; in 1885 as president of the City Council; and between 1888 and 1894 he served three times as mayor of Colorado Springs. As mayor, he sought to secure a water supply for Colorado Springs, purchasing water rights on Beaver Creek and laying the foundation for the construction of the Strickler tunnel on the west slope of Pikes Peak.

Irving Howbert

John Potter

Dr. Anderson, another Southerner, established a medical practice in Colorado Springs in 1874. In those early days, his patients were mostly ranchers. "The antelope were very plentiful in those days and I remember driving through herds of twenty to thirty thousand many times." Dr. Anderson once suggested a radical cure for some of his consumptive patients: "Drink a lot of whiskey, get on a horse, and ride like hell." Anderson liked to drink large quantities of whiskey himself and during the Civil War rode with Colonel John C. Mosby, a dashing Confederate who led stealth attacks on the Union Army. After the war, Dr. Anderson went on a notorious drinking binge in Manitou Springs with William Tecumseh Sherman, a famous Union general who cut a swath of destruction through the South on his march to the sea. As the former enemies toasted each other, Dr. Anderson no doubt thought of the Union bullet he still carried in his body. Local author Bob Hoff writes that Dr. Anderson subsequently developed tuberculosis and always believed that the disease was triggered by the wound. But Dr. Anderson was unsure whether the wound itself stimulated a "quiescent" form of the disease, Hoff writes, or whether he had contracted the disease from a contaminated bullet itself or the instrument that failed to fish the round from his body.

Dr. Samuel Edwin Solly, a lean, graceful aristocrat who dressed with impeccable style, decamped for the Springs after contracting tuberculosis in London. He was a close friend of General Palmer's and a graduate of London's Royal College of Surgeons. He was tall and courtly, with a rich soothing voice and lively intelligence, writes author Marshall Sprague, and soon became a ranking specialist in the cure of consumption. Dr. Solly's wife, Elizabeth, would devote much of her time to helping Mrs. Wood. She, too, reportedly had tuberculosis.

There were few medicines with which to treat serious infectious diseases, so it was not surprising that the physicians and laypeople alike put so much stock in the curative properties of climate. While the climate may have helped some consumptives, the rigors of the journey, the uncomfortable and cold surroundings, may have hastened the death of others. A few brave souls warned against Liller's brash and effusive claims, including his competition down the road in Pueblo. Wrote the *Pueblo People*:

> We are opposed to the efforts that are being made to populate Colorado with incurable invalids and her graveyards with imported corpses. It seems to us radically wrong to hold out inducements to invalids – consumptives and others – which we all know cannot be realized either here or elsewhere on the face of the earth. Every train brings to Colorado people who bring with them a tattered fraction of a diseased lung, and who are led, by extravagant representations, to believe that a few weeks' residence here will put them in possession of a new set of breathing apparatus as sound and capacious as a blacksmith's bellows. They are disappointed – they die, and straightaway the report goes abroad that the climate of Colorado is not salubrious and is quite unfitted for persons of consumptive tendencies. This is the practical result of our own misrepresentation. Under these circumstances, it will not be long before Colorado graveyards will be dismal testimony to the fact that Colorado air will not raise men from the dead.

The prophecy was borne out by newly arrived residents such as Albert Pearson, a young organist who had hoped to study music in Germany, but instead found himself "banished" to the Springs following an unfortunate sailing accident. Expecting the "Italian" climate that the town founders had advertised, Pearson was not prepared for his first winter. The snow was three feet deep and lay on the ground for more than two months. "Life in our boarding house that winter was anything but comfortable with twelve invalids for companions," he remembered. "In the early days many people came west too late to be helped, and our house had its full share of these unfortunates. The nine I met at my first meal were all dead in a little over a year."

Elizabeth Mellon Evans Solly was a member of the relief society and her English husband, Dr. Solly, was a TB specialist. Both were said to have consumption. 1901. (Colorado Springs Century Chest Collection, Colorado College Special Collections, hereafter referred to as Century Chest)

In fairness to Liller, he did caution invalids with an advanced form of the disease to stay home. "Consumptive patients may look forward to being rapidly benefited, unless the disease has been suffered to get too firm a hold before the health renewing air of Colorado is resorted to. There have been many cases in which consumptives 'in the last stage' have been brought to Colorado, and are now active professional and business men, but such instances are rare, and could probably be counter-balanced by as many in which death has been hastened by the long, wearying journey and the sudden tax upon the exhausted system resulting from quickened respiration."

Their bodies stiff and aching, veterans of the Civil War stepped down from the train and made their way to rented rooms or to the homes of friends. The soldiers carried the visible reminders of that bloody war: amputated arms and legs, gouged-out eyes, and wounds that had healed poorly. Some were suffering from a strange form of paralysis. Others seemed unable to forget the horrors they had seen in battle and their preoccupation with the past was alternately called nostalgia, melancholia, or soldier's heart. "The late war had left the entire south prostrate in every way and overwhelmed in a great desolation from which there was but little hope of recovery before another generation at least," John Potter, the town's first postmaster, recalled in a 1901 letter. "In the North, a great reaction from the unnatural prosperity created by the demands of a great war for material of all kinds at high prices had taken place, and there was over production in the manufactures of nearly every kind and also in farm production. In addition to this condition of things, the disbandment of the great northern armies threw a multitude of young and active men into the fields of labor where already the supply was greater than the demand." Potter said these causes — more than any other — led to the settling of most of the western states and territories. "It was from this element of discontent in the east and south that not only Colorado Springs, but nearly every other city and town of any permanency in the west found its pioneer builders," he added.

Lithograph from *Harper's Weekly* entitled "In the Emigrant Train." Jan. 24, 1874. (PPLD)

Union soldiers or their widows received a small pension from the Grand Army of the Republic, a veteran's organization. A Grand Army representative in Colorado Springs paid visits to the sick and needy and on one occasion foraged up a pair of "smoked glasses" for a blind member. For those veterans who were unable to live on their own, old soldier homes had been established throughout the country, including one in Monte Vista, Colorado and another in Cheyenne, Wyoming. The auxiliary of the Grand Army, called the Women's Relief Corps, was also active in the Springs. "Sickness and old wounds and lack of work began to make cruel ravages in the Veterans ranks," remembered one female officer. "Where then would the veterans turn for help but to the loyal women of America, the women who had so bravely stood by them in the bitter past?" Many of the Southerners came from Missouri, Kentucky and Tennessee. "There was no unfriendliness between these two elements," said Potter. "In the true American Spirit, the animosities engendered by the war were relegated to the great battlefields on which they culminated, and those who had but lately confronted each other in the strife of battle now met to work shoulder-to-shoulder for the best interest of all."

The economy boomed until Sept. 18, 1873, when a financial house in New York failed. Credit dried up. Businesses and consumers stopped buying goods. Farm prices collapsed. Factories and mills went silent. The causes of the financial meltdown were varied and complex, but most historians blame the rampant speculation in railroads and real estate that occurred following the Civil War. The effects of the 1873 Panic would ripple down through the economy and be felt for the rest of the decade.

Aided by the thousands of miles of new railroad track, the great river of travelers swelled with jobless men. Leaning their backs against the swaying boxcars, they dreamed of the new life in the mythical land that lay just over the horizon. "Unemployment was endemic to the new industrial order," writes labor historian David Montgomery. The unemployment rate nationally surpassed 16 percent of the labor force during the Panic of 1873, he adds, and the periodic waves of unemployment would continue as the United States transitioned from a rural to an industrial nation. "Shifting seasonal demands, crippling illnesses caused by industrial poisons, and alternating spasms of relentless work and forced idleness caused by the drive of each employer to capture as much as the market as possible – all these made for long days without income," he writes.

In Colorado and other western states, the boom-to-bust cycles of mining and railroading and the seasonal nature of farming and timber harvesting also helped to contribute to a mobile army of under-employed, seasonally employed, and unemployed workers. "Each surge in construction sent railroads and the firms that built them scurrying to secure the most tractable and inexpensive labor force possible," historian Thomas Andrews notes. "When the track-laying booms inevitably crested, then crashed, 'large numbers of men' found themselves thrown 'out of employment.'" Compounding the problem was the extremely turbulent

Miners were paid three dollars a day for a shift lasting anywhere from eight to ten hours. 1879. (PPLD)

relationship between owners and workers that resulted in acrimonious strikes and lockouts and blacklists. Between 1881 and 1905, reports author J. Anthony Lukas, there were some 37,000 strikes in the United States.

Though Colorado Springs had no industry to speak of, the town would not be immune to the wrenching effects of industrialization or the frequent economic downtowns. In the decades to come, thousands of unemployed men would knock on the doors of the relief society. They were called tramps, vagabonds, vagrants, wanderers, beggars, n'er do-wells, hoboes and finally, the homeless.

AspenPointe Health Services

This clinic was one of the two original components of AspenPointe, c. 1950s.

"We calculated last year that we served over 5,000 people without funding. It's amazing."
Nancy Craney

With roughly 300 employees, Health Services is AspenPointe's largest division and provides clients of all ages a full compliment of behavioral health services, ranging from inpatient treatment for people in acute crises to traditional out-patient therapy, to education and wellness programs. It's spread out across multiple locations throughout Colorado Springs. The Acute Care Facility, also known as the Lighthouse, is located at 115 Parkside Drive and provides short-term inpatient care for people who are a danger to themselves or others or who need to be medically stabilized. Child and Family Services, located at 179 Parkside Drive, offers a continuum of counseling and psychiatric services for children and their families. And Adult and Rural Services, located at 875 Moreno Avenue, focuses on teens, adults and seniors and provides one-on-one therapy sessions, group therapy, case management, as well as educational classes and art programs.

In all, the various programs and services offered by Health Services results in 150,000 unique visits annually. "So much is expected of this company because it's the largest nonprofit in the area," said Nancy Craney, who formerly served as vice president and has since taken another job. "We calculated last year that we served over 5,000 people without funding. It's amazing. It's a story most people don't know."

Health Services provides:

- **Screenings and assessments.**
- **Counseling.** Includes individual therapy, group therapy, case management, family therapy and adult substance abuse treatment.
- **Specialized therapy and services** for families and caregivers of infants and toddlers with mental health or behavioral health challenges.
- **Childcare consultation** for educators and childcare workers regarding young children with significant behavioral issues.
- **Therapeutic after-school, spring and summer camps.**
- **Adoption, foster and kinship care.**
- **14-week parenting group** that targets reduction of aggression and behavioral issues in children between the ages of two and eight.
- **A classroom program** that meets twice a week in the schools or childcare setting and helps children build social skills and learn to manage their anger.
- **Outreach to the homeless** mentally ill.
- **Outreach to prisoners** with psychiatric illnesses.
- **A 12-hour course called Mental Health First Aid,** which trains people to help individuals with mental health problems or in a mental health crisis until professional help arrives.

Health Network & TeleCare

Sitting behind two widescreen computer monitors at his office at 6208 Lehman Drive, Michael Allen looks more like an air traffic controller than a mental health professional. He doesn't direct jumbo jets, but as vice president of Health Network & TeleCare he needs the same nimbleness to keep this segment of AspenPointe aloft. "We connect payments, people and providers," he says.

Health Network is essentially a managed care company for local and state governments and businesses. It consists of a network of about 400 credentialed and contracted providers who help people suffering from mental disorders, substance abuse problems, family issues, and even physical ailments. For providers, it offers an array of services, from care coordination/case management to claims adjudication, payments and appeals processes. TeleCare, which is a subsidiary of Health Network, provides professional telephonic support to people suffering from depression, asthma, diabetes, heart disease, substance abuse disorders or chronic pain.

Allen, a licensed clinical social worker and a certified addictions counselor, spent a decade counseling tough populations like doctors and lawyers addicted to drugs and adolescents with severe behavioral problems. Then he decided to go into management and returned to Colorado State University and earned an MBA. "With counseling, I felt like I could help people one at a time but in management I felt my influence was going to be bigger."

"We connect payments, people and providers."

Michael Allen

Many of the clients who receive help through Health Network or TeleCare are low income and lack health insurance. "The way we structure our contracts, all the money comes from the payer. The patient doesn't pay anything for our services. The federal, state and local governments pay us for the services for these at-risk populations and we provide them at no cost," he said. "That's the beauty of having multiple contracts. I can find a dollar here and a dollar there so the client doesn't have to worry about it."

With the economic downturn, he has seen an increase in homeless people, as well as former professionals who now are now on Medicaid. "It's not the typical people you would expect to see," he said. Below are some of Health Network's activities:

- It is the Managed Services Organization, or MSO, for seven counties in and around the Pikes Peak region. It serves those who have no insurance or other resources to cover substance-abuse-disorder treatment. Health Network connects the clients to providers and pays for their care. Serves 4,800 clients annually.
- In a related contract, Health Network administers the Access to Recovery grant in partnership with the state Division of Behavioral Health. This program connects those with no insurance or other way to pay for substance-abuse-disorder services with the care they need, including funding. This grant covers the entire state and serves 2,200 clients annually.
- Health Network has a contract with El Paso and Teller County Departments of Human Services to administer their behavioral health services for families involved in the child welfare system. Serves approximately 1,900 clients annually.
- Health Network is a partner in the Regional Care Collaborative, or RCCO, for El Paso, Teller, Elbert and Park counties. Called the Community Care of Central Colorado, the collaborative coordinates care for Medicaid patients, linking them to healthcare providers that hopefully will become their "medical home." Health Network provides an array of services, including fiscal management, data support, provider contracting, care management and a comprehensive telephonic service center for patients and providers. The regional care collaborative is part of a pilot program and Allen thinks that's where the healthcare system is headed. "It's the integration of behavioral health with primary care," he said. "This is full-person health, which is great. We're working with docs, hospitals, Peak Vista and large Medicaid practices."

Enterprises

As vice president of AspenPointe Enterprises, Jonathan Liebert oversees about 130 employees and roughly half of his workers have some kind of mental or physical disability. That would give any ordinary businessman the jitters, but Liebert knows something about his employees that would come as a surprise to most employers. "We call them chronic attenders. They're great workers. They are an untapped labor force."

Youthful and dark-haired, Liebert describes himself as a "social entrepreneur," that is, someone who fixes large and small social problems that have been broken for a long time. In the process, he and his organization hope to save the community millions in tax dollars. "You take the best in business and the best in nonprofits and change the world," said Liebert. "Now is this easy? Heck, no. It's actually harder. I've got to run a business and incorporate the mission. Oftentimes those two things are in conflict."

One of the most successful examples of a social enterprise is TOMS Shoes, which gives away a new pair of shoes for each pair purchased to people in more than 50 countries, including Albania Cambodia, Liberia, Sri Lanka and Tajikistan. AspenPointe Enterprises, with a capital 'E,' has multiple business lines and training and education programs to help the disabled, the homeless, at-risk youth, seniors and veterans. As the company recently explained on its website, "A social enterprise exists to solve some type of social issue, but instead of seeking funding in the traditional charitable sense, these businesses seek to use the powerful economic engine of capitalism to fund their missions. While many entrepreneurs make charitable contributions or run 'socially responsible businesses,' a social enterprise is differentiated in that their social aims are primary, and their profits are secondary."

Perhaps the most easily understood is the AspenPointe Café. Its primary mission is to help train people for jobs, yet it's also a viable restaurant and catering company and competes with other similar businesses for customers. "Social innovation works. How do I know it? Look around this room," Liebert said one morning gesturing at the customers in the café. "Some of these people are here for the food. A lot of them are here for the mission. Everyone who walks in this door is voting for this concept with their wallet, which is really cool."

"Social innovation works. How do I know it? Look around this room."

Jonathan Liebert

After taking some time off to travel the world, Liebert realized it was time to get a real job. His father, who had worked for Pikes Peak Mental Health for 25 years, was getting ready to retire and encouraged Liebert to apply to the organization. Liebert followed his father's advice and got a job working as vocational and housing coordinator at the mental health center. Eventually he was promoted to vice president of Enterprises.

In the old sheltered workshop model, Liebert said, 99 percent of the workers were disabled. "That creates a very disabled environment. People are a product of their environment and they were learning a lot of disabled coping mechanisms. From the beginning, we said we're going to do a competitive placement model, which says 'I'm going to work with you, but I'm not going to give you a job based on your disability. I'm less interested in what you can't do. I'm interested in what you can do. Tell me what your strengths are. Tell me what your hobbies are. And I'll help you get a job. And, oh by the way, I'm going to help you write a resumé but I'm not going to help you get a job. I'll facilitate your getting a job.'"

The principles resonate with both Republicans and Democrats. "Becoming a social enterprise is a game changer. We changed how we told our story," Liebert said. "The other phrase that I like to use that I've coined on my own is, 'It's using capitalism for good not just for gain.' It's a powerful economic engine that nonprofits have not tapped into. Making profit for it's own sake has also gotten us into trouble. You just can't grow and grow and grow. It's time to get back to the basics of why businesses were

created two or three hundred years ago. It was to build communities where people could flourish. You can make money and also solve social problems."

Lately, the organization has begun to think about what it can do about obesity, which is a huge problem both locally and nationally. "You want to solve the healthcare crisis? Solve obesity. It's the gateway to heart disease, diabetes and cancer. All the things that are killing Americans. Don't cure it, solve it," he said.

One way of determining how much value a social enterprise holds for the community is through social return on investment, or SROI, which attempts to measure the value of, say, reintegrating a long-term unemployed person to the workforce or helping a returning veteran find a rewarding career and heal from the wounds of war. By doing so, the organization indirectly helps to eliminate some of the costs that would normally have been shouldered by the government. Put another way, tax users become taxpayers. Enterprises estimates that its total social return on investment for 2012 was more than $20 million. "In the long-term, I'll know I'm successful when I'm out of business," Liebert said.

Business Lines

- **The AspenPointe Café.** Trained 97 people in fiscal 2012. Twenty students completed all four tiers and nine placed in jobs. Went from $33,500 monthly loss to $2,900 average monthly profit in six months. Increased catering by 189 percent compared to same six-month period in fiscal 2011.
- **Custodial services.** Longstanding AbilityOne disabled worker janitorial contract at the Denver Federal Center and new one with FAA at Rocky Mountain Regional Airport. Provided janitorial services at 17 AspenPointe properties and four YMCAs in the Pikes Peak region. Contracts with the Colorado Division of Military Affairs, the Colorado Department of Transportation, and the State of Colorado Integrated Document Solutions.
- **Furniture and Assembly Services.** Space planning and installation and warehousing of modular office furniture. Manages Government Furniture Reuse Program for Peterson Air Force Base.
- **Maintenance Services.** Provides commercial and residential maintenance and landscaping services.
- **Career and Development Services.** Teaches interview skills, job search strategies and resumé writing.
- **Education Services.** GED preparation classes and testing.
- **Creative Expressions.** Teaches students a variety of art techniques and uses art as therapeutic tool.
- **Peer Navigator.** Aids veterans and family members with job placement, housing, education, healthcare and behavioral health needs.
- **Youth Directions.** Helps youngsters who get in trouble with the law make amends to their victims, teaches them better coping and life skills, explores careers and job opportunities.

3

Catching at Straws

J. Elsom Liller should have known that his articles praising the Springs' health-restoring climate would reach the ears of rich and poor alike. Yet, he professed alarm on Jan. 11, 1873, upon discovering the first cases of "absolute destitution." A man with three small children and a consumptive wife arrived in the Springs with only 25 cents in his pockets. And another extremely ill consumptive was about to be evicted. "The landlord of the house in which he was staying had told him he must turn out unless he paid his board-bill, and that he had no earthly means of raising the money, and had no idea what he was going to do."

There were also colonists "apparently possessed with the insane idea that they only had to come here and let money fall into their pockets, have spent what little money they brought with them, and now in the dull season of the year, find times hard," he reported. "We hope that next winter we shall have very few of this class; one season's experience should either set them earnestly to work and to economize, or send them back whither they came, and the next spring and summer's crop of colonists we intend to warn in good time." He continued:

> It will doubtless strike anyone as folly for such people to come here in such hap-hazard style; but they are drowning men catching at straws, and are worthy of sincerest sympathy. Such, it may be expected, will always come, and will come in increasing numbers; and, ere long, we believe that a benevolent people all over the States should be asked to contribute for the erection of a Public Hospital at some point in the Territory for their reception. But, meanwhile, we must endeavor to bear the burden of those who are amongst us, and seek to relieve their pressing necessities.

Concerns for the needy were temporarily swept aside by a tremendous windstorm. Buildings were flattened, the front of a livery stable was ripped off, the top of a buggy found its way into the blacksmith's shop, and a man living on Cascade Avenue was obliged to hire a bricklayer to build him a new chimney before he could "indulge" in breakfast.

Rebuilding began immediately and those who could afford it constructed their homes using stone or brick. The town founders suggested residents build rental houses or set aside rooms for visiting invalids and tourists. "We urge attention to it, not so much on account of the pecuniary benefit, which will be derived,

as for the bearing it will have on our future success as a place of resort for health and pleasure seekers," the newspaper advised.

Mrs. Wood's husband began construction on two "villas" at the corner of Pikes Peak Avenue and Weber Street at a combined cost of $5,000. One of the carpenters he hired was Winfield Scott Stratton, a hollow-eyed and melancholy man who had arrived in town in 1872 and purchased a lot with a $300 bankroll he had stashed in his pocket. Stratton was a superb craftsman and in great demand, but preferred to spend his time hunting for gold. Given to alcoholism and fits of rage, Stratton had disagreements with three of his business partners and once engendered the wrath of the El Paso County Humane Society for beating a burro with the handle of a pick ax. From its inception, the town had a soft spot for animals and the newspaper reported disapprovingly that the head of an eagle had been found in the street. "We should rather like to 'put a head on' the person who went out eagle shooting for no better purpose than to throw away what he had bagged. If eagles are not wanted even for stuffing, pray let them be allowed to exist; they are not over-plentiful hereabouts." The El Paso County Humane Society waged fierce campaigns against shippers of livestock and chicken who overcrowded their railroad cars. It also fought tirelessly against the practice of docking horses' tails and using the wings of birds to decorate ladies' hats. The Humane Society did not limit its efforts to animals only; in its formative years, it also sought to protect women abused by their husbands, children abused or abandoned by their parents, and elderly men who were destitute.

By Nov. 29, 1873, a "Society of Ladies" had been formed to raise funds for charity. "We have people amongst us who are in want of the necessaries of life and who are too sick to obtain them by work. The efforts of such a society should, therefore, be well supported by our citizens," the newspaper wrote.

The 1873-1874 holiday season found the Utes selling buckskins and buffalo robes. The following February, prices had dropped and a good buffalo robe could be had for five or six dollars. A Young Men's Christian Association was formed and D. Russ Wood was elected to the board of trustees for Colorado College, which was in the midst of raising money for a building.

On Feb. 6, 1875, the newspaper announced that the Colorado Springs Relief Society had been organized five days earlier at Colorado College. Its main function was to provide the needy with food, shelter and clothing. Once those needs were met, it sought to help people become self-sufficient again by finding them work. In the coming decades, records would show that the majority of its applicants were single men who were sick or unemployed and families impoverished by illness and death.

The town's railroad builders, mining kings, bankers and businessmen financially supported the relief society, but it was their wives and daughters who nurtured it and were involved in its daily activities. At that time, there were few acceptable outlets available to educated women and they poured their energies into charity work. Women such as Mrs. Wood and Mrs. Solly and Mrs. Lennox carried beef tea and pigeons and crates of cherries to the poor; hired nurses and doctors; found jobs for their clients, and often dispatched their own servants to put households in order. They also organized fund-raisers and attended monthly meetings and kept the organization alive through severe economic downturns. "In this town, as in all others, there are some who are given to mere pleasure seeking, and whose time is spent as it was so many years ago in seeking and telling 'some new thing.' But these are not the women of who I wish to write," remembered Elizabeth Cass Goddard, a wealthy and prominent woman who hailed from an old New England family. "There is a large element, composed of bright, intelligent, philanthropic, public spirited, high minded and cultivated women, and these do much toward molding public opinion and giving character to the town. They are always busy and their work continues from January to December."

Elizabeth Cass Goddard was a leading figure in Colorado Springs society and was involved in many charities, including the precursor to AspenPointe. 1901. (Century Chest)

Elizabeth Cass Goddard was the grand dame of Colorado Springs society and moved west because she had a son in ill health. Both her son and her husband died, but Mrs. Goddard remained active in many local charitable and social organizations. "The blue blood in her veins flowed from fifty-six colonial ancestors, including her eminent grandfather, Lewis Cass, who was a brigadier general in the War of 1812 and later ambassador, governor, senator and presidential candidate," writes Judith Reid Finley.

The original relief society consisted of two women from the Congregational Church, two from the Methodist Episcopal Church, two from the Baptist Church, two from the Presbyterian Church, two from the Cumberland Presbyterian, two from the Episcopal Church, and two from the Unity Church. The Rev. E.A. Taft was president, the Rev. P.A. Rice was secretary and a Mr. McIntire served as treasurer.

Mrs. Wood, along with six other women, were appointed to the "Prudential Committee," which doled out food and clothing. "Winter pants and coats are particularly needed," the newspaper reported in that first announcement. Mrs. Wood wrote that not long after the society was organized, a "Union Thanksgiving Service" was held in the Presbyterian Church and the collection taken up and the proceeds placed in the bank for the use of the society.

The following year, 1876, the members held a meeting at the library and decided to divide the city among canvassers who would solicit monthly subscriptions of 10 cents each. Seven women volunteered, including Mrs. Wood and Mrs. William S. Jackson, whose husband was from Philadelphia and was a friend of General Palmer's. Their efforts were apparently not very successful. Wrote the newspaper, "It is full time for the ladies of this place to reorganize their Relief Society. We hear there are several cases of destitution in town, and there will be many more, as a large number of invalids who come here are afflicted with poverty as well as sickness."

Victorians on a wildflower expedition on the Colorado Midland Railroad. 1908. (PPLD)

A meeting was held a week later and Mrs. Wood was elevated to president. She would be faced with many challenges, money being foremost among them. When she took over, the coffers of the relief society were almost empty and the organization appealed for donations. "The society is being called upon to give relief much earlier this year than any previous one, and they anticipate that they will have many poor families to care for during the winter," the newspaper wrote. "In order that they may be able to render assistance when called upon, it is hoped that our citizens will come forward and subscribe whatever they may be able to pay at once as the society funds are very low indeed."

By the end of the 1870s, the United States as a whole was recovering from the recession. Although agricultural products had once comprised the United States' primary exports, the exports of tools and machines were increasing. Steel forks, hoes, rakes, shovels, hammers, and edgers were being exported to England and Europe. Wire fencing, iron bars and water pipes were going to South America. More than 100 locomotives made at the Baldwin Works in Philadelphia had been

"Many working women in the east who would have come west for the large wages could not be persuaded, even by their friends who wrote to them from here, that we were quite safe from sudden Indian raids and attacks from wild beasts if we ventured out doors."

MRS. ELIZABETH SOLLY

shipped to Brazil, Russia, Australia or Peru. Saws, files, nuts, bolts, rivets and locks were also being exported.

"During the four decades following the war, the fabrication of the metal machinery, rails, and utensils on which a modern economy rests became a mechanized factory process," writes historian David Montgomery. "The United States census, which counted only 55,000 machinists in 1870, listed 283,000 of them in 1900," he continues. "Machine-made machinery allowed the country's industrial output to outstrip that of England by 1885."

In Colorado, the appetite for coal grew as smelters, ore processing facilities, brick kilns, glass works, and sugar beet factories and countless other enterprises sprung up along the Front Range. Day after day, the Denver and Rio Grande chugged north with its railroad cars brimming with black coal. An editor in Pueblo questioned Palmer's monopolistic hold on the coal market, claiming he charged rates that were so high they could be "viewed in no other light than that of an extortion." But in Colorado Springs, Palmer was revered as he shared his immense fortune with the city, donating land for parks and schools and charities.

Locally, the economy was booming. "At the present time, lots and lands are higher in price than ever before, and none are being sold except for immediate improvement. The houses now being erected are all good structures, ornaments to the town, and if not to be occupied by the builder are rented at once for a year or more in advance," the newspaper reported. The rise in prices, it went on to say, was not due to speculation. "So far as we can learn not a lot has been sold for months to a party who simply wishes to hold it for an advance. All are to be immediately improved in a substantial manner. Although many new houses have been recently built, and a hundred others more or less enlarged, it seems almost impossible to supply the demand for houses and rooms. Our streets are lined with persons seeking such accommodations and fifty good-sized houses could doubtless be rented at good rates as rapidly as they could be built."

The members of Colorado Springs' upper class came together for ice cream socials, skating parties, hunts, and balls. Author Amanda Ellis writes that meals were large and elaborate, especially at Thanksgiving, when, in addition to turkey, the menu might include fresh oyster soup, mackinaw trout with egg sauce, boiled ham, calf's tongue, corned beef and cabbage, roast loin of beef with oyster dressing, venison, pork and beans, and scrambled eggs.

Along with the housing shortage, there was also a shortage of servants to cook and clean and wash and iron the innumerable articles of clothing belonging to the town's well-to-do. "The servant question was a trying one – not being enough to go around," remembered Mrs. Elizabeth Solly. "Many working women in the east who would have come west for the large wages could not be persuaded, even by their friends who wrote to them from here, that we were quite safe from sudden Indian raids and attacks from wild beasts if we ventured out doors. Many a delicately nurtured lady became familiar with unaccustomed household labor – most likely to her benefit both in health and appreciation of what to expect from others."

There were still stubborn pockets of poverty and the question arose as to whether El Paso County needed an almshouse, or poorhouse. Similar institutions already existed in large Eastern cities and in Great Britain. The newspaper opposed the idea because it was too costly. "We say costly, because in the experience of authorities in counties older than any in the state of Colorado, these almshouses have almost invariably cost roundly in the course of a number of years, no matter how scanty have been the accommodations or bill of fare. The county has pauper expenses, however, but certainly not to the extent that would obtain if she possessed even a makeshift of a poorhouse." Besides, the newspaper added, Mrs.

Wood and the relief society were capable of handling the city's less fortunate citizens. "The society wants to be assured that persons applying are not unworthy of the charity they ask. This point established, the relief society delights in extending the needed assistance so far as possible."

The relief society eventually established the Helping Hand Wood Yard at 23 W. Cucharras Street. The wood yard not only provided applicants with an actual way to earn money for food and clothing and shelter, but also served as a "test" to separate the "worthy poor" from the "unworthy poor." If an applicant was willing to work, then the society was willing to help him. If he declined, the organization was likely to send him on his way empty-handed. During that era, poverty was often associated with social deviance or character flaws and many cities had similar "work tests" and wood yards. Men and women and even able-bodied children were viewed with suspicion if they weren't working. So-called tramps were particularly loathed because they neither worked nor had families. In an 1878 *Scribner's* magazine article that was re-published in the *Gazette*, one physician recommended they be rounded up like cattle and placed in workhouses:

The "incorruptible" Matt France. (CSPM)

> The tramp is a man who can be approached by no motive but pain – the pain of a thrashing or the pain of hunger. He hates work; he has no self-respect and no shame; and by counting himself permanently out of the productive and self-supporting forces of society, he counts himself out of his rights. He has no rights but those which society may see fit of its grace to bestow upon him. He has no more rights than the sow that wallows in the gutter, or the lost dogs that hover around city squares. He is no more to be consulted, in his wishes or his will, in the settlement of the question as to what to be done with him than if he were a bullock in a corral.

Historian Kenneth L. Kusmer, who in 2002 published a groundbreaking history about the homeless in America, said, "Part of the hostile reaction to tramps and beggars in the late nineteenth century was outrage over the fact that these outsiders had seemingly rejected male responsibility by embracing a vagabond lifestyle free from the bonds of marriage and family."

The "incorruptible" Matt France, who arrived in Colorado following a 43-day trip in an ox-drawn wagon, led the fight to establish a home for the poor in El Paso County. France, another Virginian, served two terms as mayor of Colorado Springs and was also an El Paso County commissioner for many years. His wife was very active in the relief society.

In 1880, the commissioners purchased a small cottage and three and a half acres of land on the east side of El Paso Street between Boulder and St. Vrain streets for a county home. At the time, the site was far from the town center and there were few neighbors. Additional rooms were built onto a small cottage that existed on the property, and several years later, a much larger two-story building was erected. By the time the commissioners sought to build a more commodious facility, the surrounding area was populated and nearby residents rebelled against the plan. The same battle broke out at other potential sites around town. Finally, after "many sleepless nights," the commissioners purchased the Liebig Ranch, which consisted of a farmhouse and 525 acres outside the city limits and south of Bear Creek. The Colorado Springs Relief Society often sought to place the destitute and sick at the county farm. Some went willingly but others preferred suffering and death to what they perceived as an ignoble ending.

4

Microbes and Men

By the 1880s, the Colorado economy was booming again thanks in part to the discovery of silver. The population of Colorado Springs was about 4,500 and it still had the feel of a small village. The newspaper wrote about horses that had escaped colic and horses that had escaped capture. Sprinkling carts watered the dirt streets and "illuminating gas" produced by coal was distributed to stores and offices and the "better class of dwellings." The Antlers Hotel, located at the west end of Pikes Peak Avenue, had replaced the vermin-infested Colorado Springs Hotel and boasted a hydraulic elevator, fine china and linens.

Tuberculosis sufferers from around the world continued to flock to Colorado Springs. "From the 1880s to the 1940s, tuberculosis treatment was the community's only major industry," writes Matt Mayberry, a historian and director of the Colorado Springs Pioneers Museum. "Nothing else came close to attracting as many residents and jobs as TB."

In 1882, Robert Koch, a bespectacled and bearded scientist, delivered a lecture in Berlin that would challenge the very foundation upon which that "industry" was built. The great German scientist had isolated the bacterium that caused tuberculosis and brought a virtual laboratory into the lecture room to prove it. "If the importance of a disease for mankind is measured by the number of fatalities it causes," he began, "then tuberculosis must be considered much

more important than those most feared infectious diseases, cholera, plague and the like. One in seven of all human beings dies from tuberculosis. If one only considers the productive middle-age groups, tuberculosis carries away one-third and often more."

When he was finished, the audience was too shocked to applaud. To make visible the microorganism responsible for killing more than a billion people was a monumental achievement. Viewed under the microscope, the rod-shaped microbes resembled flecks from an eraser. "The great majority of all cases of tuberculosis begin in the respiratory tract, and the infectious material leaves its mark first in the lungs or in the bronchial nodes," he wrote. "There can hardly be any doubt about the manner by which they get into the air, considering what excessive numbers tubercle bacilli present in cavity contents are expectorated by consumptives and scattered everywhere."

Although the culprit had been found, the world would have to wait another sixty years for effective drugs. In Colorado Springs, meanwhile, doctors continued to tout fresh air and sunshine as a cure. One of the most renowned was Dr. Charles Fox Gardiner, who developed a canvas tent for consumptives that resembled a teepee. Gardiner was a sickly, pampered child born in New York City whose blue-blooded ancestors arrived in New England in 1632. "Long before I had long trousers I led a man-of-the-world life when I should have been in school. I went everywhere, saw everything, sat up late and was as wise to all the sin and scandal of a big city as any adult," he said in an oft-quoted passage.

Gardiner, who never weighed more than 110 pounds, was determined to become strong and spent nine years in "violent exercise." He worked out for two hours a day at a gymnasium on New York's Twenty-Eighth Street, took boxing lessons, learned tumbling and bar work from members of Barnum's Circus, went on long hiking trips in the Catskill and White Mountains, took up long-distance running, camped out with only one blanket, learned to use a rifle and an ax, and make fire in the rain. "And gradually, by years of practice, hardened my thin, frail body so that, although I was not big and strong, I was very active and could tire out many of my stronger friends."

The relief society continued to aid impoverished homeless men, tuberculars and other poor people. It reached out to the YMCA when it was trying to find jobs for young men, tapped the Grand Army of the Republic when it came across Civil War veterans, contacted the school district when it discovered truant children, and called upon the Humane Society for help with abused animals and abused human beings. It also contacted the doctors of Colorado Springs when a client was desperately ill or needed to be hospitalized.

Despite its efforts, by 1884 public interest in the organization had dwindled and a reorganization was undertaken. Mrs. Wood was re-elected president and immediately asked the church pastors to announce from the pulpit an emergency meeting for the following Wednesday in the lecture room of the Presbyterian Church.

Dr. Charles Fox Gardiner, 1901. (Century Chest)

The purpose of the society, notes Article II of the constitution, was "to aid the poor, the homeless and the sick of the city, and so far as possible to obtain employment for those able to work."

The purpose of the meeting, the newspaper wrote, "was to effect some organization for work among the poor, as there are at present some distressing cases which require immediate attention."

Mrs. Wood credited the Rev. Mr. Vail, pastor of the Baptist Church, with providing $125, the largest donation it had ever received to that point. "In a short, but pointed address, he made an appeal to the congregation telling them that there was suffering and distress among us which must be relieved and the philanthropic were called upon to practice their profession of general benevolence," she wrote.

The relief society in 1885 found itself once again pleading with the public for help and called for another meeting in the reading room south of the post office. "There is at present time a great deal of sickness and destitution in our village which demands the prompt attention of all Christian people," the newspaper wrote. "The funds of the Colorado Springs Aid Society have all been used and to avoid the disgrace which neglect of this suffering would bring upon us, something must be done at once."

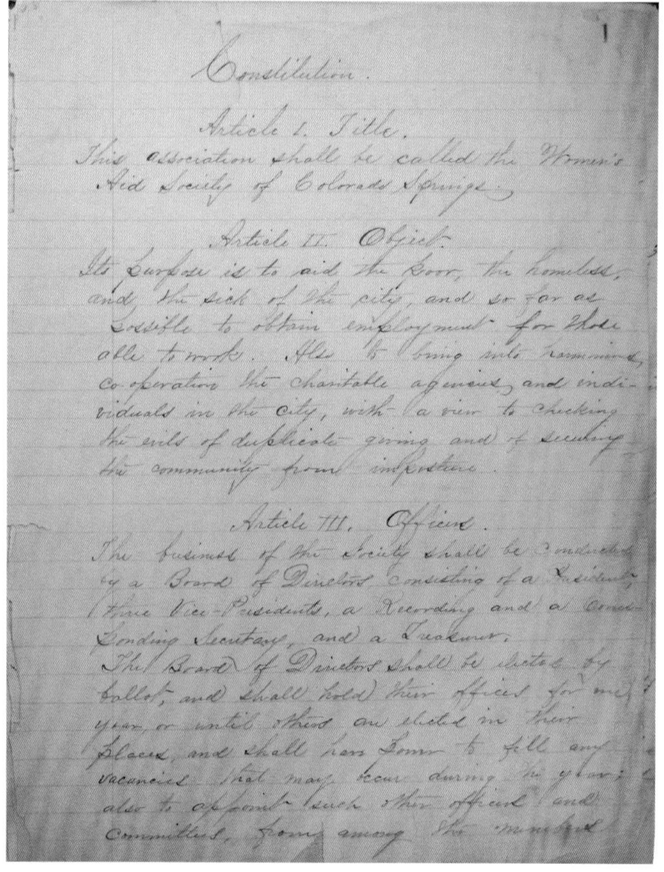

1

Constitution.

Article I. Title.

This association shall be called the Women's Aid Society of Colorado Springs.

Article II. Object.

Its purpose is to aid the poor, the homeless, and the sick of the city, and so far as possible to obtain employment for those able to work. Also to bring into harmonious co-operation the charitable agencies and individuals in the city, with a view to checking the evils of duplicate giving and of securing the community from imposture.

Article III. Officers.

The business of the Society shall be conducted by a Board of Directors consisting of a President, three Vice-Presidents, a Recording and a Corresponding Secretary, and a Treasurer.

The Board of Directors shall be elected by ballot, and shall hold their offices for one year, or until others are elected in their places, and shall have power to fill any vacancies that may occur during the year; also to appoint such other officers and committees, from among the members

The society underwent yet another reorganization in 1887 and its name changed to the "Women's Aid Society." Mrs. Wood remained as president and a lengthy constitution written up. In this document, the continuing evolvement of the organization can be seen, as well as its emphasis on finding work for its clients. The purpose of the society, notes Article II of the constitution, was " to aid the poor, the homeless and the sick of the city, and so far as possible to obtain employment for those able to work." The second half of that same article makes clear that the society viewed itself as the city's leading nonsectarian charity and intended to coordinate donation efforts and to protect the community from unscrupulous applicants. Or, as the constitution puts it, "to bring into harmonious cooperation the charitable agencies and individuals in the city, with a view to checking the evils of duplicate giving and of securing the community from imposture."

The board of directors included a president, three vice presidents, a recording secretary, a corresponding secretary and a treasurer. Memberships were open to anyone in the city. Annual dues were one dollar and a $25 donation constituted a "life membership." There were a number of standing committees, including a visiting committee, finance committee, registration committee, clothing and sewing committee, committee on printing and committee on employment.

The members of the visiting committee were to investigate each applicant, determine if aid was needed, and provide moral support to the families. "Members of the Visiting Committee shall endeavor to see each poor family personally, not only providing for bodily wants, but as far as possible offering sympathy and

Facing page: Building at northeast corner of Tejon and Pikes Peak Avenue. 1901.
(Century Chest)

THE ROBINSON DRUG CO.
Only One Night Out
Buffet and Dining Cars
PRESCRIPTIONS
A SPECIALTY.
CIGARS.
POSTAL TELEGRAPH-CABLE CO.
RESTAURANT
TAILOR

kindness." The employment committee was to "receive applications from those seeking employment, and aid them as far as possible in securing it." And the sewing committee was charged with making clothing from donated materials and organizing a sewing club if they so desired.

The dues-paying members of the society were a virtual Who's Who of Colorado Springs society. Participants included Mrs. Wood, Mrs. Howbert, Mr. and Mrs. Lennox, Mrs. Solly, and Mrs. France. Also represented were Mrs. Orlando Metcalf, whose husband was a Pittsburgh steel baron; Mrs. L. R. Ehrich, whose husband was a wealthy New Yorker and had a fine collection of Dutch and Flemish paintings at his home on North Cascade Avenue; Mrs. Joel Hayes, the daughter of Confederate president Jefferson Davis; Alice Cogswell Bemis, whose New England husband had made a fortune in the manufacture of textile bags, and Miss E. A. Crowell, the sister of pioneer Benjamin Crowell, El Paso County's first treasurer and longtime business partner of Irving Howbert.

Benjamin Crowell, writes Howbert, was undoubtedly "the man who exercised the greatest influence in El Paso County affairs from the time that he arrived in Colorado City in 1860 to the end of his life. " The son of a sea captain, Crowell had been born in 1835 at Manchester-by-the-Sea, Massachusetts, and headed west during the Colorado gold rush of 1859 after "his health had become somewhat impaired." Howbert and Crowell and a man named J.F. Humphrey invested in a silver mine in Leadville called the Robert E. Lee. When they struck a fabulous vein of ore, they built a small house over the shaft, erected a barricade and personally stood guard over it for several months. With some of the profits, the trio then teamed up to build the Colorado Springs Opera House on Tejon Street.

In 1888, the society was in good financial shape, taking in $1,237, which included $356 in membership dues, $630 from the proceeds of a concert, and about $110 from local churches. It expended roughly $63 for coal; $133 for groceries; $13.50 for medicine; $26.50 for dry goods and $45 for the room rent of Miss Keep, who apparently oversaw the storeroom where the donated goods were kept. Many requests for help were coming from young men and the society's board of directors voted to confer with the YMCA to see what could be done. It had been paying seven dollars a week to hire nurses for the poor, but the practice had depleted the treasury and the members voted to stop it.

Mrs. Wood's long tenure was coming to an end and in a paper entitled "Work Among the Poor," she wrote of the young schoolteacher and the freighter with the badly frozen arm. "The object of the society then, as now, was to lend a helping hand when sickness or any calamity befell a family and destitution followed, and also to provide some way that the poor be able to assist themselves. In some instances my trouble in their behalf has been rewarded; in others it has been a signal failure." While writing her paper, Mrs. Wood's eye was caught by a lovely ruby-colored vase that she had recently taken out of storage and placed on a shelf. Shaped like a jug, it caught and refracted the rays of sunlight. "To this little jug there hangs a tale of sadness and distress which had almost passed from my memory," she began:

> With its return came the remembrance of a severe winter day, a miserable, cheerless room, a bed with a sick woman lying upon it and an infant beside her and several other children near. Only for the kindness of a poor washer woman, who gave the clothes from her own bed and flannel that her own children used, I think they must have frozen. I attended to their wants and when the mother was again able to minister to the wants of the family, the husband, a delicate man, was taken frightfully ill with pneumonia. Still they lived through all this trying season and when the father recovered, work was procured for him. One day when going to see them a little girl of eight years of age ran to meet me and placed this ruby jug in my hands. I did not like to take it from her as I thought it must have been some cherished memento of former days, but she seemed so distressed with my refusal that I took it home with me.

The following year, the society voted once more to change its name, this time to the Colorado Springs Aid Society. Mrs. Wood, who would have been about 70 years old, was in poor health and relinquished the presidency. She would die five years later from pneumonia.

5

The Invalid's Wife

In 1890, a commanding woman named Anna Osborne Hagerman became the new president of the Colorado Springs Aid Society. She was handsome in a dark, austere way, with a straight brow, determined mouth, and hair parted down the middle and pulled tightly back from her forehead. Anna was the wife of an extremely wealthy railroad builder and mine owner named James John Hagerman. Like D. Russ Wood, he was a Canadian and had come to Colorado Springs because he had tuberculosis.

Mrs. Hagerman had two sons who were required to attend church on Sunday and read the Bible in straight-backed chairs when they came home. Afterward they would take a trip to the cemetery where their father would warn them, "That's where you end up." Before they succumbed to that fate, one would become a prominent businessman and the other would go on to serve as governor of New Mexico.

Anna Hagerman was a member of the society's finance committee during Mrs. Wood's final years as president. Upon assuming the presidency, Mrs. Hagerman demonstrated a tough-mindedness and lack of sentimentality that was equal to her husband's. When a woman on Willamette Street died, her destitute husband, a former Union soldier, asked the aid society to advance him $15 so he could buy his wife a shroud. "Agent consulted Mrs. Hagerman – President – who decided that we must use what funds we have for the living and that it would be unwise for us to establish a precedent of that nature."

As always, there were pockets of poverty in Colorado Springs and the newspaper reported that there was an "unusual amount" of suffering due to the influx of farmers fleeing a drought in the Midwest. For many people in Colorado Springs, it was a time of great prosperity. Electric lights had been introduced and there were 79 subscribers to telephones. The resort hotels were filled with fashionable invalids. The railroads were building again and thick veins of silver had been discovered in Leadville. On Tejon Street, customers could order manicures, facial massages and scalp treatments. Umbrellas trimmed with ivory or pearl sold for five dollars at a store on Bijou Street.

The Hagermans built a showplace at 610 North Cascade Avenue, which one author said made General Palmer's residence resemble a "gardener's cottage." Winfield Scott Stratton, gloomier than ever over his inability to find gold, was recruited to do the woodwork and cabinetry. The library, drawing room, dining room and bedrooms were constructed with different woods, including oak, maple and mahogany. The hallway was ornately carved and the exterior walls constructed from peach blow sandstone.

Anna Hagerman, president of aid society. 1890s.
(Colorado Room Information Files, Colorado College Special Collections)

James John Hagerman had begun his career as a clerk in a Michigan shipyard, which built sidewall steamers that plowed the Great Lakes. He met Anna on the *B.F. Wade* and they married and settled in Milwaukee. He rose through the ranks of the shipbuilding firm and eventually invested in a mining company that owned rich deposits of iron, which were in great demand by railroad builders. In a few years, he was a millionaire and counted among his friends such nineteenth-century moguls as Andrew Carnegie, Henry Phipps and Russell Sage.

In 1882, at the age of 44, he began hemorrhaging and was diagnosed with tuberculosis. "I was a sick man during all that busy time. I never saw a well day from start to finish," he remembered. Hagerman sailed for Europe with Anna and the two boys. He consulted a leading tuberculosis specialist in London and then traveled to a renowned clinic in Davos, Switzerland. The family spent winter months on the French Riviera and summered in the Swiss and Austrian Alps. In 1884, they returned to the United States, sold their Michigan home, and headed for Colorado Springs. Hagerman was unimpressed with the so-called Sarasota of the West:

> The town was as dead as Julius Caesar. The old-timers were blue and discouraged. There was no business worth mentioning and little hope for the future. Real estate could be bought for a song. The deposits in the two little banks were insignificant and few of their loans could be collected. Although I liked the climate the town was so depressingly dead that we almost decided to try Denver, but we finally made up our minds to Colorado Springs, believing it to be the best place from a health standpoint.

Small, blunt-spoken and bearded, Hagerman was an irritant to General Palmer and the town's old guard as he flung himself about town in a shawl and hot pepper plaster. "A rich, ambitious, restless invalid," sniffed Philadelphia blue blood William S. Jackson. Hagerman retorted that Jackson had a mind "that conformed to the narrow gauge" of Palmer's railroad.

"He cared nothing for society or for any frivolous amusements," Percy Hagerman wrote of his father. "Such leisure as he had during a life of incessant work was given over mostly to serious reading. He surrounded himself with good books in beautiful bindings and with attractive pictures, which he owned not as a fad, but because he loved them." Though Hagerman had little use for religion, he had a strong belief in a Supreme Being, the son added. As Hagerman's health began to improve, he found the idleness "irksome" and plunged back into mining. " The air was full of stories of new mines, he liked mining, and the first things in which he became interested were some mining ventures in Leadville and Aspen," his son wrote.

By the mid-1880s, Hagerman had also assumed the presidency of the Colorado Midland Railway Company. The initial plans called for the railroad to go up Ute Pass, cross the Continental Divide, and then head toward Salt Lake City and the Pacific Coast. Not surprisingly, the building of the Colorado Midland sparked a bitter turf battle with the narrow-gauge Denver and Rio Grande, which Palmer had lost control of some years earlier due to the machinations of Jay Gould. Hagerman induced Sir William Lidderdale, the Governor of the Bank of England to become an investor, as well as pioneers Irving Howbert and Benjamin Crowell and others.

The passenger cars were well built and luxurious. The drawing rooms were finished in mahogany, the smoking rooms in English oak, the ceilings of richly decorated white wood. The seats were upholstered in maroon and gold plush and the floors covered with thick carpets. The trimmings were silver-plated and the passenger cars warmed by small heaters placed in closets lined with incombustible material. "The windows are unusually large, so as to give the best possible view of the scenery in passing," the newspaper added.

"The Colorado Midland was an epic effort to defy the laws of gravity," writes author Marshall Sprague. "And the crowning wonder was that the Midland was slammed through by the sheer driving will of a very small and very sick man who had come to Pikes Peak to die." Sprague, a TB sufferer and town booster himself, glosses over the human suffering that occurred during the building of the Colorado Midland. The environment was so punishing that the railroad in 1887 opened a hospital on West Colorado Avenue for its hordes of ailing laborers.

James John Hagerman was a feisty businessman who sought to recover his health in the Springs.
(Colorado Room Information Files, Colorado College Special Collections)

Dr. Anderson was named chief surgeon. During one horrific railroad accident, seven men were killed outright and another 60 injured.

Hagerman sold the railroad in 1890 to the Atchison, Topeka and Santa Fe at a price, which "let him and every other investor who cared to participate out at a substantial profit," wrote Percy Hagerman. "My father was the largest stockholder in this as in nearly every other enterprise in which he was ever interested. He never asked a friend or investor to put any money into a scheme which he was not backing heavily with his own money. He also stood to win or lose more than anyone else. He was glad to get out of the Midland as the work of carrying it on was too heavy a strain and too much of his fortune was at stake in it."

From left, unidentified man, George Buckman, Irving Howbert, James John Hagerman and Mrs. Charles Noble, on first run of the Shortline Railroad. March 23, 1901. (CSPM)

Hagerman turned his attention to the difficult problem of de-watering a silver mine in Aspen called the Mollie Gibson. As the miners plunged deeper, they discovered silver of such purity that they were awestruck. "It was a sensational strike, probably the richest silver ore ever shipped in such quantity from any mine in the United States," Percy Hagerman wrote. Within a year, the mining company paid off debts, purchased additional property and paid out $1 million in dividends. A third of the profits went to Hagerman. The rest went to investors. "Colorado Springs people, familiar with the history of the place, all feel a deep sense of gratitude to Mr. J. J. Hagerman, to whom in late years it owes more of its prosperity than any other," wrote the *Gazette*.

While her husband focused on his railroad and mining ventures, Mrs. Hagerman continued with her charity work. To raise funds for the aid society, she organized a benefit concert that featured piano and violin solos and Verdi's "Storm King" sung by the Methodist church choir. "The exact amount realized from the entertainment has not been announced yet, but the rapid sale of tickets has assured the ladies of a neat little sum." Some influential new women were elected officers of the aid society. One was Mary Slocum, the wife of the Rev. William Frederick Slocum, president of Colorado College. The Slocums had met in the factory town of Amesbury, Massachusetts, where they had crusaded for better conditions for mill workers, who were mostly girls and young women from farms who worked in factories for 12 hours a day or longer. Another new officer was Mrs. Mary Needham Gregg, the wife of the Rev. James Bartlett Gregg, a Harvard-educated trustee of Colorado College, and pastor from 1882 until 1909 of the First Congregational Church. The Rev. Gregg arrived for his job interview in the middle of a snowstorm, encountered another snowstorm during a drive in Cheyenne Canyon, fought a bitter wind returning to town and waded through a foot of snow to get back to the depot. Despite the inclement weather, he liked Colorado Springs and eventually accepted the job. His challenge, upon arriving in town, was to find a place to live. "There was no room large enough to put our piano; none high enough to set our bed, or large enough to contain my library."

Day after day, people knocked on the society's door asking for help. On Dec. 22, 1890, a young man named William Clune came looking for clothing. A society official described him as "hard-looking," but nevertheless gave him a coat and advised him to look for work. The Church family, who lived on Rio Grande Street, was grappling with typhoid fever. Family members were given clothing and fresh bedding and the charity tried unsuccessfully to find light work for the eldest son.

Mrs. Janery, who resided on Kiowa Street, had lost her husband a few months earlier. She had three children and was desperate to find work. "Seems a superior case – woman has evidently seen better days." The aid society found her work as a washerwoman. "She does her work nicely but is not always prompt about sending work home or calling for it."

To better acquaint the public with its efforts, the society began publishing monthly statistics in the newspaper. During the month of January 1891, 42 families had been aided and four had been turned away after being deemed "unworthy." Temporary employment was found for 10 people, permanent employment for four others, and two people had been furnished transportation to the homes of relatives who could care for them. Roughly 178 garments and 12 pair of shoes were distributed. Twenty cases, or nearly half of the monthly caseload, involved illness.

In a large public gathering held in the Methodist Church, a Mrs. Jacobs made a "stirring address" and urged the organization to create a central office and hire a professional "agent." "This method, having long been thought desirable, but impossible from lack of purse was after this meeting made possible by the election of seven gentlemen to act as an advisory board and assist in the raising of money," the newspaper reported.

The society took possession of Room 22 of the Bank Block and hired Louise Schnapp, who had five years of experience working for charities in New York City. Miss Schnapp was a highly opinionated woman who turned away many able-bodied men who knocked at the door because she thought they were "imposters." The society's officers nevertheless approved of her approach. "I think there are none of us but feel that this was a wise movement and are satisfied that all calls have been promptly, justly and kindly attended and that imposters have been discovered and to a large extent baffled," wrote Mrs. Charles Eldredge, recording secretary.

The Rev. William F. Slocum was president of Colorado College and his wife, Mary, was active in the charity. (Colorado Room Information Files, Colorado College Special Collections)

Miss Schnapp was a whirlwind of activity. In the first nine months of 1891, she wrote, 673 visits had been made; 163 families had been assisted; employment found for 107 people; 93 sick patients aided; 1,261 garments distributed; six people admitted to hospitals; five nurses provided; four people received transportation to relatives; 15 cases were found to be unworthy of aid, and 58 single men were sent to the wood yard to work for board and lodging.

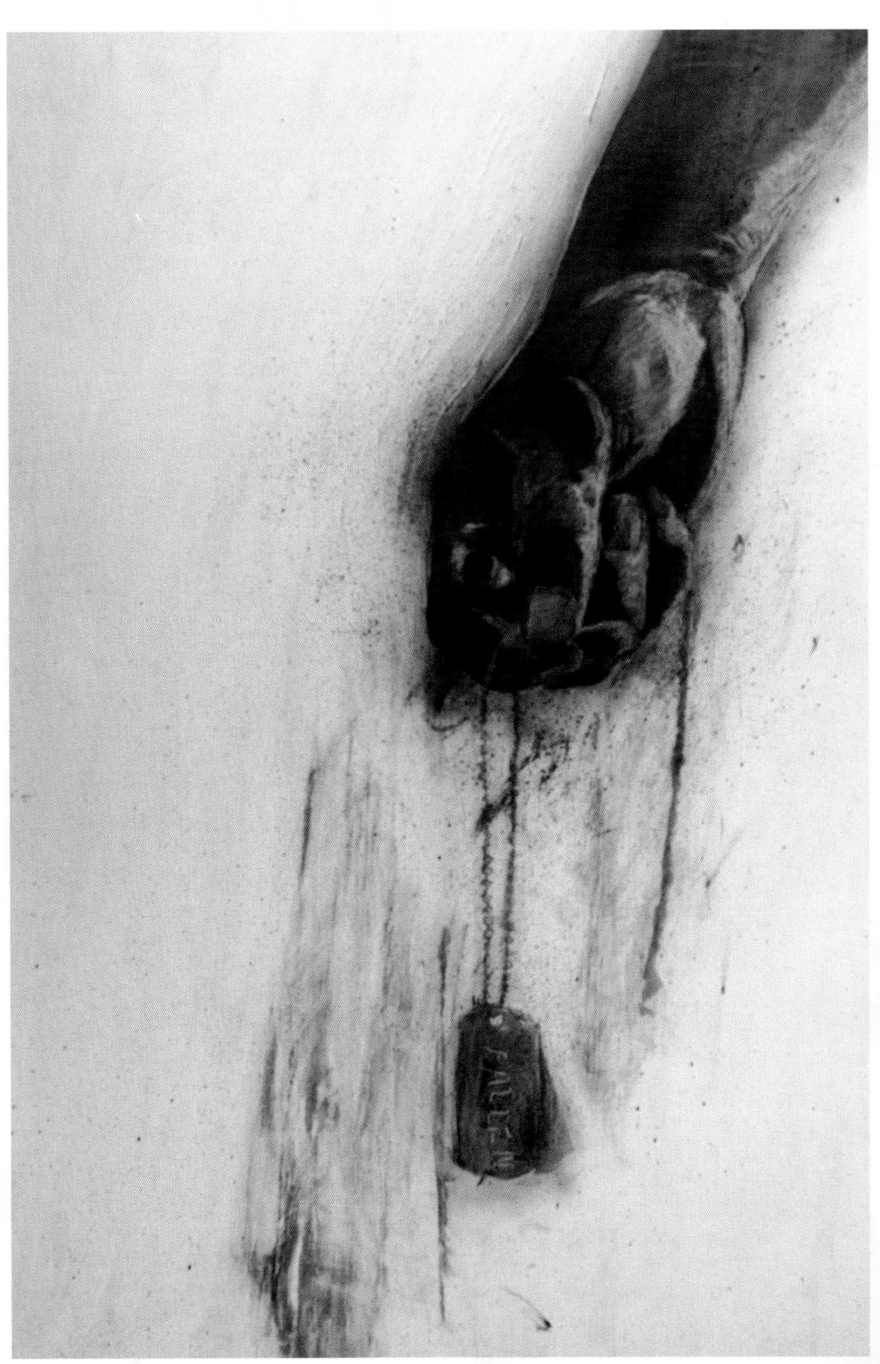

War Re-Imagined

Nothing is so terrifying as a blank canvas, except maybe filling it and seeing war made visible. Week in and week out, in studios spattered with paint, soldiers confront anger, guilt, and pain they've carried from tours in Iraq, Afghanistan or Vietnam. When they begin to put those emotions onto the canvas, healing seeps in. "I am able to see the invisible being healed," said Isaac Torres, an Iraq veteran, at a 2012 AspenPointe event called Spotlight on Hope.

The artist-soldiers include former snipers, sappers, pilots, and Humvee drivers. They might be suffering from combat-related post-traumatic stress disorder, traumatic brain injury, the loss of a friend to suicide, or even sexual assault. On one afternoon, the group included a young medic, who suffered from rage attacks and blackouts. Another was a former drone aircraft operator who was being "med-boarded" from the Army. His buddy, who was still in Afghanistan, had committed suicide the day before.

Expressing buried feelings can be explosive, cathartic and scary. Fortunately, they have an experienced person to guide them: Kim Le Nguyen, AspenPointe's Creative Expressions Program Manager. A talented artist in her own right, Nguyen grew up in war-torn Vietnam and knows the binding power of old ghosts. "The mind is so complex," she said. "The art is something tangible with their wound, their stress, their nightmare. It's something they can hold onto and say, 'I'm broken here.'"

Nguyen conducts art therapy classes for Fort Carson soldiers at Colorado Springs' Fine Arts Center. She also helped establish an art therapy program for veterans at the Cottonwood Center for the Arts in a partnership with the Colorado Springs Vet Center, a specialty mental health clinic sponsored by the U.S. Department of Veterans Affairs Readjustment Counseling Services. "Painting is like dreaming," she said. "When you go to war, you experience extreme trauma. Your body and your memory and your psyche hold it. Your dreams try to balance it. That's why you have nightmares. The art takes images from the dreams and makes them visible."

When Saigon fell in 1975 and the Viet Cong marched into the city, Nguyen's father, a soldier in the South Vietnamese army, removed his uniform and ran back to

Kim Le Nguyen, Creative Expressions Program Manager

his family, who were hiding in a foxhole in the barracks. The family packed everything they owned onto a Honda scooter and headed south toward a fishing village where relatives lived. When they got there, the village was chaotic and partially abandoned and smelled of dead fish. They moved into an empty house where they stayed for eight months while the family plotted its escape. On Dec. 19, 1975, Nguyen and her family left on a boat with about twenty other people. In the middle of the ocean a storm blew up and the boat's engine died. "It was December. We were all wet and cold. They tried to fix the engine. They gave up and went up to put up the sails."

A huge wave knocked her father overboard. All the passengers, including 13-year-old Nguyen, rushed to the side of the boat. They were screaming and crying. Someone shined a light and she could see her father's head. He was wearing an Army coat and boots. Then three huge waves rose and fell between the drowning man and the boat. "Just three waves and we couldn't see him anymore."

Amid the wailing and crying, her mother told the children to say their contrition prayer and prepare to die. But Nguyen had the childish notion that since God had already taken her father, he would spare the rest of them. For a long time, she hoped that another boat would pick him up and that some day the family would be reunited. But that was not to be. On Christmas Day of 1975, they landed in Malaysia. After months there, eventually they were allowed to immigrate to California. Nguyen learned English and went on to college. She had a knack for painting and drawing,

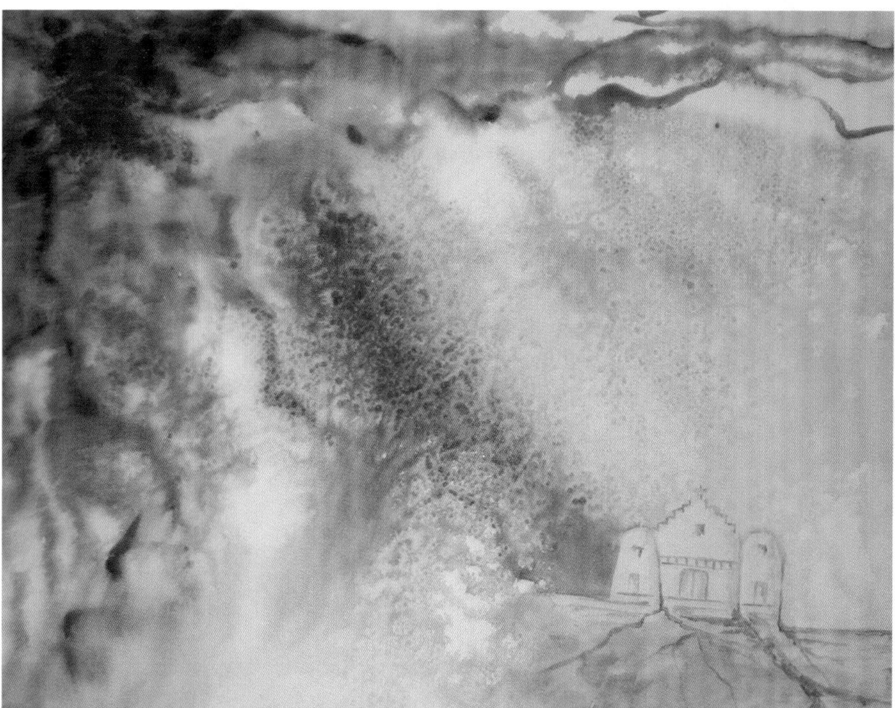

and made images of herself lying in a coffin. During one of her classes, an art therapist made a presentation and she realized she had been doing therapy on herself. "I was expressing my depression, my grief, my loss," she said. She subsequently went to Louisiana State University where she got a master's degree in art therapy.

In the classes for the soldiers, Nguyen usually begins by demonstrating some sort of technique and then gives the students a project to work on. At the conclusion of the class, she will interpret the artwork. That's often when the important stuff happens. One student was a former sniper who had done three tours, beginning with a peacekeeping mission in Kosovo. He had developed paranoia, guilt, and anger. He painted a picture with some white in it. Nguyen interpreted the white as his desire to return to innocence. The interpretation was accurate and he opened up and told his story, how he saw himself as a hero assigned to protect women and children and wound up becoming a monster. "I wanted to hug him. I wanted to protect him. But how can I protect him from the nightmares?"

Some of the artists have discovered that they have genuine talent and are now showing their work in galleries or attending art school. Nguyen said she and the soldiers together put on about 20 shows a year. Once a piece is done, oftentimes a soldier doesn't want to see it again and donates it to the program. The art can be provocative, dark and edgy. Sometimes the pieces sell and sometimes they don't. "People like pleasant looking paintings. A lot of those paintings express raw emotions."

t. St.
unter
Smith #710 W. Pikes Peak
clothing
el
ion Coal & Ice Co.)

~~Sante Fe Row~~
of Clothing

Fe Row.
thing
and clean

Rio Grande
iseases and
er past record
ndicate her
Mrs. J. Lennox

Newman Mrs Susan, (colored) Feb 12 – #6 Sante Fe Row.

The Agent found Mrs N. out at work, (Monday is the only day she has any regular work); found the daughter Zella (aged 14) the one who applied at the rooms Feby. 9 – at home with the two smallest children – (the two oldest boys, aged 12 and 10 respectively attending the Liller school). The house was upside down and uncleanly; they had very little food, but secured sufficient fuel along the R.R. tracks.

The Agt. reminded the girl that if the ladies should call and find the house so unclean, there would be little disposition to help them until they made better use of their brooms. The agent called half-hour later to see if his advice had any effect and found a decided improvement. The girl (Zella) is an unusually bright colored girl and should either be in school or be in some home where she would be taught "how to do". There are conflicting reports about this family but considering the fact that the mother works when she can and keeps two boys in school, the agent is of the opinion she should receive some further aid.

Feb. 14 – Sent them an order of groceries, a sack of potatoes, and gave them a reference to #204 N. Weber St. where a second girl was wanted.

Feby. 17 – Mrs. N. asked for some old clothes for children – gave her several (10) small pieces – under and outer garments.

Sinclair. Mrs. M. C. Feb. 12. #13(?) Arlington St. (mar. Willamette (?))

Mrs. Called and asked for shoes for herself and

6

Chronicles of the Poor

Rich and poor alike suffered from ill health in Colorado Springs, but the poor suffered more. They were the largely invisible army of workers who kept the town running and left no trace when they were gone. Their ranks included a Civil War veteran who foraged for watercress on the railroad tracks, a red-knuckled washerwoman who had lost her husband and was prematurely aged from having so many children, a youth who shoveled coal into the boilers in the basement of the Antlers Hotel, a young Irish woman who cleared the table in the dining room of a mansion on Cascade Avenue.

The suffering of the wealthy was ameliorated by doting servants who ironed their clothing, cleaned their homes, saddled their horses, drove their carriages, stoked their furnaces, and prepared nourishing meals rich in protein and dairy products. When the pain was too great, they summoned the elegant Dr. Solly to administer derivatives of opium. "They possessed the means to enjoy expensive leisure or luxurious ill health and they had no interest in regular employment," writes author Marshall Sprague.

By contrast, impoverished families tried to nurse each other and physicians were called only when death was imminent. The poor were exposed to more industrial poisons, more dangerous machinery and more contaminated water and food. They also contracted infectious diseases like tuberculosis, typhoid, smallpox, scarlet fever, and whooping cough more frequently. Some lived in canvas tents that rented for six dollars a month, others in two-room shacks that rented for $10 to $15 a month. They were often hungry and cold. Wives died during childbirth. Husbands deserted. Children who did not succumb to diseases were often sent to orphanages.

The men were ice cutters, cheese makers, paperhangers, bricklayers, carpenters, cooks, cobblers, hostlers, cigar makers, hay cutters and wagon drivers. The women were laundresses, cooks, servants, dressmakers, milliners, nurses, teachers and boarding-home operators. Three of the aid society's bound ledgers from the 1890s have survived and the perilous lives of the city's poor are recorded on their pages.

When an individual applied for aid, food and fuel and clothing were provided immediately. Then a thorough investigation was undertaken. This often included talking with neighbors and examining cupboards to make sure the applicants weren't "imposters." Oftentimes, if a resident was discovered hiding a

"Young unmarried man – boilermaker by trade – but willing to do any kind of work. Rather neatly dressed and of rather pleasing manner and appearance. Referred him to Y. M. C. A. – Employment Bureau."

couple of chickens in the backyard or were overly presumptuous in their demands, aid was withheld.

Only the "worthy poor" got help. But figuring out who, exactly, was worthy was often a subjective decision. Miss Schnapp often based her decision on physical appearances. Women who were "peculiar," smelled of "liquor," or were "untidy," were viewed with suspicion. Men who were "impertinent" or "hard looking" faced the same scrutiny. By contrast, if the applicant had a "good honest face" or was "modest in manner," aid was often forthcoming.

The organization helped one man land a janitor's job at the *Gazette,* procured for another a part-time position with Irving Howbert, got a third man hired on as a hostler at General Palmer's Glen Eyrie estate, and procured yard work for a fourth. The society also found pupils for a woman who gave music lessons and employment for other women as laundresses and nurses.

In May of 1891, Miss Schnapp paid a visit to a couple who lived in the 600 block of East Willamette Street. The man had been a soldier in the Union Army and the woman had suffered some type of paralysis, which may have been caused by a stroke or what was referred to at the time as apoplexy. "Woman acts as though she were under the influence of some drug or liquor or as though she were weak-minded," she wrote. One physician recommended the woman be sent to an asylum but the husband would not hear of it. Finally the man was referred to Dr. Strickler "with the view of having wife removed to county hospital, or sent East to her people. Dr. Strickler refused to act, however – sent man off." When the couple was evicted for not paying rent, the husband pawned his silverware and rented a tent in the south part of town. The wife's health continued to deteriorate and she died at the end of the month.

That same month, Miss Schnapp paid a visit to another Civil War veteran named Warren Kneeland and his wife. Mr. Warren, she wrote, was a "most reputable and intelligent man" who had sustained partial paralysis while serving in the Civil War. His wife, Martha, was extremely ill. "Old lady found to be very sick when visited – in sort of stupor – does not look as if she could possibly live – too sick to move – in a few days case will be decided one way or another." The society supplied the couple with a half-ton of coal, made arrangements for medicine, and brought in a woman to care for Martha. Eventually a son was located in California who said he would be happy to take in the couple. A donor offered to loan them $50 and the society put up an additional $14 – enough to purchase two, one-way tickets to California. Before leaving, Mr. Warren promised to pay back the money when he received his back pay and pension from the Grand Army of the Republic. Miss Schnapp saw the couple off on a 4:10 train. "Man had promised faithfully to write us upon his arrival in California but not a word has been heard from him yet."

Not long after this, an Englishman named John Heathcote rapped at the door. He was a former clergyman fresh off the train from Denver and smelled of alcohol. "Looks dissipated – has vile odor about his person. Agent offered him work in Wood Yard, by which he could earn his meals and lodging – but he decided not to trouble the Soc'y any further. Left office – came back in about an hour – said he had found work but would need heavy flannel shirts to do it in! Wanted to know if we could give him some. Agent saw at once that it was all a ruse to raise money for drink and refused the shirts – and again offered Wood Yard work – which man refused."

James and Stella McKinney, who lived at 107 E. Cimarron Street, were plagued by sickness and bad luck. Stella was a consumptive and James, who had a "tendency to consumption," had been sick with the grippe. The couple was dependent upon their fourteen-year-old daughter, Carrie, who earned $15 a month carrying messages for the Western Union Telegraph Company. Unfortunately, the daughter had come down with the measles and the family was penniless. "They left their home in Nevada City, Missouri, three years ago to seek health in the West but lost everything traveling about from place to place," wrote Miss Schnapp. The family was sent groceries and medicines and eventually the money was raised for a railroad ticket to send the wife back to Missouri, where she died a few months later.

Alexander Walsh, who was 17 years old, had lost both legs when he was nine during a railroad accident. He lived alone and had been earning two to three dollars a week selling newspapers. Now he wanted to go to school. School officials were willing to provide him with free books, but estimated that Alexander would need an additional $1.50 a week for living expenses. A school official wrote the aid society and asked if it would be willing to help out. "The ladies have decided that we cannot, as a society take up the case as there is no destitution and the matter is entirely an educational one," wrote Miss Schnapp. Fortunately, some local officials helped raised six dollars – enough for one month's schooling – and the youth was "doing very nicely."

Mrs. M.A. Sinclair, a washerwoman, had gotten in trouble with the Humane Society for failing to feed a "wretched looking" horse that she drove about town. Mrs. Sinclair, who had four small children at home, claimed she was too poor to feed the horse. So the charity sent her groceries and also 100 pounds of oats for the horse." Following are other excerpts from the ledger books:

January 2, 1891. D. E. Sherrod and wife, 709 S. Weber Street. Both husband and wife are deaf mute. 3 children – all of who can speak and hear. Man once owned a large shoe store and was well to do; boot and rubber factories have ruined his business...have placed woman's name on our Employment List and brought case to attention of Mrs. France Ch'man Ward 3 – who has decided that case is one for aid by way of work only.

Jan. 10, 1891. Vandener family. Tent at Rio Grande and South Weber. Husband has been ill – but no better. Mrs. France has made inquiries in town as to man's record and finds it good. She reports that man thinks he could get work in some barbershop if his clothes were good. Agent will send him some clothes and Mrs. France has ordered ¼ ton of coal for them. Jan. 13 – Gave man a suit of clothes, some white shirts, and woman a pair of shoes and a warm wrap. Jan. 15. Agent found that man has been promised work in a short time and woman has secured cleaning of 4 rooms and 2 halls at P. U – which will bring her in $22 per month. Case now self-supporting.

Jan. 22, 1891. Edward Gearity, North Tejon Street. Came here from Kansas City night before last – young unmarried man – boilermaker by trade – but willing to do any kind of work. Rather neatly dressed and of rather pleasing manner and appearance. Referred him to the Y.M.C.A.—Employment Bureau.

Jan. 27, 1891. Barney family...woman has inflammatory rheumatism...Mrs. Buckman has herself sent beef for beef tea and Mrs. Solly will send one of her girls to help them with the work of getting their house in order. Feb. 18th...man has put up a little shop on back of lot and has found some odd jobs at carpentering—but not much of anything as yet. Need coal very badly...Eldest boy earns a little selling papers...man found work for a time at $3.00 and wife is going out regularly once more to work.

Feb. 2, 1891. Ayres family. Woman came to say husband still idle. Has tried everyplace for work – but without success. They are now destitute. Woman has pawned her watch and other things. They manage about fuel by picking up on RR track – but need food. Woman cannot do any work at present. Has a heavy cold – sore throat and chest and will be confined in March...March 9. Called – found man still at work on Prospect Lake, now Nettie very bad with St. Vitus dance—needs constant attention.

Feb. 16 1891. John Taylor. 18 years old. Came with ticket from Mr. Willard – 18 East Kiowa Street to whom he had applied for aid. Says he left his home in Rockford, Ill. – 3 months ago – to try life in the West. Has been through Texas, Arizona and other states – could find no work and has now come down to the level of a common tramp – but has a good face and it is evident that there is much good in him; he only asks work in order to get enough money to return to his mother in a respectable condition. Agent gave him a note to take to Glass Works and other places – ask for work for boy – who is willing to work for board and lodging at present; Promised in note to fit boy out with decent clothes – if a line were sent to the effect that employment – will be given him. Boy returned same day with a few lines from Mrs. Rice, of Home Restaurant – Colo. City – in which she offers the lad work for his board and lodging for the present and intimates, that, if he, proves honest and trustworthy– there will be an opening for him in a week or two when he will receive regular wages. Agent provided him with a complete outfit of clothing, as clothes he has are filthy and only fit to be burned up. Gave him some good advice and trust the lad has learned a valuable lesson. Feb. 21st—Agent called on Mrs. Rice and learned that the lad never returned to her for the work! Case should be reported in the papers and people be warned against the fellow.

April 6, 1891. Andrew Ross – single – no home. Same old story –wandering about country -- wanted shoes and clothing.

April 11, 1891. Thomas Foster – single – homeless – just out of County Jail – asked very boldly for trousers and shirts – and was most inclined to be impudent when refused; evidently accustomed to begging and seemed to think he had a divine right to be cared for by others. Offered him work in Wood Yard – took note – but went off muttering – very plain that it was not work he wanted.

Sept. 23, 1891. Mrs. Prudence Gilliam, Pine Street and Sherman. Came from Denver where she lived twenty years...She was rather bold and forward in manner and had a very disagreeable peculiarity about the eyes – a way of closing them and not looking one straight in the face; she claims that she is not strong and only capable of doing day's work...received word from Denver that woman is a "common pauper" – has been receiving aid from county since '84...Some years ago she adopted 2 children from the Co. Hospital – a boy and girl and these have been her stock in trade; she used to send them out begging and when she found that steps were being taken to prove her unworthy of her charge – she did better. She was at last refused aid by the Denver Charitable societies and now she is trying a new field.

May 26, 1892. Moses and Rosanna Burleyson. Alley off East Kiowa St. Mayor Sprague reported man very sick – not expected to live. Agent called at once – found Dr. Strickler attending him; wife said they are not in need of aid now – have plenty of coal – and groceries, too – she thinks she will take him home to Missouri to die – she has also written to his people for money for that purpose. May 31st. Sent some groceries on 28th – neighbors having reported them destitute of provisions. June 1st. Man died at 1 p.m. today; man's brother arrives from Mo. Tomorrow and remains are to be shipped to Missouri; wife and child go also. Agent furnished her with a pair of shoes and two pairs of stockings.

July 23, 1892. Christian family, back of 317 E. Willamette, wife and six small children, just buried two others who died with diphtheria – 3 more now down with it. Wife expects confinement soon. Very poor—but said to be honest and industrious and worthy. Man has had to give up his work; neighbors have been aiding and they are only in need of bedding – as so much of what they had was burned by doctor's orders.

Written in the Books

The story of Colorado Springs -- and to some degree the larger story of the settlement of the West-- can be read in the leather-bound casebooks of the Colorado Springs Aid Society. Three casebooks from the 1890s have survived and are sitting in the Pikes Peak Library District's Special Collections. There are two small casebooks and a much larger and heavier casebook that probably remained in the office. The entries are written in long-hand, probably with quill pens in rooms illuminated by gas lights and heated with coal. They represent just a small portion of the four feet of documents that make up a collection called the Pikes Peak Family Counseling and Mental Health Center, a precursor to AspenPointe. Other items in this rich collection include donor lists and minutes from the early meetings, as well as scrapbooks, newspaper clippings, and annual reports dating back to 1880s.

Leafing through the casebooks is like looking directly into the past – a time in Colorado Springs and elsewhere – when a Dickens-like poverty existed alongside opulent wealth. In the nineteenth century, the city's affluent women kept the organization alive. Meetings were often postponed because of the frigid weather or lack of a quorum. On Nov. 26, 1887, a handwritten entry states, "The afternoon being very cold, only a few ladies were present and the meeting was adjourned to the following Saturday." Oftentimes the meetings resembled religious services. A local minister frequently gave an address followed by the singing of hymns, the recitation of Scripture, and the reading of papers or poems.

An "agent," roughly equivalent to a modern-day social worker, was hired around 1890 and followed a family's progress for several years and recorded their troubles. The McGrath family was typical. "She is decidedly English. He is of Irish parentage," the agent wrote of the couple. Mr. McGrath was a carpenter by trade who at one time was employed at General Palmer's Glen Eyrie. He had come to Colorado Springs for his health and no doubt had tuberculosis. During one visit, the agent found their home to be surprisingly tidy. "Although the furnishing was scant everything was in excellent condition and from outside of house would have thought there was every comfort within." Unable to find work, Mr. McGrath drowned his troubles in drink. On Feb. 27, 1891, the agent wrote, "McGrath was brought home beastly drunk on Saturday night last – having spent his entire week's wages for drink. Children without food – family completely destitute." Three of the five children were placed in an orphanage, but were returned home a few months later. Eventually the local authorities cobbled together money for train tickets to send the family to New York where the man hoped to find work. Dr. Strickler gave them a $13 ticket to Chicago, a friend pitched in $5, the mother sold her furniture for $20, the relief organization donated $7, and a railroad company gave them a half-rate fare, which left the family with exactly $1.25 for "incidentals" for the trip.

As recently as 1947, a roomful of the charity's documents still existed. That year, Mary Edmonds, who took over the organization following World War II, decided it was time to "thin" the collection. "Apparently this is the first time that such a sorting of these records has been attempted. So far she has gone thru the records of 4,000 cases," the newspaper reported. The article went on to say that records not deemed to be historically significant were to be burned.

Two decades later, Sharon Williams, a staff member at the mental health center, stumbled upon a cache of documents in an old shed behind the center's administration building on Eighth Street. Next, she received a tip that led her to a vacant house where a woman associated "with some charity mental health clinic" had once lived. "Searching through a mouse-infested closet, Ms. Williams found a battered, water-stained box and in it a score of historically valuable materials," the newspaper reported. "It was like a fairy tale," Williams exclaimed.

DRUGS
WHOLESALE & RETAIL

7

The Beauty and Burden of Gold

Winfield Scott Stratton was about 45 years old, white-haired and gaunt, when Fourth of July 1891 dawned bright and cool on Pikes Peak. He had had a vision in the night and as soon as the sun was up he rushed up a west-facing slope filled with briars and boulders and staked two claims, the Independence and the Washington, which would become two of the richest gold mines in U.S. history. Stratton would become wealthy, much too wealthy. "Too much money is not good for any man," he would later say.

With Stratton's discovery, Colorado's second gold rush began. Speculators and miners poured into the Springs from throughout the world. Within three years, 150 mines were operating in the Cripple Creek district. With gold production set to increase from $2 million to $120 million in the ensuing decade, the Springs economy boomed like never before, writes author Marshall Sprague. There were three separate mining exchanges. Bank deposits increased ninefold. Fifty new millionaires were minted. So many residents built homes along Wood Avenue that it became known as "Millionaires' Row," Sprague goes on to say. William Lennox and his wife, Anna Belle, also built a palatial new home, but theirs was located at the northeast corner of Yampa Street and Nevada Avenue. "It is the finest house in Colorado Springs and the most beautiful. It cost, with furniture, seventy thousand dollars," Anna Belle wrote. That would translate to more than $1.7 million today.

Facing page: North view on Tejon Street between Huerfano Street and Pikes Peak Avenue. 1901. (Century Chest)

Winfield S. Stratton

The mine owners from Colorado Springs could be divided into roughly three groups: First, there were the established businessmen like Irving Howbert, William Lennox, James John Hagerman and others. Second was a group of well-educated young men from the East who were dubbed the "socialites" and included future philanthropists Spencer Penrose and Charles Tutt. The third consisted of working-class Irishmen like James Doyle and John Harnon and Jimmie Burns, who built a gorgeous theater on Pikes Peak Avenue that featured a marble foyer, floating balconies and a hand-painted mural in the lobby. And then there was Winfield Scott Stratton – the

Tea at the Lennox House at Colorado College. Undated. (PPLD)

king of the gold kings – who allied himself with the Irishmen.

Nearly all the wives of the mine owners were active in the charity. When not attending meetings, they had households and servants to oversee. A typical day might consist of breakfast between 8 a.m. and 9:30 a.m. followed by a trip to the kitchen to inspect the refrigerator where foodstuffs were kept cool by large blocks of ice. The matron would telephone the grocer to place an order, dress in a woolen skirt, a close-fitting bonnet, boots with thick soles and low heels, and walk downtown to pick up the goods. "During this little expedition cheery greetings are exchanged and quite a bit of social life is brought with the morning walk," wrote Elizabeth Cass Goddard.

The charity's monthly meetings were often followed by luncheons. The fare was simple and started with slices of grapefruit or oranges followed by a clear beef soup served in cups. The main dish might consist of chops, prairie chicken, a wild bird, turkey, or small pieces of tenderloin of beef, followed by salad, molded ice cream and a cup of black coffee served in the parlor or on the porch. Afternoon teas were also a popular way of entertaining and the hostess generally called upon her friends "to pour" and to receive guests. "Formal dinners are very elegant affairs, with elaborately decorated tables and the ladies in full dress," said Mrs. Goddard. "Two or three maids, neatly attired in black dresses, white aprons, and small white caps wait upon the table."

Some of the wealth from the gold mines trickled down. Jobs sprang up in ore processing facilities and smelters, in stores and restaurants catering to the newcomers, and in the mining camps themselves. As the gold rush continued, the aid society reported a large drop-off in assistance. In one month, for example, only nine families were assisted and 70 garments given away. But there was the flip side to the boom times; miners who were killed or maimed; young women left with a brood of children and no way to support them, and individuals stricken with infectious diseases in the high-altitude camps. Some of the poor came looking for Stratton himself, including one fellow named J.A. Clark from Fort Collins who wanted to see if Stratton was interested in buying a fishpond in Cheyenne, Wyoming. "Neighbors think him insane," an aid society official wrote. "He certainly is a little off. A meal ticket and small grocery order given as he said he positively had nothing to eat and no money." The ledger books show Stratton did provide some applicants with work, or clothes, or small amounts of money.

The acerbic Miss Schnapp resigned in 1893. About that time, another financial calamity was approaching. The federal government decided to repeal the Sherman Act, which caused silver to plunge and provoked a deep recession. "Our people are in debt," complained William Palmer. "Wages are being reduced, incomes topped or diminished, men being discharged, while many of the 'well-to-do' who formerly could have assisted their neighbors or the unemployed to tide over a season of disappointment or misfortune, are now uncertain whether they will themselves come out 'even with the world.'" Silver kings like Horace Tabor went broke overnight. But others, such as James John Hagerman, were able to offset the losses by gold mine investments.

Residence of Wm. Lennox.

Unemployed silver miners headed to the Cripple Creek District looking for jobs. The prevailing wage in the gold mines was $3 a day for an eight-hour shift, though some miners received $2.50 and some shifts were for nine or ten hours. With a surplus of labor, some gold mine owners declared they were implementing 10-hour workdays with no commensurate increase in the prevailing wage. James John Hagerman, the peripatetic invalid, sought a compromise, saying he was also implementing the ten-hour day but the workers would have an hour off for lunch. The compromise failed to mollify the miners and they promptly went on strike. They were led by the Western Federation of Miners and a miner named John Calderwood, a sociable and mild-mannered man who began working in Scotland's coal mines at the age of nine, emigrated to the Pennsylvania coal mines at age 17, and was reportedly blacklisted for being a member of the Molly McGuires, a secretive group of Irish miners once active in Pennsylvania's coal country and involved in violent conflicts with authorities.

The miners and the mine owners came from starkly different worlds. "The geographic distance between owners and miners marked class differences much more profound than space could measure," writes historian Elizabeth Jameson. The mine owners living in Colorado Springs were largely Protestant and Republican and made their living through banking or business. By contrast, the miners in Cripple Creek were largely Catholics, had Democratic or Populist leanings and made their living through physical labor. About a third were Irish, which at that time was a particularly loathed ethnic group. "Sullen, malicious, conscienceless, with no capacity for enjoyment save in drink and the lowest forms of debauchery, they are filling our prisons and reformatories, marching in an ever-increasing number through the quiet country, and making a reign of terror wherever their footsteps are heard," a nineteenth-century writer observed.

The El Paso County Sheriff's Office asked Gov. Davis H. Waite, a pro-labor

M. Ry
Cornishmen at Tunnel No 4
Manitou Co

"The strike had lasted 130 days, the longest and bitterest of all American labor disputes up to that time. It plunged the Springs mine owners – including the ex-invalids, playboys, and aesthetes – into a harsh world of spies, intrigue, blacklists, propaganda, injunctions and terrorism."

MARSHALL SPRAGUE

Populist, to send the state militia to Cripple Creek. Waite obliged, but found the area to be peaceable, so the troops were withdrawn. The mine owners then met with the sheriff, told him they intended to bring in a large number of non-union miners, and asked if he could protect them. The sheriff responded by saying that El Paso County didn't have the money to hire more deputies, so the mine owners subsidized the hiring of 1,200 deputies, many of whom were former Denver police and firefighters.

As the newly deputized men approached their destination, the Strong Mine shaft house exploded and the train in which the deputies were riding promptly retreated. In a clash a couple of days later, two men were killed — one from each side — and several were wounded. Six strikers were arrested and taken to Colorado Springs. In retaliation, the strikers captured three workers from the Strong Mine and held them as hostages for the six imprisoned men. At Hagerman's request, William Slocum, president of Colorado College, the Rev. Edward Evans-Carrington, and Charles Collais, president of the Trades Assembly, went up to Cripple Creek to negotiate a peace settlement and make arrangements for the exchange of prisoners.

Afterward, Waite and Calderwood traveled to Colorado College to negotiate a settlement. While they were inside Palmer Hall, a mob of angry residents surrounded the building and the two were forced to flee out a back door to the depot. Eventually an agreement was reached. But the newly minted deputies were still spoiling for a fight and went on the offensive in Cripple Creek, cutting telegraph and telephone wires and imprisoning reporters. Waite called out the militia again, this time to protect the miners. After a tense period, the miners surrendered their weapons and the newly deputized army stood down.

Facing page: Laborers constructing tunnel on the Colorado Midland Railway. c. 1886. (PPLD)

To this day, there is controversy over who blew up the Strong Mine; two miners were charged and convicted, but were subsequently pardoned by a Republican governor. And William Lennox and Springs merchant Ed Giddings, who leased the Strong Mine, later alleged in a lawsuit that the mine owner himself had arranged the explosion in order to get out from under the lease. Wrote author Marshall Sprague, "The strike had lasted 130 days, the longest and bitterest of all American labor disputes up to that time. It plunged the Springs mine owners – including the ex-invalids, playboys, and aesthetes – into a harsh world of spies, intrigue, blacklists, propaganda, injunctions and terrorism." What's more, he adds, it brought tremendous prestige to the Western Federation of Miners, which in a few years would become the most powerful labor organization in the United States.

The labor unrest in Cripple Creek may well have had a negative impact on the aid society's bottom line. For the first time in its history, the organization reported a deficit of about $250 for the twelve- month period from October 1894 to October 1895. Despite the great fortunes being amassed, public begging was common. To discourage it, the organization decided to give Springs residents meal and lodging vouchers to pass out: "In July it was decided to try the plan adopted in Denver and many other cities of supplying meal and lodging tickets for any of our citizens to give to tramps, in place of feeding them at the door, or giving them money. Arrangements were made with one of the restaurants for meals for 10 cents each, and with one of the hotels, in the south part of town, for lodging for 15 cents. It is hoped that many of our citizens will make use of these."

The society also noted with sorrow the passing of the estimable Mrs. D. Russ Wood in the spring of 1895. "The society has lost one of its firmest friends – Mrs. D. Russ Wood – one who, perhaps more than any other in the city, gave

The Mining Exchange. 1901. (Century Chest)

herself to personal work among the poor. For years before the Aid society was formed, much of her time was spent in the homes of the unfortunate, kind words of sympathy and helpfulness always accompanying her generous gifts."

By the end of the 1890s, Colorado Springs had a moderately robust economy and a population of about 21,000. Of these, 1,500 people belonged to labor unions. As a result of the 1890s recession, the attitude towards organized labor had grown more positive throughout the country and between 1897 and 1904, union membership increased nationally from 447,000 to 2,072,700. The unions were especially attractive because they offered sick benefits and funeral benefits at a time when there were few safety nets. In Colorado Springs, unions existed for blacksmiths, tinsmiths, carpenters, brick masons, stone masons, stone cutters, granite cutters, plasterers, painters, electricians, hod carriers, cornice workers, lathers, plumbers, roofers, barbers, clerks, cooks, waiters, streetcar employees, motormen, conductors, domestics, printers, engineers, firemen, stage employees, teamsters, expressmen and newsboys.

"At the present time there is a disposition among wage earners both in the organization and out to adopt more or less the Socialist idea of thinking and conducting affairs, but it does not at all times predominate," wrote carpenter and union member Charles G. Collais, a mediator in the Cripple Creek strike. The unions pledged $2,500 toward construction of a new YMCA building. "While there is very little religious sentiment among organized labor, yet there seems to a disposition and a desire to counteract evil influences that are at work around our young men and to assist them to higher and better lives," Collais added.

As a result of the labor unrest, an eight-hour day had been established. Miners earned $3 a day; carpenters, $3.50; plumbers, $4; brick masons, $3.50; stone masons, $5; hod carriers, $4.50; building laborers, $3; painters, $4; common laborers, $2.50; teamsters, $2; electricians, $4, and tinners, $3.50.

As the city grew, the workload of the aid society increased. A report for the year ending 1898 showed that it had processed 427 applications. More than 1,200 garments were passed out, 92 grocery orders filled, 47 orders for fuel written up. Some 300 visits had been made, 108 families aided, and 40 deemed unworthy. The society helped 80 people find employment.

Still, there were problems. "In spite of the avowed objects of the society as stated in the constitution, other agencies and societies were giving help, duplicating was common and the unprincipled were preying upon the charitably disposed of the town," writes Manley Ormes, who himself contributed money to the organization.

Facing page: Bank Building, northwest corner of Tejon and Pikes Peak Avenue. 1901. (Century Chest)

LAW OFFICE
ATTORNEY
HOLBROOK &
FIRST

TB patient suns himself on a rooftop at Cragmor Sanatorium. 1925. (PPLD)

8

Are You 'Tubercular?'

As the nineteenth century drew to a close, ragmen in horse-drawn wagons rolled down the alleys calling for old clothes and scissors grinders hailed housewives from sidewalks. There were 21 police officers and 17 firemen in Colorado Springs and the two departments had a combined budget of about $44,000. Thoroughfares were still unpaved and a debate raged about parking, lighting and streets. One expert, Charles Mulford Robinson, secretary of the Municipal Art League of America, said that the destiny of Colorado Springs was to be "the Switzerland that beckons the multitudes of the east across the rolling prairie of their own great country." Given its lofty destiny, a street should not just be a street but a "salon de reunion," he argued. "That is, you should make it an out-of-doors room, inviting people to loiter there, to sit in the sunshine and enjoy the views."

Tuberculosis sanatoriums dotted the city. They ranged from Spartan-like tent colonies, to the Y-shaped Glockner that admitted sunlight into every room, to the ultra-luxurious Cragmor that had its own greenhouse, stables and dairy and was once dubbed as the "most desirable" sanatorium in the world. "Colorado Springs began to welcome new TB treatment centers," writes historian Matt Mayberry. "They were typically established along the outskirts of town, where they slowly began to surround the community. This ensured that the city would receive a financial boost related to TB, while keeping the contagious patients and their actual spittle at a distance."

One Eastern newspaper, however, warned that the great concentration of tuberculars in Colorado Springs was turning it into a "plague spot" instead of a pleasure resort. In a town in which residents had once added rooms onto their homes to accommodate invalid guests, TB patients now found it increasingly harder to find a place to live. Separate boarding houses sprang up for consumptives. One physician recalled driving around town all day in a horse and buggy before he found a place to rent. "The question, 'Are you tubercular?' was always asked, and the affirmative sent him on his quest again," writes historian Manley Ormes. Colorado Springs had no sanatorium for the poor and the charity knew one was desperately needed. Wrote one official:

> "There is no more pitiful case in our town than that of a sick man or woman unable to work, forbidden to work by his doctor, yet without means to enter one of our

5558. Glockner Sanitarium, Colorado Springs, Colorado.

existing sanatoria. They are, alas! a menace to the community as long as they wander about from place to place. They are lonely, friendless, feared by those near them, and yet we still hesitate about supplying a place where they might recover, or at least die comfortably. It is a terrible indictment of our Christianity, of our common humanity. We only allow it to continue because we hide its existence from our eyes. At present the attic of St. Francis Hospital (and this is no criticism of St. Francis but of us), or the Poor House, or the chance care of someone in a lodging house is all this rich community offers to the poor consumptives.

Dr. Charles Fox Gardiner, the courageous 110-pound physician who had scaled a mountain to treat a badly injured miner, was residing in a comfortable home at 224 Pikes Peak Avenue. He breakfasted at 8:30 and then saw patients in his house until 10:30. "I then drive about town seeing my patients, as the town is built largely with lawns about the houses and the environment decidedly rural and country-like, and as many of the people I treat are cultivated and refined, the task I have in my daily work is neither arduous or disagreeable."

Dr. Gardiner and other physicians in Colorado Springs generally charged $2 for an office visit; $3 for a house visit; $10 for the first-time examination of the chest, and $5 for a second. Most physicians drove a horse and buggy. "A few use motor carriages, but electric are not practical here yet, and steam freezes up in cold weather, while gasoline makes a noise and unpleasant smell. A few (one or two) ride horseback and I did regularly for a number of years," he added.

Dr. Gardiner usually dropped in at the El Paso Club to see the patrons and then returned home about 1 o'clock. He ate lunch and then continued to see patients in his home until about 4 o'clock. Afterward he went driving again, often taking his wife for a trip to the Broadmoor or Cheyenne Canyon. "This life in Colorado Springs from a medical man's standpoint is not burdened with the work and anxiety of a medical man's life in a large city like Philadelphia or New York."

Dr. Gardiner still believed passionately that the city's climate could cure tuberculosis. "Our patients come from all over the world to be cured in the dry air and sunshine. This is a cure in a large percent of cases of consumption during the first stages of the disease, and in fact today we rely in all countries on plenty of food and fresh air as a cure."

Dr. Samuel Edwin Solly, who helped found Cragmor, also remained devoted to the climatic cure. "Thank God we are now beginning to turn from drugs to the methods of nature for the cure of our patients," he wrote. "In the treatment of tuberculosis in this city the best doctors give very few drugs ...but trust to keeping our patients — when they will allow us — both day and night in the open air."

For Dr. Gardiner and Dr. Solly and countless other physicians to admit that they were wrong would discredit their writings and much of their advice to patients. What's worse, the physicians afflicted with TB themselves could have spread the disease to their patients when they leaned in to inspect a sore throat or to listen to a pair of wheezing lungs. The best that could be said is that they had followed the advice of Hippocrates and had tried to do no harm. Breathing fresh air was certainly better than inhaling the fetid fumes in an over-heated room or a dust-filled factory.

Two men seated outside of a Gardiner tent. 1913. (PPLD)

Dr. Anderson in 1901 rejected Koch's assertions outright. "The foolish talk of some of our pseudo scientists and younger medical men, that we are contracting phthisis [tuberculosis] from the expectorated sputum of consumptives is the vilest rot and nonsense," he fumed. "In my 27 years of practice here I have seen not one case of phthisis contracted in this climate and I believe firmly when you read this one hundred years from today that your 'best stock' in trade will be your antiseptic climate."

Four years after Dr. Anderson penned those lines, Koch received the Nobel Prize for his discovery. In his acceptance speech, Koch emphasized again that the disease was spread through contaminated sputum and that cleanliness on the part of caregivers and TB sufferers alike could reduce its spread. Koch also questioned the efficacy of sanatoriums. The so-called cure touted by sanatoriums was really a "recovery of earning capacity," he asserted. "But from the standpoint of prophylaxis there is no gain in this, since a patient who is not completely cured but is only improved to the extent that he is capable of earning again for a while, later develops the condition of open tuberculosis, and succumbs to all its consequences." Nevertheless, the idea that a person could not contract tuberculosis in Colorado Springs was so deeply embedded in the city's identity that the health department continued to go to great pains to note in its monthly reports that nearly all cases of tuberculosis were contracted elsewhere.

9

The Gordian Knot

In 1899, the aid society changed its name to The Associated Charities, a name it would keep until after World War II. Its offices were located at 21½ East Bijou Street and it boasted a telephone with the number 473B. Edward Evans-Carrington, one of the peacemakers at Cripple Creek, oversaw the daily operations. Born in Wales in 1847, Carrington was a restless, complicated man who wore a neatly trimmed beard and a pince nez.

In Philadelphia, he had risen to become vice president of Peirce College of Business, a highly respected institution that is still thriving today and was established after the Civil War by Thomas May Peirce to help veterans get jobs in mercantile houses. It was one of the first institutions in the country to offer shorthand and "type writing" for women. While at Peirce, Carrington developed a lifelong friendship with Simon Guggenheim, who would become a Colorado senator and philanthropist and president of the powerful American Smelting and Refining Company.

Upon arriving in the Springs in 1880, Carrington worked first as an accountant for El Paso County, then gravitated into the ministry and finally established an undertaker business with his two sons. At the age of 53, he would collapse and die on a Denver street corner during an evening stroll, the victim of apparent heart disease. He was considered so prominent that his obituary would be featured on the front page of the *Gazette*, next to an article about Commander Robert E. Peary's effort to find the North Pole.

Carrington oversaw the charity during a turbulent period in the nation's history. Corporations were growing more powerful, the gap between rich and poor was widening, and a new generation of journalists called 'muckrakers' was writing about social injustices. In the cities, revolutionaries, socialists, anarchists and anarcho-syndicalists stood on soapboxes and exhorted workers to demand higher wages and better working conditions. In their ragged clothing and battered hats, they were nearly indistinguishable from the labor-loathing tramps, who were much reviled by men such as Edward Evans-Carrington. The attitude was common among self-made and prosperous men, writes historian David Montgomery. "It was easier for the more fortunate members of society to blame such sufferings on the 'ignorance, indolence and immorality' of the poor. They believed that this was a land of 'self-made men,' in which earnest effort could carry any ambitious youth up the ladder of success."

At the charity's first annual meeting in the fall of 1899, the city's gold barons and wealthy businessmen were well represented. Officers and board members included Irving Howbert, Winfield Scott Stratton, William Lennox, J. R. McKinnie and Elizabeth Cass Goddard. Mayor John R. Robinson opened the meeting by decrying the twentieth century's gross era of "money-making." Two local ministers spoke briefly and then E. G. Lancaster, a professor at Colorado College, took the podium.

In his address, Lancaster talked at length about the differences between pauperism and poverty. Paupers were parasites who lived off the work of others, he explained. By contrast, the poor were decent human beings who had been impoverished by disease or other misfortune. Jesus Christ belonged to the poverty class, Lancaster said, but the man who never intended to do a day's work was a pauper. "The man who consumes and does not produce is a pauper," he said. "Poverty is no disgrace, but pauperism is an unending awful disgrace to anyone who can descend so low as to be willing to suck the juice out of the orange (which is the world) without supplying more juice for the orange." Unfortunately, Dr. Lancaster said he had discovered a "nucleus of pauperism" in Colorado Springs:

> One man told me he would not give anything to the Associated Charities because there was a poor family in this city for whom nothing was being done by the organization. I decided to investigate this family and I did straightaway. I found a husband who might possibly be past work but I think he might be able to do something; a woman who was perfectly strong and healthy and two or three small children. I went to the coal dealers and asked them if they knew this family, and they told me that the name was well known to them as the name of the mayor. I investigated further and found that this family was being supported out and out by one rich man, and was also receiving aid from the city, two churches, one fraternal society, and three individuals. The work of Associated Charities in a case like this would be to stop this waste of charity and take steps to prevent the children of that family being brought up to a life of pauperism.

Colorado Springs didn't have the sprawling factories and teeming tenements of London, New York and Chicago, but it still had its homeless, its destitute, and its sick poor. Some influential thinkers had applied Charles Darwin's evolutionary theories to politics and sociology, arguing that poorhouses, wood yards and alms-giving only perpetuated social problems, which, if left alone, would cure themselves by extinction. "Social Darwinists," as they were called, believed society was like any other organism and survival belonged to the fittest. By contrast, Karl Marx had predicted a widening gulf in classes that would lead to the eventual demise of capitalism and he argued for a more paternalistic form of government. Professor Lancaster summarized the two schools of thought:

> The first view is that held by [Thomas] Malthus and his followers. They say, 'Let nature take its course.' We are not responsible for bringing men into their present condition. Let nature take its course. Nature does not furnish any soup kitchen, wood yards, hospitals or institutions of like character. The other view is that held by Karl Marx and the socialists who go so far as to demand that the state must provide for the poor. They say the state should act as a loving father and take care of each of its children. The science of charity is the Gordian knot of the social problem of the age. It refuses to be untied. I believe that a mistake has been made by both schools whose views I have quoted...We can't leave the problem to nature. The animals of the lower kingdom do that but man has a higher conception of life than that. We are our brother's keepers. I don't believe in the socialist view. Making a personal application of this view to myself, I can't expect Colorado Springs to feed me. I can't expect the state to care for me when I've made a failure of my life. The state doesn't owe me a living unless I earn it.

In a page seemingly taken from a Charles Dickens novel, Lancaster warned against a ring of organized paupers who were preying on the respectable residents of Colorado Springs and elsewhere. "Boys are sent out to beg and steal and get money in any way. They are trained to it," he said. "Nearly all the paupers are organized for their work. There is a big trust which controls street corners, etc., and which regulates the movements of beggars from place to place, carrying out the work on a strictly business basis. And the beggars from Maine to California are controlled by this syndicate, so it is a poor scheme to give money to beggars at the door or on the street. This big trust is sucking existence out of the toil of honest workmen. If the people of Colorado Springs would decide to stop their promiscuous giving tomorrow, and do their charity through the Associated Charities, all this would be stopped so far as this city is concerned."

Reflecting the organization's continued development, the Associated Charities published for the first time a modern-looking annual report, which included a detailed breakdown of receipts, expenditures, liabilities and donors. In 1899, the organization received about $2,191 and expended $1,846. The salaries for the Rev. Carrington and Miss McDowell totaled $453 and comprised the largest single expense. The organization also spent $384 on office rent, fixtures and supplies; $314 on rail tickets for clients; $227 for provisions and coal; $141 for hospitals: $73 for board and lodging, and $66 for clothing, and $45 for rent relief.

Office of
The Associated Charities
21½ E. Bijou St,
Colorado Springs, Colorado
July 29. 1901

To the Citizens
of Colorado Springs
of the Twenty first Century

Greeting:-
I am to write you, across the wide expanse of a century, of the charity organizations of our city, as they exist today; including not only what is actually being done but, also, the plans of contemplated expansion as well; thus conveying to you what our largest ideas of public charity are.-

All the churches and fraternal organizations of the city do more or less charity work, within the limits of their own membership; and considerable money is spent by them in that way during the year.-

But the only charity organization that is representative of the

"It is surely wiser to help people to get beyond the need of charity, than, as someone puts it, to 'merely tide them over into next week's misery.'"

Reverend Edward Evans-Carrington

"We need a cottage for women, sick, homeless and perhaps penniless. We need a cottage for invalided men, such as are not proper cases for the hospital," Carrington said. "We need a corps of registered and fairly well trained nurses, especially such as are interested in the sick corps. We need a guild of friendly visitors – not inquisitors – and that means only the bringing together of the many ladies in our city who are already actively engaged in that work, with others who would gladly identify themselves with so Christ-like a ministry."

Carrington stressed the cooperative nature of the organization and its desire not to supplant other religious or fraternal groups. "We have co-operated with the clergy, the police authorities, the county commissioners, the Humane Society, the Red Cross Society, the Needlework Guild, and YMCA," he wrote. "It is our aim not to supersede but to coordinate existing charity agencies, organized and private, and we are extremely anxious to bring about the closest possible relation." As an example of that cooperation, he pointed out that the charity discontinued its employment bureau after receiving complaints that it was interfering with other employment agencies. However, it still continued to procure temporary employment for its clients.

In an effort to explain the expenses, Carrington said it was unwise to judge the charity by the amount of direct aid given. "It is surely wiser to help people to get beyond the need of charity, than, as someone puts it, to 'merely tide them over into next week's misery.'" As an example, he described a woman who had been cared for continuously by the organization at a cost of about $500. "In less than three weeks we had the good woman in her own rented cottage keeping house with her son. This was done at a cost to our organization of only $10 in cash, but who can place a value on the time and thought of the agent involved in the case?" He added, "Every case is carefully and, let me say, considerately investigated; and while direct relief is always given, when necessary, and given promptly, it is our rule to require every applicant, where and when practicable, to earn by service of some kind whatever material aid is rendered."

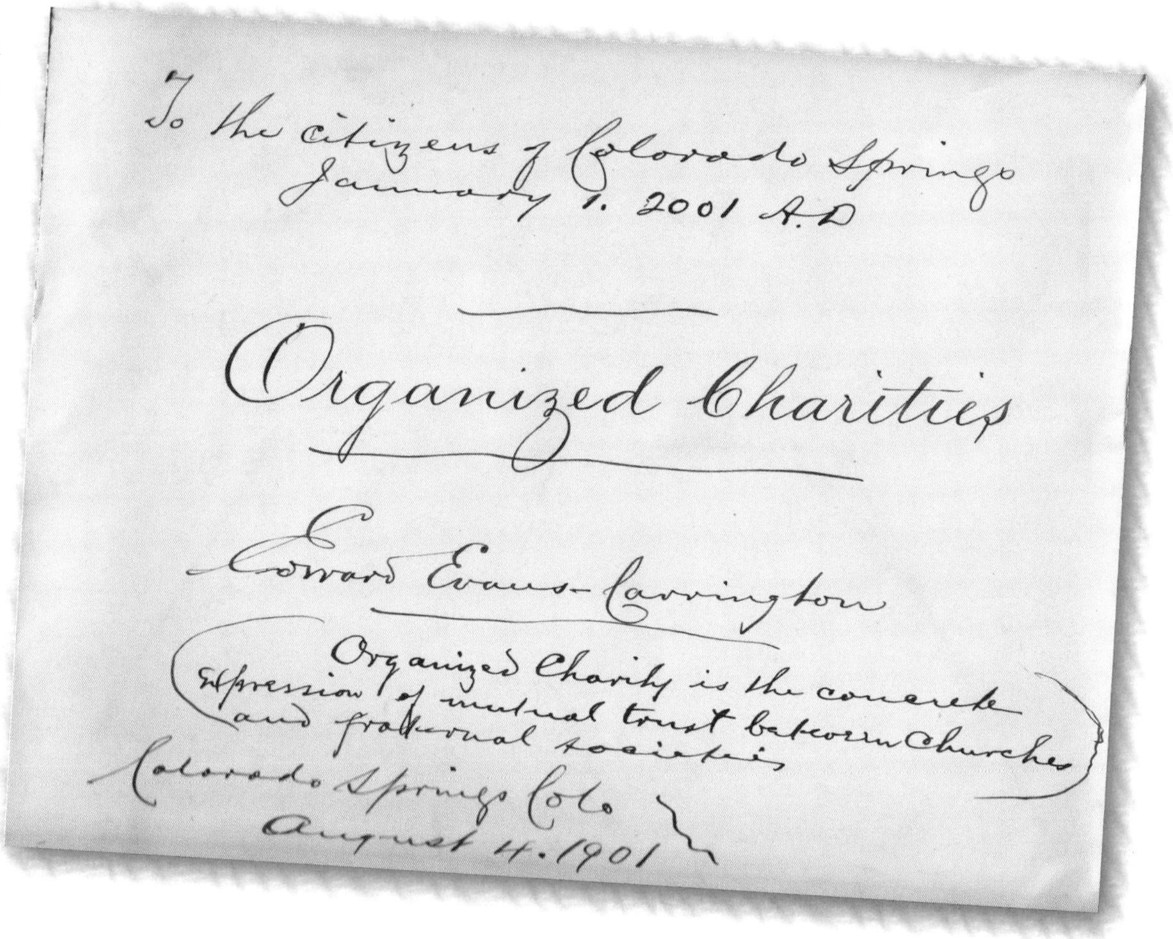

The Garden

Like a green spit of land, the garden rises from what was once a barren and under-utilized corner at 220 Ruskin Drive. Butterflies float over the raised green beds, yellow tomatoes ripen, and sticky vines of zucchini and pumpkin spread across the ground. Like many of AspenPointe's enterprises, the garden does double, triple, even quadruple duty. First and foremost, it's a working garden and supplied 770 pounds of fresh produce in its first season, including lettuce, spinach, carrots, tomatoes, basil, herbs, cucumbers and squash. Although the majority of the produce goes to the AspenPointe Café, a portion also goes back to the community and to volunteers. It's also used as a teaching tool and a recently erected geodesic dome allows for year-round gardening. During the first summer, culinary art students from the café made regular treks to the garden to sample the herbs and teens enrolled in youth programs discovered for the first time the taste of tomatoes still warm from the sun. Jonathan Liebert, vice president of Enterprises, said he also hopes to teach youngsters marketing skills by having them sell the produce at farmer's markets and other outlets.

First, though, they have to get acquainted with the fresh-grown vegetables themselves. "A lot of kids who are used to getting things at Costco or King Soopers don't know where their food comes from," said Elise Bowan, a professional gardener

hired by AspenPointe. "They don't even know what a lettuce leaf or a spinach leaf is. And it's like, 'What? You want me to eat that?'"

Bowan, who studied sustainable agriculture in college, knows that community gardens can actually change lives. She saw it when she was in Americorps and working in an urban garden. "Those families went from eating Fritos to making homemade soups. Families with six or seven children would be harvesting the food and the mom would be talking about how they made zucchini bread and soup. They were on food stamps and they changed. I saw it."

Bowan, who is a mother of two and has her own small plot, usually lets visitors find their own way in the garden. Sometimes she will send the guests on a scavenger hunt to find something yellow or something sweet or something salty. "I like them to go to whatever it is that attracts them and talk about that. I think it's important for them to have an interactive experience in the garden. There are so many smells. There are so many things to taste and touch."

The garden is also a therapeutic tool and some clients find relief just by digging in the dirt, feeling the hot sun on their backs, or simply sitting on a bench inhaling the green scents. "It can be so healing, whether they have a mental illness or a physical disability, just to be in the garden breathing the fresh air and feeling good about themselves," said Adah Rodriguez, former program director of Education and Youth Services.

The garden, which is open to the public at specified times, also builds good community relations and helps reduce the stigma surrounding mental illness, said Dr. Fred Michel, chief medical officer. "The community nearby might not like the idea we have clinical services in this building but when they see that there's all these things going on, it's more like a community center than a mental health center."

Bottom line, though, the garden is a refuge. "I think gardening is something that is not political. It's good for everyone," said Bowan. "It doesn't matter the political party, the religion. It's a place you can walk into and none of that matters."

Elise Bowan says gardens can change lives.

10

Beggars Begone

On May 2, 1900, a new hotel opened in Colorado Springs. Unlike the Antlers, with its luxuries and liveried carriage drivers, the hotel was a functional affair and the guests were rousted out of bed at dawn. Still, the men who tramped through the city were grateful, especially on nights when the thermometer plunged below zero.

The "City Hotel" was the first overnight shelter for homeless men in the state of Colorado and was located in the old jail at 10 W. Vermijo Street. The El Paso County commissioners had agreed to rent it to Associated Charities for $1 a year. Various merchants donated building materials and union members helped with the remodeling. There were 14 beds and the men were required to bathe first before being admitted. Then, wrote the Rev. Carrington, "The guest's clothing is treasured in the disinfecting room for the night, and he is furnished with clean night suits and slippers."

Associated Charities also purchased the Helping Hand Wood Yard at 23 West Cucharras Street for $275. Able-bodied men who applied for relief were expected to chop wood if they wanted a bed for the night. Many often worked extra hours for shoes and clothing, Carrington wrote, adding that wood-chopping not only brought in income for the organization, but helped to "arrest" the deterioration of a person's character.

Similar wood yards and lodging houses existed throughout the country. The facilities were often grim and the food inedible. In Kenneth Kusmer's history of homelessness, a writer describes at length the conditions in a Boston lodging house. After the man disrobed and his clothes were taken from him, he was ordered to take a bath in a tub of

Phone 516 A. Coal Orders Taken.

Colorado Springs, APR 21 1900 1900.

M F M Calvin

221 E Willamett

BOUGHT OF

Helping Hand Wood Yard,

All Kinds of WOOD

Kindling, Stove Wood and Grate Wood.

TERMS CASH.

Settlement must be made on or before delivery.

23 W. Cucharras St. Uptown Office 'Phone 473 B.

2 sacks Kind .50

Charge to Mather

murky, unchanged water. At dawn, he was ordered out of bed and his clothing, still damp and clammy, was handed back. "When I was dressed, an axe was given to me and I set at work in the yard. The breakfast, to which I was allowed to go after two hours of wood-splitting-and-piling was served at a well-scrubbed counter in a cheerless room. It consisted of a hard, ship biscuit, an enormous bowl of soup and several "hunks" of bread. The soup was ridiculously thin and so peppery that it nearly blistered my tongue."

Carrington was hopeful the City Hotel and the wood yard would put an end to the tramp problems. "There is now no excuse for street begging. Any man who wants work and is able to do it can get it at the wood yard. He is given three square meals a day and a good clean bed on which to rest his weary limbs at night," he said. "But if good-natured people keep up the practice of encouraging beggars at the door, our plans and purposes will to some extent be defeated." Carrington's frustration with citizens who gave freely to beggars was typical of organized charity workers, writes Kusmer. "The tramp and beggar were the very negation of the charity reformers' cultural system, and charity professionals expended a great deal of time and energy attempting to combat them." Carrington also exhibited the streak of "authoritarianism" that Kusmer describes in many turn-of-the-century social workers.

Associated Charities continued to evolve and grow as an organization. By 1900, in addition to its large board of trustees, it had created six standing committees. The charity's income had tripled to $7,223 and its expenditures were also $7,223. The city had increased its contribution from $300 in 1899 to $1,000 in 1900.

In 1900, 392 requests for aid were the result of sickness; 187 were prompted by joblessness; 82 applications came from the elderly; 103 cases involved other misfortunes; 20 involved alcoholism, and 10 were deemed "shiftless." Thus, the charity's own statistics show overwhelmingly that most people sought help because of misfortune or illness and not because they were lazy.

One time-consuming task involved verifying the backgrounds of people who sought "charity tickets" from the railroads. "To the sick, who have to return to their homes, and to their friends here, this is a great boon," Carrington wrote.

Warmly dressed men play a board game in Acacia Park. Jan. 8, 1908. (PPLD)

"Our plan makes it entirely unnecessary and inexcusable for any man to go abegging, even for a bed; and as I have said, it serves as a test of a man's worthiness – a man who is able to work and will not, is a proper subject for police attention and the rock pile."

REVEREND EDWARD EVANS-CARRINGTON

"Not only are the sick attended to at this end, but we have arrangements with charity organizations in all the large centers by which the sick are met at the depot and every attention paid to them."

In 1901, the charity purchased two lots on the northeast corner of Vermijo and Sierra Madre streets behind the City Hotel for a new Helping Hand Wood Yard. Carrington said the wood yard had made a "fair profit" and the proceeds were used to feed the men who worked there. The City Hotel supplied 10,198 meals and 3,633 nights of shelter. Carrington said he had observed the men carefully and was happy to report that no "pauper spirit" had materialized. "If our city is to be kept free from pauperism, the disease, for such it is, must be attended to in its incipient stages. It is no disgrace to be poor and poverty we shall always have with us; but, while it is a sacred duty to succor the needy, it is a crime to encourage pauperism by haphazard dole-giving."

Carrington noted that the Salvation Army provided cheap lodging for 10 cents a night, but said he would not do that. "It encourages the lazy and criminal element to loaf around town, and gives the hobo the excuse of begging a dime for a bed – sometimes begging it from an army lass at that," he said. "Our plan makes it entirely unnecessary and inexcusable for any man to go abegging, even for a bed; and as I have said, it serves as a test of a man's worthiness – a man who is able to work and will not, is a proper subject for police attention and the rock pile."

By 1901, Associated Charities had some of first rudimentary components of what a modern-day social services agency would look like. For example, when someone requested aid, a charity employee called a "registrar" would make a personal visit to the home and gather all information possible. Returning to the office, the registrar would then talk the case over with the manager and together they would decide on a course of action. The decision was entered on a record card under the heading "suggested treatment." Once a week a "case committee" composed of three people would meet to review the case and decide what further action should be undertaken. Carrington said the organization was also in need of women to make home visits. The visitors would have tasks that would bear some resemblance to modern-day social workers:

> Her duty, then, is to get in personal touch with the whole family if at all possible; study the causes of the trouble and seek to influence them in such a way as to help them to help themselves out of their condition. It may be necessary to move the family from one neighborhood into another; to find employment for such members of the family as can work; family wars may have to be smoothed over; wayward children may have to be taken in hand; drunkenness and other forms of dissipation may have to be dealt with; and last, but by no means least, religious obligations must be emphasized. An up-to-date visitor will hold on to such a case for weeks and months, despite all the discouragements naturally involved in it. In the humble judgment of the writer, the best kind of a friendly home visitor is a woman of positive Christian experience & good hard sense. Not the religious sentimentalist, nor the formal & patronizing ethical culturist of our time.

Instead of merely giving away food, groceries, coal and clothing like the earlier relief society, the organization began to try to unravel the more complex problem of how the family or individual had become impoverished and how they could be made self-sufficient again. A big part of the effort – then as now – was devoted to helping clients develop new skills and finding jobs.

The organization hoped to establish a hand laundry, sewing room and diet kitchen for women. "The laundry is to answer a double purpose: to provide a certain amount of work for a class of women, of whom we have not a few; and a training school for high-class laundry work, such as a woman can do at her own home. The diet kitchen is intended as a training school, and to enable us to furnish suitable food for the sick poor. This we regard as the nucleus of a School of Domestic Science. If possible, we want to add right away, a department of Industrial Art such as high-class artificial flower making."

Carrington described some imposters who had been foiled by the charity's detective work. One case involved a widow, neat of appearance and seemingly respectable, who came in and asked for money for a train ticket to Kansas to visit her six children, whom she hadn't seen in nine months. The charity made some inquiries and discovered she had abandoned the children and that they were scattered through Kansas in "wretched surroundings." Delving further, Carrington found that the widow had just come from the town to which she wanted to return. "She had forfeited control of her children and of course we could not help her," he wrote.

The next case involved a tradesman who said he had a wife and a sick child and could not find work. The charity found a job for him, but he quit for some unspecified reason. Then it offered him work in the wood yard. He refused twice and on the third occasion made a feeble effort, earning about one-third as much as a 65-year-old man. The tradesman, as it turned out, had been going around town telling his sad story and had been given $50. "But he had to labor for what he got from us!" Carrington exulted.

Carrington dubbed the third case "Forgot the Potatoes." As he was working in the office late one night, a man came in and told him his mother had sent a load of potatoes for the City Hotel. "I had never heard of her, but of course thanked him very cordially and told him where to take the potatoes the next morning. He then left the office, but in less than a minute came back and asked me to lend him 85 cents," Carrington wrote. "I noticed he was not an abstainer and my suspicion was aroused, so I told him we did not keep money in the office over night, and that I was very sorry. The potatoes have not yet materialized. Two days after, I saw the man on the street, I tried to intercept him but he dodged into an alley and I lost my man."

Breadlines were common in cities during economic downturns.

Carrington went on to describe people who were genuinely in need of help. One day a woman came into the office so distressed she could barely speak. The family had experienced much sickness and death and had been forced to borrow $50. The note had come due and they were unable to repay it. Eviction loomed. The charity stepped in and paid the note. "I will bring you the interest, sure," the woman said, tears of gratitude in her eyes. "You pay what you can on the principal and don't worry about the interest," Carrington responded.

At the1901 annual meeting, Dr. Urdahl, a professor of social science and economy at Colorado College, gave a speech on "Individualism and Pauperism" in which he applied the concept of the division of labor to charity. "It used to be the case that this charity question was handled by individuals, each man doing something for his neighbor, but we have come to see that we must socialize our charity, that we must have a sort of machine for handling this problem, such as the Associated Charities here." Citing advances in medicine that had made such practices as bloodletting obsolete, Professor Urdahl went on to say that the science of charity had likewise advanced. "So in handling the pauper question, bread and money were considered the remedy, and it was the universal remedy in all cases. Now we have found that bread and money cannot solve the question. Work, friendly assistance and sometimes imprisonment are needed for the solution of the problem."

11

The Bobtail and Ragtail of the Earth

Suffering from cirrhosis of the liver, trusting only a few old friends, Winfield Scott Stratton died in 1902. He had become a virtual recluse in his final years, but remained a great friend to Associated Charities, serving as a trustee for three years and contributing generously. In 1899, he contributed $925, or nearly half the total expended on clients. In 1900, he gave $1,355 and in 1901, he gave $1,060. When he died, Associated Charities, Colorado College and the City of Colorado Springs no doubt hoped he would leave a sliver of his fortune to them.

Instead Stratton established a home for the elderly poor and dependent children and named it The Myron Stratton Home in honor of his father. Stratton instructed his executors to make sure the residents would not be "clothed and fed as paupers usually are at public expense, but that they shall be decently and comfortably clothed and amply provided with good and wholesome food and the necessary medical attendance, care and nursing to protect their health and insure their comfort."

As soon as the will was made public, a great roar of indignation went up from the public and from newspapers across the state. "The bobtail and ragtail from the ends of the earth will arrive to take up residence here and acquire a home," warned one influential citizen. "To perdition with the poorhouse! We don't want it," thundered the Denver *Post*. A weekly magazine that catered to the Colorado Springs' wealthy residents put it more tactfully: " To leave practically his whole fortune, estimated at $10,000,000, to found a gigantic poorhouse is certainly unwise." The comments reveal the mixed feelings that the community harbored toward the poor and that were reflected in the charity's ledgers and annual reports. Fear was no doubt a factor. With all the panics and recessions of the nineteenth century, no one felt financially secure, not even General Palmer who worried in 1894 that the wealthy might lose their "place" in the world. Then, too, radicals on street corners throughout the United States continued to proclaim from their soapboxes that the nation's wealth belonged to the workers who produced it. But the capitalists who owned the mines and factories were just as insistent in claiming the wealth belonged to them.

Myron Stratton

"To leave practically his whole fortune, estimated at $10,000,000, to found a gigantic poorhouse is certainly unwise."

Stratton's will underwent more than a decade of legal challenges. One of the men who defended it and made sure Stratton's wishes were carried out was attorney David Strickler, the son of Dr. William Strickler, who had attended to many of the charity's patients. Stratton biographer Frank Waters writes that the younger Strickler as a boy had accompanied his physician father on many trips to the poor farm and was determined to make sure that the Stratton Home differed "widely from the dreary buildings, meager unwholesome food and squalid surroundings he had seen in childhood."

Myron Stratton Home. 1930. (PPLD)

Stratton, a workingman himself, was a moderating force in the ongoing tension between miners and mine owners in the Cripple Creek District. A year after he died, a far more violent labor dispute began. This time a Republican, James Hamilton Peabody, was sitting in the Governor's Mansion and he was "no friend" of unions, writes historian Elizabeth Jameson. During the intervening decade, the Western Federation of Miners had been busy signing up members. And the mine owners had been engaged in a ruthless competition among themselves to integrate their holdings and gain control of transportation and processing facilities so they could wring more profit from the gold they took from the ground.

The 1903-1904 dispute was marred by violence on both sides. A cable in the platform of Stratton's Independence Mine was cut on Jan. 26, 1904, and fifteen non-union miners fell to their deaths. And on June 6, 1904, an explosion on the platform at the Independence depot of the Florence and Cripple Creek Railroad occurred, killing thirteen non-union miners and injuring six others.

In the aftermath, writes historian Elizabeth Jameson, "The employers provoked what could only be called mob violence." Union offices and stores were sacked and nearly 200 union members rounded up and held in a bullpen. Later, mass deportations were undertaken in which union miners were loaded onto trains and taken to Denver or to Kansas or to the New Mexico state line. They were ordered off at gunpoint and told never to come back. Most never did. "Rioting, dynamiting and anarchy has had its day in Colorado," the governor declared.

Back in Colorado Springs, Carrington was in his fifth year as manager for the aid society and was becoming exhausted from the "coming in contact with the dark side of life almost incessantly." The organization had established a "tent colony" for poor tuberculars at a cost of $268.37. The City Hotel had been renamed the

"We have this year, through the agency of the wood yard and the home, been able to do much more effective work in putting men on their feet and in a position to earn a living than during any previous year."
Reverend Edward Evans-Carrington

City Home and in 1904 furnished 13,264 meals and 3,869 nights of lodging. The Helping Hand Wood Yard was operating at a loss, but Carrington said it remained vital as a work test. "But for this provision our streets would have been invaded by beggars for meals and lodgings," he said. "We have this year, through the agency of the wood yard and the home, been able to do much more effective work in putting men on their feet and in a position to earn a living than during any previous year, several having stopped their roaming career and now are doing well for themselves."

Carrington also condemned counties who dumped their sick poor on other counties by purchasing train tickets for them. Under the law, the originating counties were obligated to reimburse the receiving counties, but few paid the bill. "El Paso County," he said, "gets more than her share of this class and the temptation to 'pass them on' is proportionately strong." Fortunately, Carrington had noticed a drop in transients applying for help. He attributed the decrease to the 1904 World's Fair in St. Louis, Missouri, but it's also likely that men steered clear of the Springs because of the ill will from the strike.

On the facing page, children living in the Myron Stratton Home line up for a snack, 1951. Above, an elderly couple in a residence, 1930. (PPLD)

Carrington relinquished his position sometime between 1904 and 1907. About that time, the United States was rocked by another economic spasm after two men tried to corner the copper market and depositors withdrew their money from the banks that had financed the plan. Stock prices tumbled and banks and trust companies went bankrupt. As in previous economic crises, the effects rippled out, leading to the closures of smaller banks and factories and more people seeking help from Associated Charities.

GEN. Wm J. PALMER
THE ANTLERS
TITLE & DESIGN REGISTERED

12

Death Comes for the General

It took about two years for the effects of the 1907 Panic to reach Colorado Springs. To compound the economic problems, the mining industry was in the doldrums and railroad building had slowed down. Thousands of men were thrown out of work and the charity's caseload between 1907 and 1909 tripled. "The year which follows a panic is harder on the poor than the panic year itself," wrote Frank Bruno, the new agent. "Work is resumed very slowly, and the inefficient, which means only too largely the poor, the last to be taken on. At such a time, a small matter tends to force down the family into dependence."

Making matters worse, the city cut its contribution to the charity to $400 and the county reduced theirs to $67. But the real blow came from the death of General William Jackson Palmer, who in October 1906 had been thrown from his horse and paralyzed from the neck down. Thanks to his extraordinary wealth and round-the-clock doctors, he lived another two and a half years, dying in his sleep at Glen Eyrie on March 13, 1909. The charity lamented his passing in the annual report:

> General Palmer contributed a thousand dollars a year to our work, and nearly the same amount is still most generously contributed by the members of his family – but that is not the point. General Palmer's was a name known throughout the community as that of a friend in need. People were daily applying to him for help. A large number of those applications were sent to our office, together with the means of granting their requests, should the office deem it wise. But now weigh this thought: when the General was no longer here, to whom could all these needy people turn? A few of them apply to this or that person of wealth, but the large majority come directly to our organization, only now without the means of relieving them, which General Palmer formerly sent with the application.

Bruno didn't like the idea of spending the charity's scant resources on the so-called tramps. In fact, much like the *Scribner's* writer nearly 40 years earlier, he believed tramps should be rounded up and placed in state-run colonies where they could be trained in useful occupations. "There ought to be in this city a lodging house where men, in exchange for a meal and a lodging, should be compelled

General Palmer sitting on a gnarled wood bench with his Great Danes. Before 1907. (CSPM)

to take a bath, have their clothes fumigated, and work a certain amount each day; but, better than that, there should be in the State a farm colony to which every homeless man could be sent, and where he could be built up physically and industrially, the former by wholesome diet, habits of life and work, and the latter by being trained in some useful occupation."

Tramps, he asserted, were responsible for stealing and destroying property in the West at a cost between $100 million and $200 million each year. "Whatever may be the attractions to the individual of this sort of life, economically and socially it is vicious and borders on the criminal," he wrote. Similar colonies, or "tramp farms" were advocated in other states, reports historian Kenneth Kusmer, but none were ever established.

For the first time, in the charity's 1909 report, the word, 'homeless,' is used to describe tramps. Bruno blamed the charity's heavy caseload wholly on the "homeless man, " but what he pointedly ignored was that two-thirds of the homeless men who applied for aid were suffering from tuberculosis or other diseases.

Some 250 private and public charities throughout the country had gotten together and adopted rules aimed at discouraging the dumping of poor people on other communities. "One of the evils which organized charity is striving to remedy is the habit of passing dependents along from county to country," Bruno explained. "This gives us redress in case of dependents shipped to this place for health or any other purpose, as under such circumstances not only can the person be sent back but the costs collected." Unfortunately, the agreement did not include everybody. "It is difficult for any such an agreement to include the small country places where most of the passing along of dependents is practiced, " he admitted.

In an effort to offset the loss of income from General Palmer, the charity in 1910 had succeeded in increasing its number of donors, going from 328 to more than 700. Its annual budget was about $10,000 and 1,559 people received aid. Though the caseload was heavy, Bruno nevertheless found time to muse about the changing nature of social work. In the old days, he wrote, neighbors would chip in to help neighbors. "When a group of farmers gave a day's work to a family whose father had recently died, they were doing a perfectly legitimate and in every way praiseworthy thing," he wrote. Similarly, he went on to say, when they refused to help to the ne'er-do-well or the black sheep, the refusal came from first-hand knowledge of the person's character. But with the breakup of neighborhoods and villages and the growth of cities, it

"It was the awakening of the community to a realization that some people were preying upon its charitable instincts, and that such a parasitic life was possible because the aid was asked by a stranger."

Frank Bruno

had become much more difficult to figure out what a person needed. So early charity workers – such as Miss Schnapp — sought to separate the 'worthy' from the 'unworthy':

> It was the awakening of the community to a realization that some people were preying upon its charitable instincts, and that such a parasitic life was possible because the aid was asked by a stranger. So the first attempt by central charitable societies was to divide, to make a simple analysis of its applicants, to one of which it gave the resources at its command – food, clothes, coal, rent – usually but little more than these, and to others it refused any aid, and warned the community against them.

But that wasn't the solution either, he wrote. Dividing applicants into 'worthy' and 'unworthy' could only be regarded as a "lazy dependence upon a formula," he wrote. For the social worker, it was important to understand "how the man worked and lived when he was not in want, and the stages through which he passed from independence to dependence, what it was in the intricate system of his activities and relationships which actually gave way, and under what strain – it is an understanding of these factors which make an intelligent plan possible."

A picture from Marjory Palmer's Glen Eyrie photo album showing Palmer women with a footman and carriage. 1906. (CSPM)

Despite the efforts of organized charity workers like Frank Bruno, Americans throughout the country — including people living in Colorado Springs — continued to help tramps who showed up at their back doors or approached them on the street. Americans, if only on a subconscious level, were aware that homelessness could happen to them, writes Kenneth Kusmer. "No group, however, was immune to falling into the homeless class, because no one was safe from the unregulated capitalist economy," he adds.

Bruno departed the charity in August of 1911. He had been employed for only two years and no reason was given for his resignation. The workload was heavy, the financial resources meager and the burnout rate was high. Despite the fact that most social workers had some education, they were often paid less than domestic servants.

Peer Navigators

For many veterans, the real war starts not in the flash of roadside explosions or the sickening spiral of a gunned-down helicopter, but in the mundane world that comes after: The backed-up traffic on Powers Boulevard, the crowded aisles of Wal-Mart, the Saturday morning squall of kids and cartoons. Before, they were soldiers who had to survive. Now, they are civilians who have to survive. For some, that means finding a place to live and a job. Others may want to access their VA benefits, enroll in college, get some job training, or find a counselor for a marriage that's been severely stressed by multiple deployments. AspenPointe's created a program to help them. When someone calls and says they need help, they help. It's that simple.

"A vet grabs a vet's hand and says, 'Where do you want to go?' 'We will meet you anytime anywhere to take you wherever you need to go.' Nobody was doing that. Everyone kept pointing them to a website, a telephone number. We were the only model that said, 'We will show up and take you where you need to go,'" recalled deputy CEO Paul Sexton. "Once we did that, it seemed so simple. We had people coming back who had college benefits but were so traumatized that the exercise of driving from their house to the college to get the application was too stressful. So we said, 'We'll do it with you.' And people got better."

The program began in 2009 and was called the Peer Navigator program. For the first couple of years, AspenPointe paid for it out of pocket using money from one of its for-profit entities. It subsequently undertook a statistical analysis of 106 veterans who went through the Peer Navigator program and was able to prove that the community saved more than $5 million that might have been spent on jails, hospitals, unemployment, or other costs related to the re-adjustment to civilian life. Armed with that powerful data, it has begun receiving funding from other sources, including the USO and the Colorado Springs Veterans Trauma Court.

AspenPointe's first navigator was Rich Lindsey, a Vietnam veteran and retired command chief master sergeant who spent 28 years in the Air Force. Lindsey knows all about the difficulties coming home. When his plane touched down in San Francisco in the mid-1960s, protesters were there to greet it. "People were spitting at us, calling us baby killers. What I did was immediately go into the restroom and change into civilian clothes to fly to Boston," he said. "It was terrible. When I first got back from over there, I was angry and bitter. I wasn't the same person that I was before."

Lindsey grew up in Winchester, Massachusetts. He was the youngest of 15 children and had a happy childhood. "I don't think it could have been better." His mother, who lived to be 103 years old, owned a beauty shop and later worked as a medical receptionist. His father was in the Merchant Marine. Lindsey had seven brothers who served in the military. The oldest was in World War II when he was born and a second served in the Korean War.

In Vietnam, Lindsey was in the air police and assigned to guard an Air Force base that flew sorties every night and stored munitions for other jungle installations. The Viet Cong shelled it with mortars, rigged explosives to its gate, and attempted to infiltrate the base to blow up its bomb dump. For a youth fresh out of high school, the assaults were unnerving. Compounding the stress was the tension between races. "It was a turbulent time in the country for racial issues and it was the same way in the military."

Lindsey, who has since moved to Dallas area to be near his grandchildren, initially worked as a counselor for a nonprofit called Workout Limited where he developed a restorative justice program for youths who committed misdemeanors or low-level felonies. When AspenPointe purchased the company several years ago, Lindsey remained and eventually became the first Peer Navigator. "A lot of these young soldiers, when they come back from a tour, they won't say they have psychological problems. They're worried about their careers being affected. They just want to go home to their families. They fail to mention that they have had these traumatic experiences and that they affected them," Lindsey said. "They end up getting in trouble with the law because they have a flashback and aren't thinking like they normally would. Sometimes they think they're back in Iraq or Afghanistan. We've had cases where a young soldier will clear a neighbor's house in the middle of the night thinking they're clearing a house in Iraq or Afghanistan."

Catherine Mayberry, Peer Navigator

Soldiers who have been in combat situations and have suffered some form of abuse in their childhood, or who have alcoholic parent, are at higher risk for developing post-traumatic stress disorder. PTSD can cause permanent changes in the structure of the brain and lead to an increase or decrease of hormones and chemicals that help regulate mood, sleep and learning. It can also affect civilians and children subjected to traumatic events. It's been around forever and has gone by many names. During the Civil War, it was called nostalgia, melancholia, or soldier's heart. In World War I, it was dubbed shell shock. In World War II, it was referred to as combat fatigue.

A severe anxiety disorder, PTSD can cause nightmares, insomnia, depression, fits of rage, substance abuse, and even domestic abuse. One high-ranking general has recommended the word, 'disorder' be changed to 'injury' and Lindsey thinks it's a good idea. "It's just like a wound. I think it would make a huge difference to these young troops. No one wants to feel like they have a disorder, but anyone can get an injury and that would ease their reluctance to seek help."

AspenPointe estimates that its program, which is available to veterans of all ages and all eras, has served more than 500 veterans, but Lindsey thinks the numbers are higher. "It's the role of the Peer Navigator to know where the agencies are and get these people hooked up with organizations that can help them. It doesn't matter what the problem is. There is some place where it can be fixed," he said.

One Vietnam vet in his mid-seventies had lost his dentures and couldn't afford to replace them. Lindsey found an organization that would help him get new dentures. "He was so grateful. He called me every week to thank me. It made such a difference to the quality of his life," Lindsey said.

With the wars winding down, the armed forces have been trying to cull their ranks and any soldier who gets in trouble could wind up with a type of discharge in which they're not eligible for VA benefits, Lindsey said. "Some of them are coming out with literally nothing," he said. "Young people are being discharged with no warning, with very little time to get their stuff together. So when they come out, they're already in a pickle."

Lindsey said the effects of the two wars will be felt throughout the United States for decades to come. Those effects will be even greater in places like Colorado Springs, which has five bases, including Fort Carson, one of the nation's largest Army posts. "I've always said, 'This isn't just an Army problem, it's a community problem because these people are going to be living in the community. It makes sense for the community to get involved and support these people and ensure that they're treated right and get the help they need and recover as much as they can from these maladies."

The after-effects of the two wars are already being felt, particularly upon the Veterans Administration, where there is a backlog of one million claims, according to a March 2013 article in *The Economist*. Roughly half of the 1.6 million soldiers who served in Iraq or Afghanistan have filed for disability benefits, the magazine added.

Said Paul Sexton, "I don't want to be sitting on my porch with my wife when I'm seventy years old and see a newspaper article saying twenty-five years ago we were in a war and we did nothing and look at the devastation that happened to an entire generation. I want the article to say, 'Thank Goodness. Twenty five years ago when these wars were going on, somebody was paying attention.'"

13

Echoes

With the departure of Frank Bruno, the charity hired a husband-and-wife team named Daisy Lee and Wood Worcester. The couple represented a new generation of social reformers who believed society had a role in creating poverty. Married three years earlier in New York City, the Worcesters were an idealistic and educated couple who collaborated on a number of papers, including one that examined the plight of cotton mill workers. In their annual reports, the preoccupation with indiscriminate alms-giving and so-called imposters is gone. Instead they wrote extensively about the underlying causes of poverty, such as juvenile delinquency, child labor, desertion, poor housing conditions and inadequate education. "Endless duplication of relief, fraud, begging and pauperization, are the least of the evils," Wood Worcester wrote in one report.

Worcester favored the establishment of a bureau near the train station where newcomers could get information about tuberculosis, as well as the location of disease-free hotels and boarding homes. Saranac Lake, a resort in the Adirondacks for both tuberculars and tourists, had a similar bureau. Worcester wrote that he was often asked by the dying why they had not been told how to take care of themselves or how to avoid contagion. "Such statements as these, repeated again and again, by the sick and dying, have impelled us to urge upon the community some immediate action."

Wood was born in 1871 in Oberlin, Ohio, and would have been about 40 years old when he took the job in the Colorado Springs. He attended Ohio State University where he earned a bachelor's degree in philosophy in 1898, a law degree in 1901, and a master of laws degree in 1903. Daisy was born in 1882 in Kentucky and would have been about 29. She was a 1905 graduate of Vassar College and had also studied at the New York School of Social Work. She enjoyed gardening, debating, public speaking and reading. Her husband was an accomplished writer and his skill is evident in the charity's annual reports.

The couple may have met at the Department of Labor where they had both worked as "special agents" between 1907 and 1909. After that, the Worcesters spent a year working at the Woods Run Settlement House in Pittsburg, Pennsylvania. The settlement movement, which began in England in the 1880s, strived to alleviate poverty caused by industrialization and to help new immigrants assimilate, explains a Harvard University website. Run by idealistic young people like the

"Why are they here? What makes them what they are? I cannot bring myself to look upon these most pathetic of human beings as wholly responsible for their present condition."

WOOD WORCESTER

Worcesters, settlement houses were found in most urban areas by the turn of the century and offered a variety of services, ranging from educational classes to public baths and public kitchens and overnight shelters.

The Worcesters arrived in the Springs in the summer of 1911 and remained for the next four years. Wood served as agent, Daisy as visitor, and their office was in the Hagerman Building at the corner of Kiowa and Tejon streets. The workforce also included a registrar and stenographer. By the time they arrived, many of the old pioneers and businessmen who had supported the charity had retired. The organization had added some important "ex-officio members," including the mayor, the "county commissioner of the poor," the secretary of the YMCA and the secretary of the YWCA.

Wood Worcester wrote with great compassion about the people he encountered. He recalled a young man not quite 30 whom he accompanied to the railroad station. "Just sending him home to die – that is all." Another haunting case involved a mere child, barely sixteen, who, "betrayed through her innocence and her ignorance" was to be a mother in a few days. A third was a workingman, once a weaver in one of the great eastern mills, who had hoped to support his family. "He, too, has worked and starved; and now death is written on his face."

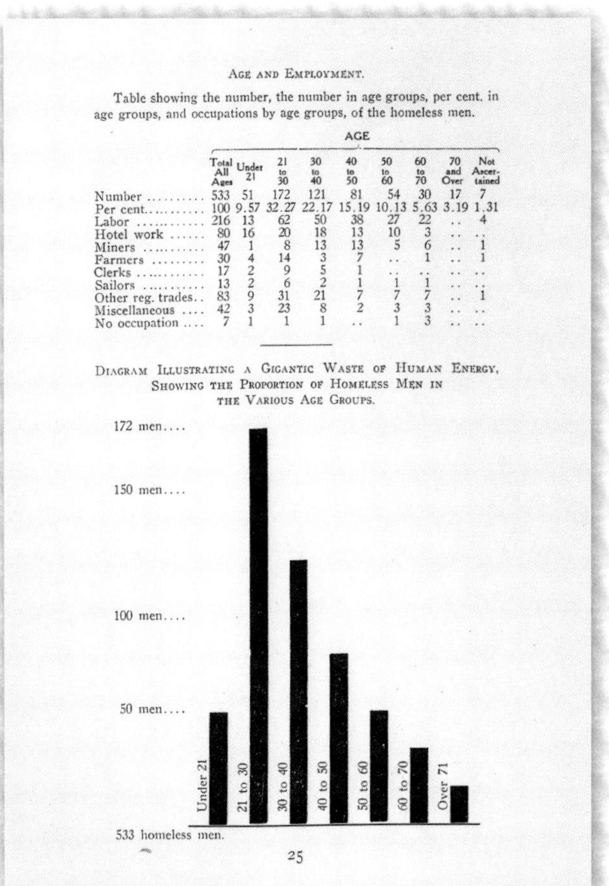

AGE AND EMPLOYMENT.

Table showing the number, the number in age groups, per cent. in age groups, and occupations by age groups, of the homeless men.

	Total All Ages	AGE: Under 21	21 to 30	30 to 40	40 to 50	50 to 60	60 to 70	70 and Over	Not Ascertained
Number	533	51	172	121	81	54	30	17	7
Per cent.	100	9.57	32.27	22.17	15.19	10.13	5.63	3.19	1.31
Labor	216	13	62	50	38	27	22	..	4
Hotel work	80	16	20	18	13	10	3	..	..
Miners	47	1	8	13	13	5	6	..	1
Farmers	30	4	14	3	7	..	1	..	1
Clerks	17	2	9	5	1	..	..	..	..
Sailors	13	2	6	2	1	1	1	..	..
Other reg. trades	83	9	31	21	7	7	7	..	1
Miscellaneous	42	3	23	8	2	3	3	..	..
No occupation	7	1	1	1	..	1	3	..	..

DIAGRAM ILLUSTRATING A GIGANTIC WASTE OF HUMAN ENERGY, SHOWING THE PROPORTION OF HOMELESS MEN IN THE VARIOUS AGE GROUPS.

25

By then, many social reform movements were underway in the United States. Filthy tenement houses were being torn down. The spread of infectious diseases from contaminated water sources was recognized and improved sanitation systems were under construction. Cow's milk had been discovered as a source of tuberculosis and dairy farms were being regularly inspected. The playground movement was gaining converts. Opposition to child labor was growing. Safer workplaces were being advocated to prevent debilitating industrial accidents. And loan associations were springing up that would not exploit the poor.

"We have no slums, no factories, few overcrowded buildings, perhaps even a minimum of sick babies and rickety children – all earmarks of poverty in our great industrial centers," wrote Wood Worcester. "Without factories, we still have echoes from the great industrial centers – victims of unsanitary workshops, of unguarded machinery, of the great and constant warfare of human life going on in the still unregulated industrial world. We have here not the problems of one city, but the problems of many, awaiting solution."

In his writing, Worcester challenged the entrenched idea that poverty was caused by "shiftlessness." For example, of the 218 families that had sought help in 1910-11, disease was present in nearly 78 percent of the two-parent homes. The "homeless man," he continued, also suffered from illness, industrial accidents, unemployment, or lack of education:

There were 533 of them last year. Of these, 19 were not really homeless, but married men with families, here in search of health. Of the remaining 514, 49 had family ties, 5 being divorced, and 44 widowers. These men, cut loose from old moorings, penniless, most of them, in need, all of them, of aid of one form or another reflect and typify some of the most serious and difficult problems of our civilization. Why are they here? What makes them what they are? Of the whole number, 344, or 65 percent were under 40, young men in the prime of life and at the high tide of their earning capacity, adrift in the world, without employment, without money, without friends. I cannot bring myself to look upon these most pathetic of human beings as blameworthy, as wholly responsible for their present condition. We who have lived for a time in the heart of our great industrial centers, see the forces at play that make for this gigantic waste of human energy. We must go back to their individual problems, to see the causes for the existence of these wanderers. Seasonal industries, irregular employment, occupational diseases, industrial accidents, defective education, are all factors entering into the production of the so-called tramp. My personal experience with these men is limited; confined to those who have come to us in the past few months. In that time, I have been particularly impressed with the fact, that an insignificant number of these men would fall into that rather vague army known as tramps unless we choose to enlarge and humanize that term.

"Where some of the poor of Colorado Springs are trying to recover from tuberculosis – within two blocks of Antlers," Associated Charities annual report, 1911.

Giving a homeless man a meal and a night's lodging was no longer enough. "Perhaps by shutting our eyes, and our hearts, and our minds, we can make the problem as simple as that," he wrote. "It is my belief that they all need, not only food and shelter, but sympathy, and courage and friends, and work, and health, and all else that is required to restore them to normal manhood."

Of the 533 homeless men who sought help, 74 had been injured in industrial accidents; 68 had contracted tuberculosis; 12 were suffering from other lung diseases; 28 had rheumatism; 10 were "mentally deficient"; nine had syphilis; seven had paralysis; 77 were suffering from other diseases, and the remaining 221 were in good health. "A big majority of these men would gladly avail themselves of the opportunity to be restored to society again as useful members, if it were in our power to offer this to them," Worcester wrote. "The sick would surely want to be cured. Many who have relatives and friends would gladly return to them, if they were able to acquire a certain amount of respectability in personal appearance, and a reasonable certainty of work in their home town."

Worcester went on to describe a young man named William Carpenter who arrived in the Springs in "pitiable shape, dirty and diseased." The charity was able to get in touch with relatives who then sent money for the youth's transportation home. William subsequently sent them back a photo of himself looking prosperous and happy. "The boy," he wrote, "wanted us to know that he was no longer a bum and a tramp."

A Boy Tramp After his Return to his Family

In 1910, the young man at left enclosed this picture of himself and a letter to Associated Charities when he returned home. It said, "DEAR FRIENDS – I send you a picture of William Carpenter who you help along am allright now and making good. har is a picture of myself. I do not look like I did when in Colorado Springs, Colo."

14

A Sanatorium of Their Own

In the old black and white photos, their faces are blurred and pale, their smiles almost grimaces as they stare into a camera that someone has arranged in a corner of a room. It's not a room actually, but a wooden porch, a creakily made thing called the "chicken coop," which admits snow and wind and starlight. Behind them stands a nurse who's also grimacing and her arms are folded behind her back like a traffic cop. The patients are swaddled in blankets, though the light has a spring warmth, and the men and boys seem embarrassed to be loafing on beds in the middle of the day.

At the opposite end of the building is the wing for women and girls. In the photo taken of their ward, they are more decorously arranged and are sitting in chairs with heavy blankets draped over their laps. Both groups of patients look worried and Sunnyrest's own statistics told the reason why: Nearly half, or 49.5 percent of those patients admitted, would die of the disease. It wasn't hard to figure out who would wind up in the latter category. They were the pale newcomers who stood in the drafty lobby wracked by coughing fits and wasted by the disease — the pleuritic grocer, the catarrhal undertaker, the hemoptoic housewife.

Like the young schoolteacher that Mrs. D. Russ Wood had encountered, impoverished TB sufferers had been coming to Colorado Springs since the town was founded. Some were stashed in the attic of St. Francis Hospital. Others lived in tents at the Poor Farm. Associated Charities itself ran a "tent colony" for a short time, though little is known about it other than it spent about $270 on the effort.

In 1908, Associated Charities began selling Red Cross Christmas seals for a new sanatorium that would be primarily for TB sufferers who could not spend more than eight dollars a week on care. Over the next two years, the charity continued to sell Christmas seals and amassed $1,452. It then created a separate and independent board of trustees to build, organize and operate the sanatorium. The trustees included Irving P. Bonbright, the Rev. James H. Franklin, the Rev. Arthur Taft, Clarence P. Dodge, Asa T. Jones and George Fowler.

Led by General Palmer's daughters – Elsie, Dorothy and Marjory — Sunnyrest became a cause celebré. Each of the Palmer sisters donated $700 and would contribute more in the years to come. Two or three times a week, a "sanatorium committee" composed of 25 businessmen met at the YMCA to strategize ways to raise funds. An exhibit of the National Tuberculosis Association was brought to the Springs. Speeches and public meetings were held. Finally, in March 1910, a public appeal was made for $25,000. In three weeks, the money had been

"We stayed on the sleeping porches with the windows open even during the winter. With 16 blankets on my bed I still woke up cold with frost in my hair and on the covers."

MORGAN JOHNSON

pledged. Fifteen thousand dollars would be used to construct the facility and $10,000 to operate it for two and a half years.

Beds would go first to Springs residents who had first or second-stage tuberculosis and could conceivably be cured in six months by nutritious food and bed rest. Any unfilled beds would then go to those residents with more advanced forms of the disease. A medical staff composed of three doctors, including the well-known physician Dr. Gerald Webb, would examine prospective patients and make recommendations on who should be admitted. In one of its annual reports, the sanatorium explained the thinking that led to the difficult decision:

> One of the early problems to be decided in connection with the Sanatorium was whether it should be a place for advanced and incurable cases, or whether it should aim to take only those for who there were reasonable hopes of permanent improvement. In so small an institution, it is obviously not possible to take both classes of patients. After some consideration, it was decided that the Sanatorium could best serve the community by taking the curable and hopeful cases, since it could thus reach a much larger number of patients and could be instrumental in restoring them to health and usefulness. Had the other policy been pursued, the Sanatorium would have become merely a home for incurables, reaching a comparatively small number of people.

Sunnyrest Sanatorium. circa 1913.
(Colorado Room Information Files, Colorado College Special Collections)

The Colorado Springs Company offered a lot on East Boulder Street, but neighbors protested, so a 20-acre parcel of land was purchased on East Cache La Poudre not far from the present-day U.S. Olympic Training Center. Sitting on a small rise, the parcel offered sweeping views of the plains and mountains. There was ample room for a vegetable garden, horses, cows, chickens and turkeys. Five nuns led by Sister Ida Tobschall were brought in to run the facility and nurse the patients. They were Kaiserwerth Deaconesses who were trained in Germany and received $15 a month in wages. Previously, the sisters had operated a large charity hospital in Buffalo, New York, and then moved to Colorado Springs where they did charitable nursing in two rental homes before taking over the sanatorium.

Sunnyrest opened on March 21, 1911. The building was a long, narrow edifice and consisted of a main building flanked by the two wings. Each wing was furnished with ten identical beds. Across from each bed was a chair. Behind each bed was a small heated room where the "porch patients" could change their clothes. "These little rooms are deemed advisable," administrators wrote, "both for the convenience of the patients and because the beds can be moved into them in case of severe hemorrhage or death – occurrences depressing to other patients in an open ward."

Located in the main building were a communal living room, a communal dining room, a kitchen, and a smaller dining room and parlor for the sisters. On the second story were the bedrooms for the sisters and an infirmary for patients who were too sick to remain on the porches.

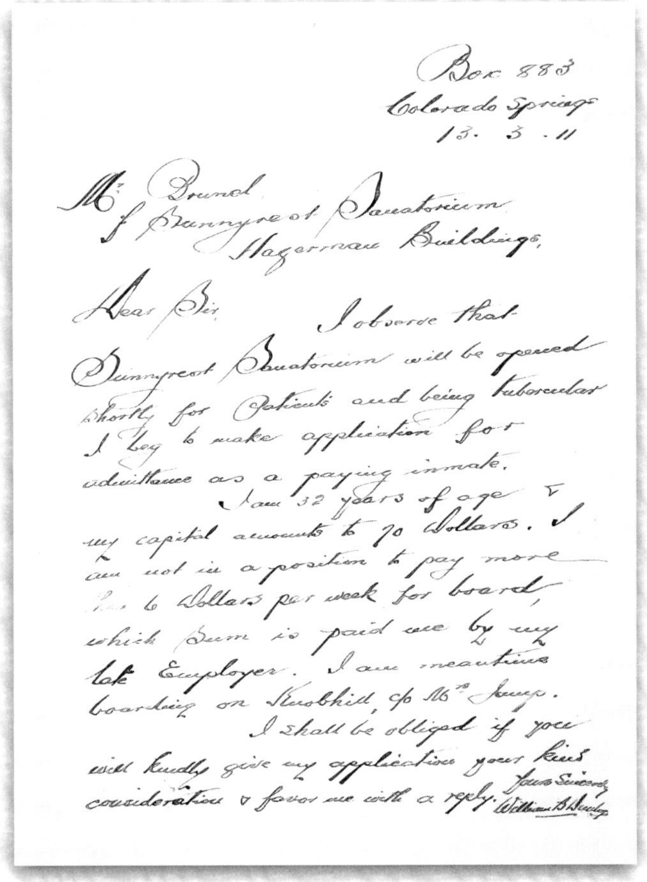

On the day of the grand opening, automobiles transported some 500 visitors from the end of a streetcar line to the sanatorium. Boy Scouts from St. Stephens Church stood at attention along the route. The building was decorated with potted plants, cut flowers and bunting. "The guests found everything in excellent condition, the neatly arranged quarters for the patients and the general reception rooms being especially attractive," the *Gazette* reported.

Various residents and organizations from throughout Colorado Springs donated furnishings for the sanatorium, as well as bedding and clothing. The items included a Graphaphone, a Regina music box, a piano, lamps, a writing desk, doilies, aprons, brooms, 26 pair of gloves, hoods and nightcaps, pajamas, a smoking jacket, hot water bags, magazine subscriptions, chickens and turkeys, eggs and oysters and "pocket electric lights for the use of patients during the long hours of the night." The sanatorium had also been offered a horse and carriage, but couldn't take possession until a barn could be built. "We should be very glad to receive more games, and if possible, a Victrola. We want to *cure* [emphasis in original text] the patients, and part of their cure depends upon our ability to keep them happy and contented, and we do not feel that any reasonable thing that will add to their happiness and comfort should be neglected," officials wrote.

By the standards of Cragmor or the Glockner, Sunnyrest was a Spartan-like environment. A former patient named Morgan Johnson said the sleeping porches were extremely cold. "We stayed on the sleeping porches with the windows open even during the winter. With 16 blankets on my bed I still woke up cold with frost in my hair and on the covers." Still, patients were eager to be admitted and a woman from Philadelphia was waiting on the steps on the day it opened. The applications poured in. "Being tubercular, I beg to make application for admittance as a paying inmate," wrote a man who was living in a rooming house not far from downtown Colorado Springs. "I am 32 years of age and my capital amounts to 70 dollars."

Many in Colorado Springs worried that Sunnyrest would attract a large number of TB patients to the city. "The experience of the past two years has proven that this fear was unfounded," the trustees wrote in 1913. "More than half the patients had been in the city longer than a year at the time of making application."

The patients came from all walks of life. Housewives made up the largest group, followed by farmers, clerks and teachers and stenographers. The patients were all relatively young. For example, in its first two years of operation, there were 10 patients under 16 years old; 11 between the ages of 16 and 20; 31 between the ages of 21 and 30; 19 between the ages of 31 and 40; four between 41 and 50, and only two over the age of 51. Contrary to what the eminent scientist Robert Koch had written, the sanatorium's medical staff had discovered that tuberculosis, at least in Colorado Springs, appeared to be a disease of early life. "There is urgent need for more adequate means of caring for those hopelessly advanced cases, which are a constant source of danger to other members of their families and to the community as a whole," officials said. "The presence of ten young children in Sunnyrest, during the past year, called attention to this situation in a pathetic manner. These children, in every case but one, were from homes where a parent, in the last states of the disease, was living in the midst of the family." Trustee Arthur Taft was so concerned about contagion that he prohibited his daughter, Rebecca, from commingling with the patients. "They feared I would contract the disease because I was so young," she remembered.

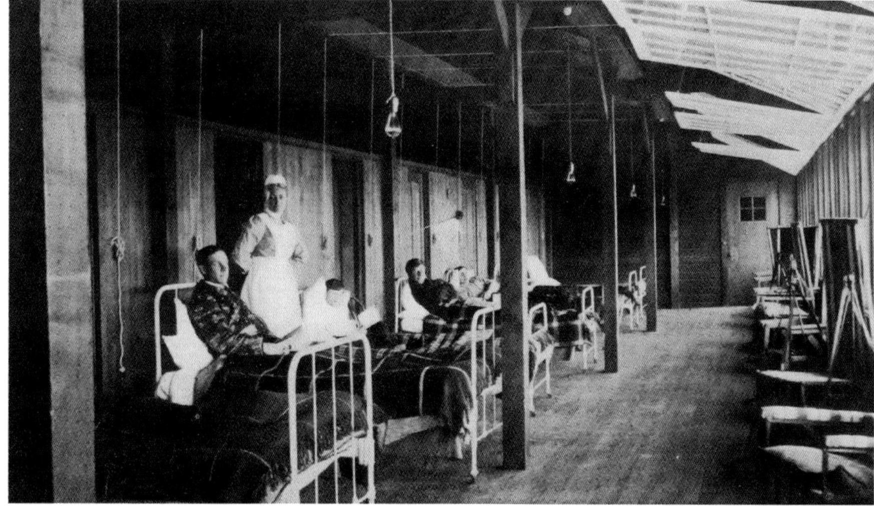

The men's porch at Sunnyrest Sanatorium. 1913.
(Colorado Room Information Files, Colorado College Special Collections)

¶NOTICE.—Patients are admitted for a probationary period of four weeks. The entire period of care per patient will not exceed six months, unless extended by the Committee on Admission as provided by its rules

THE SUNNYREST SANATORIUM
COLORADO SPRINGS, COLORADO

APPLICATION BLANK Colorado Springs
Aug-20 191 1

Name of applicant Mr F. X. McDonald
Present address 317 E. San Rafael St
Occupation Was in Restaurant Age 34 Single, married or widowed? Single
Nationality American
Number of children and ages —
Lodge Knights of Columbus
Church Roman Catholic

How long have you been in Colorado? Arrived in Denver July 11 - 1911
How long in Colorado Springs? " " " Springs " " 13 " "
What is your home address? 3408 Clark av St Louis, Mo.
How do you support yourself? — at present too ill for employment
What is your income? haven't any From what sources? Sister is paying expenses
How many are dependent on you for support? none
Could you afford to pay the estimated cost of your care, viz.: $ 8 per week? My Sister will pay same
If not, have you relatives or friends who could assist you? —
What is the maximum per week you can pay? — " " " " "
What are your habits as regards alcohol and tobacco? Don't drink or smoke
Give the name of your family physician and his address? William Porter Washington 839 N 8
Give the names and addresses of two references, preferably in your home town Mr Lou Pelta Colorado Springs
Mr John Frost 3525 Clark av St Louis Mo
Signed Frank X McDonald

Kindly mail this application direct to office of Sunnyrest Sanatorium, P. O. Box 174, Colorado Springs, Colo.

The patients did what they could to pass the time. They made crafts, enrolled in correspondence courses, learned typing and shorthand, listened to the radio, and took walks. Anna Rinker made craft items that were sold at the Broadmoor and in eight months, she had saved enough money to buy her daughter a new coat. "At first," she remembered, "I had no strength to walk at all. Then adding one block each day I was walking 33 blocks by the time I left Sunnyrest."

Many patients looked forward to weekly visits from trustee Asa T. Jones, who had tuberculosis himself and had moved to the Springs in 1886 from Massachusetts with his 20-year-old wife. Jones went on frequent horseback rides and carriage rides in the open air whenever he could. The entire family also slept on sleeping porches year-round and used heated soapstones in the winter to warm their frigid sheets. Under the regimen, his health returned and he plunged back into work. Eventually he built a house at 625 N. Cascade Avenue, which was located across the street from James J. Hagerman's house.

Jones served as a trustee for Sunnyrest from its opening until 1943 and he was also a longtime member of Associated Charity's board of directors. In addition, he was a member of the board of trustees for the Colorado School for the Deaf and Blind for 28 years and served as board president from 1928 until his death in 1945. Jones contributed generously to Sunnyrest, purchased a home for the Kaiserwerth sisters in Stratton Park, and took a personal interest in seeing that the patients were happy. On Sundays he would pull up to the sanatorium and the patients would pile into his Cadillac. "He would drive us to different houses in the Broadmoor for Sunday tea," remembered patient Herb Sheer.

"Sunnyrest was from the first a most homelike place, managed with unusual efficiency. It is the sanest and most practical effort ever put forth by our people to care for those of very slender means. Here 'Gold was changed into health,'" historian Manley Ormes observed.

15

A Winter of Discontent

In the winter of 1911–12, when Wood and Daisy Worcester opened their doors each morning, a ragged army of people greeted them. It was bitterly cold and the snow lay deep on the ground outside their office, which was still located in the Hagerman Building at the corner of Kiowa and Tejon streets. The harsh weather only added to the misery of the sick and the unemployed. Four years had passed since the Panic of '07 and many industries had shut down completely. Farmers and ranchers on the plains of eastern Colorado had experienced widespread crop failure and had sought refuge in the Springs to escape starvation.

"Probably there has been no time in the history of this city when suffering was so acute and widespread as it was last year," Wood Worcester began in his yearly report. "The industrial depression, which meant an entire cessation of work in many industries, was general throughout the country. Our city, though it has no large industries of its own, felt the effects of this general depression in the persons of 627 homeless men, who applied to us for aid."

The charity sent a few men to the Helping Hand Wood Yard to split wood, but it was mostly "made" work and cost the charity 15 cents per person. Over Christmas vacation, men shoveled snow from the lakes in the Monument Valley Park so children could skate. Several others found jobs "harvesting" ice on mountain lakes. On Dec. 23, 1911, two days before Christmas, Daisy and Wood Worcester had dealings with 34 families or individuals and wrote up case summaries that were included in the annual report.

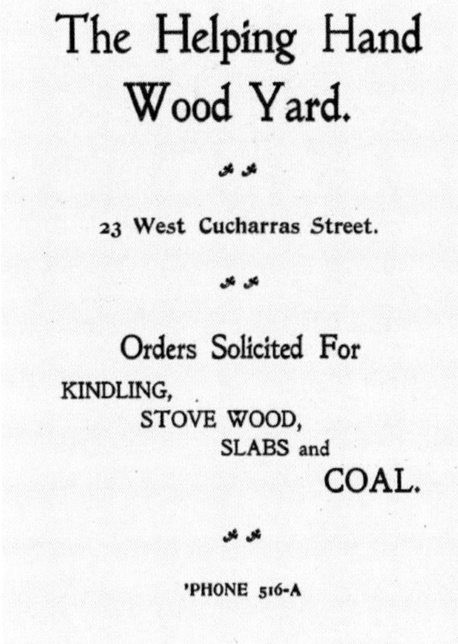

The first to show up at the office on that long-ago December day was an able-bodied man of 32 who had arrived on a freight train from Pueblo and was in desperate need of shoes and work. "We called the Free Employment Bureau to see if there was any opportunity for the man to obtain any kind of work. The reply was that there was not, and, moreover, that there were between fifty and sixty men in the office each day, all anxiously seeking employment." The man was sent to the wood yard where he worked seven hours for two meals, a night's lodging and repair of his shoes. The next day he left for Denver.

"We must face this problem with even more intelligence, with even more alertness, because of our favorable climatic conditions, which, advertised as they are, bring health seekers here from the whole country."

Wood Worcester

Later that morning, a 33-year-old man who had lost his right hand while working as a switchman on the Great Northern Railroad appeared and asked for work in the wood yard. He had done yard work about town that summer, but had earned barely enough to "maintain life." The charity sent him to Lake George to cut ice. When that job ended, the organization provided him nine dollars worth of food and lodging, which he repaid by working in the wood yard for 15 cents an hour. Later that spring he was hired by the city as a watchman.

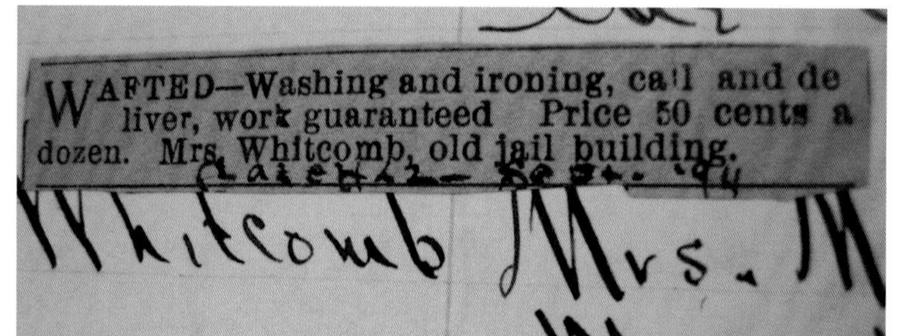
WAFTED—Washing and ironing, ca'l and de liver, work guaranteed Price 50 cents a dozen. Mrs. Whitcomb, old jail building.

A 20-year-old youth recovering from a bout of tonsillitis sought only two days' of food and lodging to tide him over until he started his new job at a nearby dairy. Like so many countless others, he had struck out for the West to seek his fortune only to find misery instead. "He would undoubtedly have succeeded without further assistance from us if he had not met misfortune. His feet were badly frozen while at work at the ranch. He was totally unfitted for work of any kind. We had to pay for his meals and lodging for nearly three weeks. At the end of that time he secured work in a restaurant and did not again apply for assistance."

A young traveling salesman was suffering from a gunshot wound that had never healed properly. The company that he worked for was willing to pay for his care if the charity could get him into a hospital. The organization arranged his admittance and found a surgeon willing to operate free of charge. The man recovered rapidly and returned to work and the company repaid the charity. "Here was an invaluable service that did not cost us a cent, but that meant life itself to the man."

Next was a 68-year-old English sailor who had jumped ship from a British merchant vessel around 1900 and entered the country illegally. The sailor had been in Colorado Springs only a short time when he had a stroke. For some reason, the El Paso County commissioners sent him to Denver where he became so ill he was hospitalized. As soon as Denver officials learned he had come from El Paso County, he was taken out of the hospital before daybreak and put on a train headed back to the Springs. The old sailor wanted to be deported to England, but immigration officials in Washington told the charity they would not deport him because he had been in the United States for too long. The County Home refused to take the man, so Associated Charities had no choice but to pay for his care, which amounted to $13 a month. Eventually the sailor was hospitalized again. The charity paid eight dollars a week for his care and he remained in the hospital until he died. In all, the organization spent $224 on his care, which was a huge percentage of its total budget. "He was aged, sick and homeless. He had no claim on any community. We could not turn him out into the streets to die," Worcester wrote.

Another man dropped by the office with a $5 donation toward a Christmas dinner for a family with 10 children. The father was ill and had mortgaged his carpentry tools. The mother had an eight-week-old baby she was nursing. The family was being supported by a 17-year-old son, who earned $6 a week, and 16-year-old daughter who earned $2.50 a week. The charity loaned the man $35 to get his tools back and he recovered his health and the family was self-supporting again.

Tuberculosis continued to burn through Colorado Springs, consuming not only human lives but also the scarce resources of the community. Since the 20 or

Public works projects like the streetcar line above helped reduce unemployment in Colorado Springs. 1895. (PPLD)

so beds at Sunnyrest were reserved primarily for residents with incipient TB, indigents with advanced forms of the disease still had few options available to them. "We, no more than any other community, can afford longer to bury our heads in the sand and, with ostrich-like stupidity, assume that our climate and natural environment render us immune to the ravages of this disease," Worcester wrote. "We must face this problem with even more intelligence, with even more alertness, because of our favorable climatic conditions, which, advertised as they are, bring health seekers here from the whole country."

Colorado Springs' climate had been advertised so effectively that some invalids believed it could raise people from their deathbeds. A Rumanian coal miner who had arrived in town with the help of $50 from co-workers "had heard that men were brought in here on stretchers who, in a few days, were able to be up and at work."

Despite regulations and legal threats, the dumping of sick indigents on Colorado Springs continued. A group of county commissioners in Oklahoma shipped a tubercular man, his wife and five children to the Springs. The charity had no choice but to care for them. "Whatever our feeling is about the injustice of this community's having to care for the sick of the whole country, when they come to us, we cannot turn them out into the streets to die," Worcester repeated.

Associated Charities spent $1,279 that winter to take care of 155 people who had tuberculosis. The organization provided them with food and lodging or paid their hospital bills. When there was no hope, they urged families to go home. One such case was a man and his wife who had come to town with a 13-year-old

"If anyone doubts that economic conditions, rather than character weakness and shiftlessness are the principal causes of the so-called tramp problem, we have only to cite the present situation."

WOOD WORCESTER

child who was extremely ill with tuberculosis. When the girl had been first diagnosed in California, the father immediately quit his job as a teamster and headed to Colorado. They established a home in Denver, but when the child grew sicker, the man decided to buy two horses and a wagon and drive his daughter through the countryside, thinking she would get well in the open air. "They got no further than Colorado Springs, when the cold became so intense they could not go further," Worcester wrote. "They stopped here just at a time when it was almost impossible to secure work of any description." The charity provided them with groceries and fuel and solicited funds to buy the girl some Christmas gifts. When it became clear that the child was dying, the family decided to return home to Ohio. The couple gave the charity the two horses and wagon in exchange for money for train tickets. Not long after they reached Ohio, the child died.

In addition to helping the people knocking at their door, Daisy and Wood Worcester also ordered food from grocers for their clients and undertook several home visits. That day, they visited a couple that had four children between the ages of two and 11. The husband, who was fatally ill with tuberculosis, had taken up homesteading on the eastern plains, but the hard work had only exacerbated the disease. When his crops failed, the family abandoned the homestead and came to town. The wife hoped she would be able to support the entire family by doing housework. The Worcesters were shocked at the "frightfully unsanitary condition" of the home and worried that the four children were infected with TB. Subsequent tests confirmed their fears. The two older children were placed in Sunnyrest for six months and recovered completely and the two smaller children were cared for in their home with the help of the Visiting Nurse Association.

"The family was at first aided by a number of individuals in the community, who, one by one, discontinued their aid, not because the family was no longer in need, not because they had proved unworthy, but because they had no real grasp of the problem and simply wearied of this family, whom they thought, as one man phrased it, they had helped quite long enough. The whole burden of caring for the family then devolved upon the Associated Charities, with the exception of $12.00 a month that the man obtained from the Odd Fellows," Worcester wrote. Eventually the husband died and the children were placed in the Odd Fellows Orphanage. The mother got a job as a seamstress at the orphanage, which enabled her to see the children daily. Their case showed that simple relief was not enough, Worcester wrote. "Our discovery that all the children had already contracted the disease emphasizes the need for an interest that goes far beyond the giving of alms."

As the terrible winter wore on, more men piled into town after hearing the city was about to begin some large public improvement projects, including putting telephone wires underground, re-laying gas mains, and paving streets. By March of 1912, the situation had grown so dire that the police department made arrangements so 50 men could sleep each night in the basement of City Hall. The police chief gave them breakfast, thinking men with full stomachs would be less likely to beg or steal. Associated Charities also supplied the men with one meal a day in order to keep them from starving. Finally, in April, the long-anticipated improvement projects began and the crisis abated. "From that time until now, it has been possible for able-bodied men to secure employment," Wood Worcester wrote. "If anyone doubts that economic conditions, rather than character weakness and shiftlessness are the principal causes of the so-called tramp problem, we have only to cite the present situation." He went on to say that the country was in the midst of unparalleled industrial activity and demand was so great for laborers that even seasonal workers had found jobs. "In contrast to last year's story, we have not had an able-bodied man apply to our office for help during the whole autumn."

Sixteenth Case*

Sixteenth Case—Call at the Office

A homeless man, age 25. The man asked for transportation to Denver. He was very ill. He claimed he could get into a home for destitute tuberculars. We communicated at once by telephone with the Home and found the man had formerly been there but had been discharged because he was suffering, not only from tuberculosis, but also from a virulent form of syphilis. It was, of course, impossible to send the man to Denver, as he had no more claim upon that community than he did upon ours. The care of the man then devolved upon the Associated Charities for 43 days, during which time we exhausted every possible resource, in order to find a place where the man could at least receive humane treatment. Although he had brought his suffering upon himself, the treatment that he had received at the hands of his relatives and various county and private institutions, marks him as one of the most pitiable characters who came under our observation. His coming presented one of those serious problems, which our organization could not solve alone, and yet at the same time imposed upon us an obligation that we could not repudiate.

The man's home was originally in a small town in a Western state. He left there when he was merely a boy, beginning the life of a wanderer. During this time he contracted both tuberculosis and syphilis. When he became too ill to work, he returned to his people. Learning of the nature of his illness, they refused to allow him to remain in their home. They had him placed in the County Farm. The officials in charge of the farm kept him for a while, isolated from the other inmates as completely as a leper would have been. Finally they told him that he must go. They offered to pay his transportation to any place that he desired. He decided to go to Chicago, as he thought that he could secure hospital care there more easily than he could in a smaller city. The County Commissioners furnished him with a ticket to Chicago and gave him $4.00 in money. He obtained admission to a hospital in Chicago. They kept him a short time, then sent him to a sanatorium for tuberculosis outside the city where he worked in the kitchen as an assistant cook. The other patients objected to this so strenuously that the officials had to dismiss him. He was turned out of the sanatorium penniless. He went to a cousin in Illinois. They lodged him in a barn for a night or two, gave him $2.00 in money, and sent him away. From that time on he was shipped from county to county, until he had been sent through practically every state in the West. He spent several months on the Pacific Coast, being sent on by the counties and various charitable institutions to whom he applied for aid, each individual's and organization's motive being to get rid of him as quickly as possible. Through our own organization twelve letters were written to his relatives and to institutions with the hope of finding a refuge for the man.

The reply to a letter written a cousin indicates pretty well the general attitude toward the man. He was looked upon as an outcast deserving but a small degree of sympathy from humanity. The letter is, in part, as follows:

> I have known of such a person for a great many years, but never had the misfortune to meet him until last fall, when he made his appearance at my home. Between my sister and myself, we fed him and gave him a place to sleep for nearly a week. We got up a small purse for him and sent him on his way, and all of us hoped and prayed that we would never hear from him again.

We at last found an institution where the man had previously been for a few months that agreed to accept him. The institution is one operated by a peculiar religious sect. We furnished the man with transportation immediately. A few weeks later, letters were received from both the County Charities and the local Associated Charities saying the man had applied to them for aid. A full report of our action was sent to both organizations. The man had voluntarily left the institution to which we had sent him. We were later informed that he was placed in the County Hospital.

There was no place that this man could claim as residence. I have already indicated the nature of the treatment that he received in his boyhood home, the only community upon which he had any possible claim. Perhaps all that we can claim for ourselves is that we lived up to the terms of the transportation agreement made with other charitable societies. How easy it would have been to grant the man's first request for transportation to Denver at a cost of $1.15! Yet, had we done so, we would have simply been another organization guilty of cruel and inhumane treatment of a helpless human being.

*Source: The Associated Charities of Colorado Springs, Sept. 30, 1912, pp. 25-26.

16

Desolating Poverty

Wood and Daisy Worcester continued their work among the poor of Colorado Springs, sometimes appalled, but never untouched by the "procession of misery" they encountered. Knocking on their door were homeless men, abandoned wives, deserted husbands, children, invalids of every age group, and tuberculars who arrived panting at the door with pulse rates of 140 and temperatures of 102.

"I believe that, in a year's time, there is no form of human suffering that is not presented to us in concrete form," wrote Wood Worcester. " Sickness and death are of daily occurrence. Prostitution, illegitimacy, venereal diseases, divorce, desertion, all of the evils that grow out of, and center about sex relationships, come into our work with appalling frequency. We hold daily converse with the vagrant and the ex-prisoner. Unemployment is a chronic problem. Child labor we must deal with occasionally; and so on through the whole list of evils that follow in the train of poverty."

The four-person office was still in the Hagerman building and was open from 9 a.m. to 5 p.m. Wood continued to serve as agent and Daisy as visitor. Alice E. Adams was registrar and Ethel L. Anderson was stenographer. For the first time, a physician served on the case committee along with a representative from the Visiting Nurse Association. Despite the improving economy, 1,467 people sought help from Associated Charities between October 1, 1912, and Sept. 30, 1913.

Homeless and impoverished invalids continued to absorb the bulk of the charity's time and resources, but Worcester devoted some space in that year's annual report to women and children. The charity helped 66 widowed women and 25 deserted mothers with small children. "Their husbands had tired of caring for them, and had simply decided to go," Worcester wrote. A new law had been passed that would give the courts authority to reunite the spouses and Worcester hoped its enforcement would act as a deterrent to prospective deserters. Deserted fathers were also not uncommon. "These are scarcely less pitiable than the mothers. One man came to us with an eleven-month-old baby in his arms. Its mother had abandoned it. Another was tramping through the country with a beautiful, two-year-old boy, from whom he refused to be separated for even a day."

There was a significant decline in the number of homeless men seeking assistance. There were 627 homeless men in 1911-12 and 344 in 1912-13. "What a picture these men present!" exclaimed Worcester. "Why are they here? What makes them what they are? What has their home life been? Here they are, hundreds of them; men adrift in the world, without employment, without money, without friends. They carry all their earthly possessions upon their backs, and these are often no more than a few tattered garments that illy serve to protect them from the cold."

Upon reviewing the records of 1,504 homeless men, Worcester remained convinced their presence was due to economic downturns, diseases, accidents, or inadequate education. Compounding the problem, he wrote, was the ease with which the men hitched unauthorized rides on the railroads. Seventy-three percent, or 251 persons, who had come to the charity for help in the past year, had "beat their way on the railroads." By comparison, only 21 percent paid for their tickets and the remaining six percent had walked or actually "tramped" into the city. A huge number of men who rode the rails ended up dead or terribly maimed, he wrote, adding:

> It is not a question of obtaining employment, for rarely, if ever, does the man who rides the freights have any sort of definite employment in view. He is hopeful of finding it in many cases, but nearly always doomed to disappointment when he comes to our city. It is usually a matter of trying his luck in a new place, or of being ordered to leave town by the police department. Certainly the public officials, who so generally indulge in this practice of ordering penniless men to leave town in fifteen minutes as an alternative to a jail sentence, cannot escape responsibility in this matter. That order is, in effect, nothing more than a command to men to trespass upon the railroads, especially in this section of the country, where miles of territory separate our cities. This is another form of 'passing on' that is accorded to the able bodied, or the partially able-bodied. It has no advantages whatsoever, for the city that orders its 'vagrants' out of town in this manner constantly receives a new supply in turn from its neighboring cities.

Homeless women and girls presented very difficult problems, he went on to say. Many of the young girls were pregnant and the organization had a difficult time trying to persuade them to keep the babies. As for the women, some "have

Statistical Report

Families.

Number of applicants	261;	days' care, 11,215
Number of families	218;	days' care, 9,228
Women living alone	43;	days' care, 1,987

Family Groups.

1. Father and mother living together	124
2. No male bread winner—	
a. Widowed mothers	32
b. Deserted mothers	25
c. Divorced mothers	15
3. Widowed women with all children under 16	19
4. Widowers with children	3

Illness in Each Family Group.

1. Father and mother living together		124
a. Father ill	37	
b. Mother ill	37	
c. Both father and mother ill	15	
d. Children ill	7	
Total	96	
2. No male bread winner		72
a. Mother ill	35	
Total	35	
3. Widowed women with children over 16		19
a. Illness	11	
b. Old age	7	
Total	18	
4. Widowers with children		3
a. Illness	1	
b. Old age	1	
Total	2	

Homeless Men.

1. Total number	533
Days' care	1901
2. Conjugal conditon—	
Single	465
Married	19
Divorced	5

ASSOCIATED CHARITIES' BRIEFS

The Associated Charities befriended 312 families last year, in which there were 554 children.

Illness caused dependency in 161 families.

There were 82 widows with children who were aided.

Deserting husbands caused 28 women with children to apply for aid.

Seventy-one per cent. of the families assisted had resided in Colorado Springs for one year or more.

Seventy per cent. of the families lived in houses that rented for $8.00 or less per month.

Eighty-one tons of coal were given to needy families.

Invalids and nursing mothers were supplied with 3010 quarts of milk.

Destitute families were given 347 grocery orders.

Among those seeking assistance, there were 348 homeless men. Ten per cent. of these were boys under twenty years of age.

These men were supplied with 1088 meals and 449 nights' lodgings.

The Associated Charities sold 1630 sacks of kindling, which furnished work to the homeless men who applied for meals and lodging.

Visits to families, 1,958. Calls at the office, 3,146. Telephone calls, 3,506.

From Associated Charities' 1914 annual report

reached the lowest depths of human degradation; victims of alcohol, cocaine and morphine, for whom there is no hope, other than prolonged institutional care." The normally sympathetic Worcester had no kind words for the "adventuresses" and "professional beggars" who were out to bilk the public with their sad tales of woe.

In the 1913-14 period, the charity made 1,958 visits to families, handled 3,146 people at the office and fielded 3,506 telephone calls. The applicants included 833 adults and 554 children. Of these, there were 348 homeless men who were given a total of 1,088 meals and 449 nights of lodging. "Poverty exists in Colorado Springs to an amazingly great extent," Worcester wrote. "A hard, grinding, desolating kind of poverty, threatening its victims with moral and physical breakdown."

Once again, he felt compelled to write about the most wretched of people – the homeless tuberculars. One man dragged himself into the office so sick that he could hardly talk. He was taken to a hospital immediately. Later, he told Worcester his story, which was typical of the multitudes that had passed through Colorado Springs. Until the man contracted tuberculosis, he had been a thrifty and productive member of society. Once diagnosed with TB, he set out for the West, tramping from place to place until his money ran out. In Denver, charity officials refused to help him because he was not a resident and a brakeman allowed him to ride out on a freight train. At Palmer Lake, he was seized by a hemorrhage and stumbled off the train at two in the morning. There he lay on the ground, without food or cover, for the next 12 hours. Finally, when some of his strength returned, he hopped another freight train to Colorado Springs. "This man had no home to which we could send him. Simple humanity compelled us to place him in the hospital and bear the cost, whatever that might be." The man didn't stay long because the altitude affected his heart. "He left again on a freight train, just as he came to us. Some other community was soon to be burdened with his care."

In October 1914, Worcester resigned to take a job with Associated Charities in San Diego. His wife, Daisy, was in poor health and had resigned the previous year. "Believing that Mrs. Worcester's health would be better in California, he resigned from the work here to the regret of everyone," wrote board chairman Arthur Taft. "During the four years of his stay in this city he had done much to solidify the position of the charity in the estimation of the people. He had worked quietly but always along the best and most effective lines. His resignation was received with sincere regret."

Daisy recovered her health in San Diego and eventually founded the Worcester School, a private college preparatory school accredited by the University of California, which operated from 1924 to 1939. She also was an instructor at San Diego State College and was a member of President Herbert Hoover's White House Conference on Child Welfare. Wood continued to work for charitable organizations and then spent four years with the American Red Cross. He ended his career as a probation officer for San Diego County.

17

The Great War

Colorado Springs regained some of its Old World serenity as the gold in Cripple Creek petered out and railroad building subsided. Only automobiles threatened to disturb the calm. Along Cascade and Nevada avenues, stately boarding homes advertised sunny rooms, balconies, steam heat, private entrances and home cooking. Some accepted tuberculosis sufferers and some didn't. "Large, sunny rooms, with sleeping porches, no invalids," states one ad.

On June 28, 1914, a Bosnian Serb assassinated Archduke Franz Ferdinand in Sarajevo, igniting World War I. As the four-year war enveloped Europe, the demand for Colorado's wheat, sugar beets and coal increased. New jobs were created, but Associated Charities didn't see much of a decline in its caseload because so many of its clients couldn't work because they were too sick, too old or had small children at home. The four-person office staff handled a staggering amount of work. As usual, homeless men and dependent families continued to consume the greatest amount of resources. In the 1914-1915 period, workers made 2,050 visits, or six a day, at cost of 30 cents per visit. Another 4,208 people called at the office, which amounted to 11 per day. In between, staffers made 4,681 phone calls and wrote more than 2,000 letters. The number of families seeking assistance remained roughly the same, at around 340, and the number of homeless men seeking help increased from 348 to 432 for the year ending Sept. 30, 1915.

Colorado Springs boarding-house residents. Most of the women were schoolteachers and the occupations of the men included train dispatcher, doctor and school superintendent. 1903. (PPLD)

With the departure of Wood and Daisy Worcester, the annual reports no longer contained

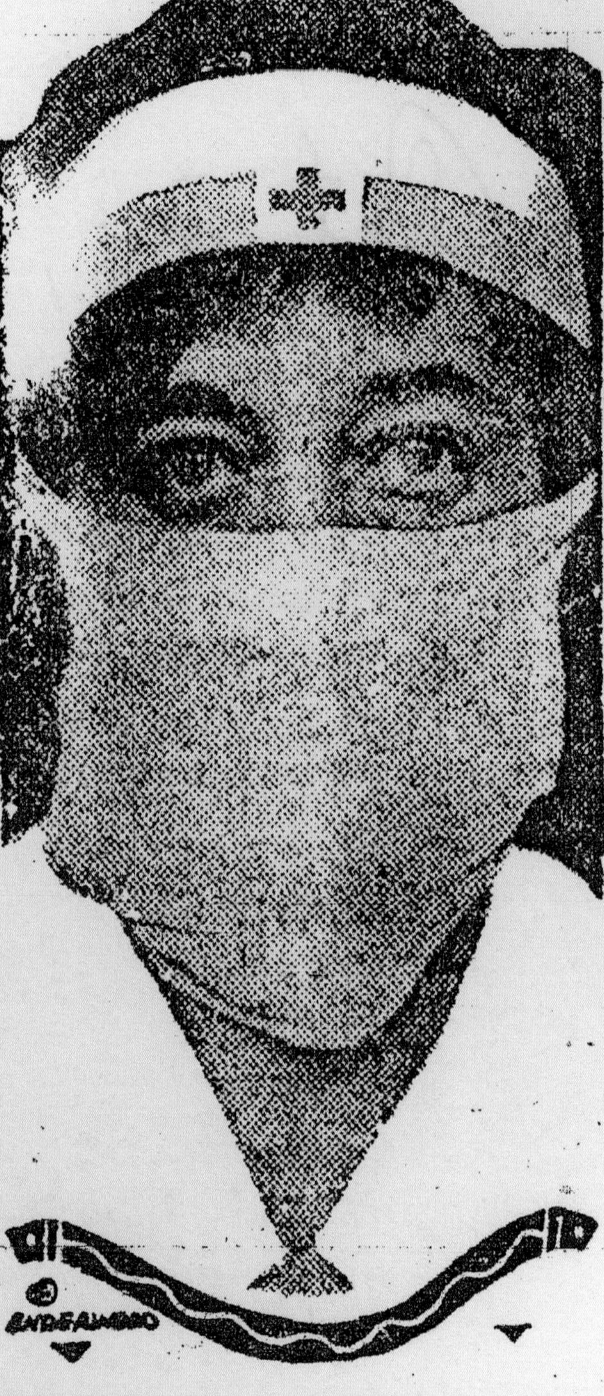

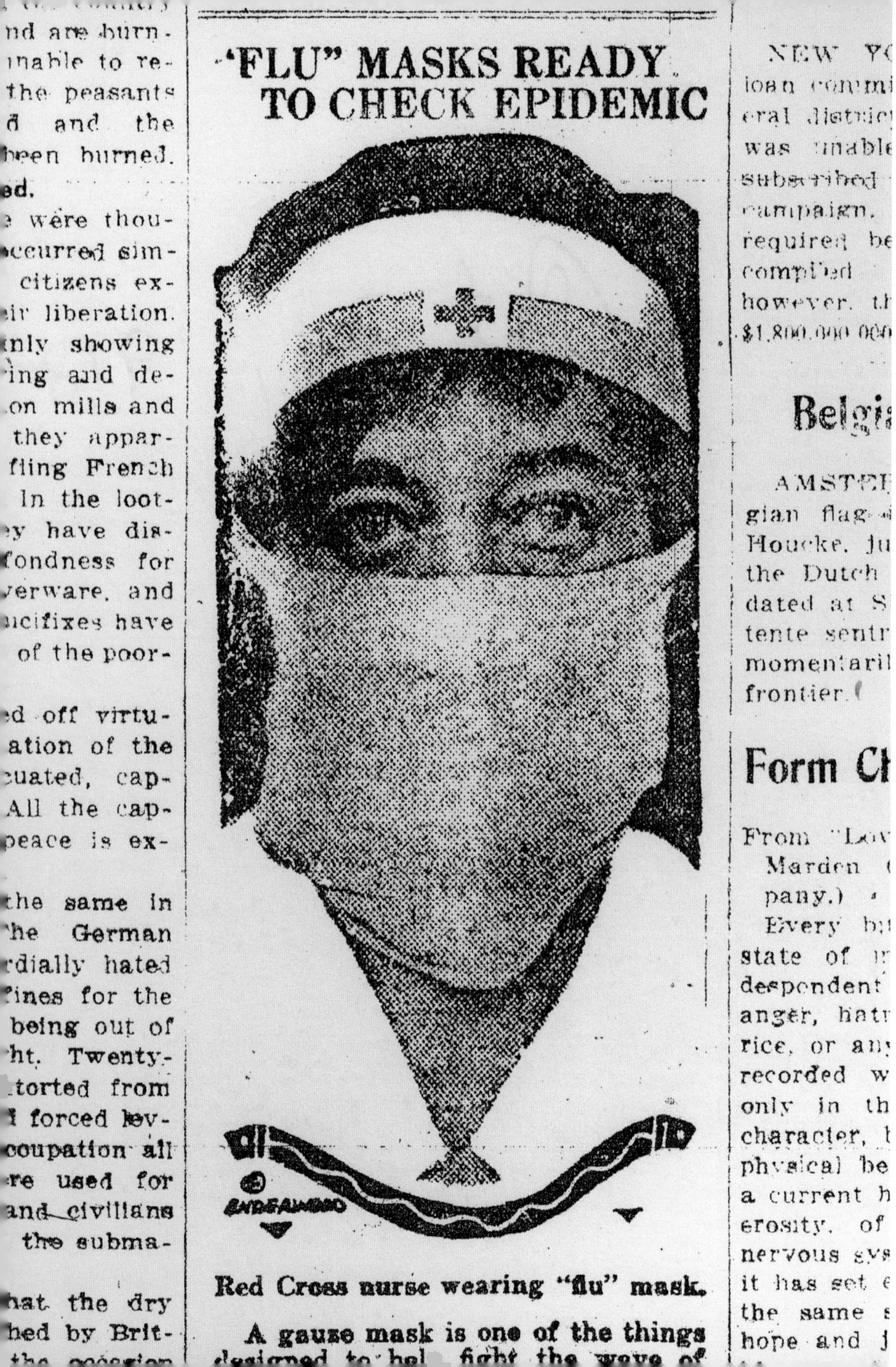

"FLU" MASKS READY TO CHECK EPIDEMIC

Red Cross nurse wearing "flu" mask.

A gauze mask is one of the things

the poignant stories of clients. Instead, they resumed the no-nonsense tone of earlier years. The new agent, I.A. Humberd, in a possible reference to Wood Worcester, said his reports would emphasize "method" rather than "philosophy" and "theory." The method would consist of: "First, The securing of data as to the problem; the resources of the family; references of responsibility; and the pledging of the people to enter into some plan to do their part. Second: Securing employment for the able-bodied members of the family, extending credit for groceries and coal; applying to relatives, to churches and to industrial unions, and give such relief as reason would dictate with all the facts in hand."

Humberd described the theoretical case of a family who comes in asking for aid. Three dollars would be given to them for relief and the charity would spend another eight dollars meeting with the family, talking to friends and employers. "Letters are written, conferences held, telegrams are sent, interviews are had. But the final result is: employment is secured; relatives and associates get together on a workable plan. Each one is led to accept his proportion of the responsibility and the family assumes its normal working conditions."

Under a new law, anyone found guilty of dumping indigents on another county could be fined $200. Additional "transportation rules" also were drawn up governing four categories of people:

> 1. The migratory man. The sick-bodied man who is in the city perhaps on the way to relatives, or perhaps, as is more frequently the case, a wandering, restless spirit. He should be checked, and either returned to the place from whence he last came, or held until relatives can be communicated with and enlisted in his care, if he should go to them. They, or we, to defray expenses as the case demands.
>
> 2. Persons who come or are sent for health reasons. These people usually hold family ties in their former homes and will return if they recover, or they will arrange for their families to come to Colorado for residence, or if they die, their bodies are to be sent back for burial. These persons should be examined, and if the case is promising, should be maintained by relatives elsewhere. If the case is hopeless, he should be returned at once.

> 3. Dependent families coming here should be returned at once unless relatives will support them, and give assurance they will not become dependent at the end of the first year's residence. Simply one year of independent residence should not be sufficient ground for subsequent relief.
>
> 4. Dependent families living in Colorado Springs may be proper subjects for transportation if through correspondence we find relatives elsewhere who will assume the responsibility of their care and keep, and the money cost of the transportation would be less than the permanent care of the family here.

Justin Hills

The charity also noted in its 1915 report that it was collaborating with the city and county to open a lodging house for men. (Documents don't say what happened to the City Hotel.) The wood yard was still in existence and the charity reported selling nearly 3,000 sacks of kindling. The following year, the Municipal Lodging House opened from Jan. 28 to April 30, 1916. Previously, homeless men had been spending the night in the basement of City Hall "practically without beds or bedding." The city contributed $575 of the $800 expended on the lodging house. "The men, unless sick, are required to work for their meals and lodging in the wood yard, and in this way a small revenue is derived," the 1916 report states. The charity received roughly $130 from kindling sold, which almost offset its share of the operating costs.

In 1916, a new agent named Justin Hills was hired to oversee the charity. Hills was an associate of General Palmer's and moved to Colorado Springs in 1903. Hills would remain for nearly three decades and bring great stability to the charity as it struggled through two world wars and the Great Depression. Under his leadership, the organization would begin to transition from an old-fashioned charity to the behavioral health and counseling organization that most people recognize today.

The winter of 1916-17 was a hard one on the city's poor because of the huge increase in food prices due to inflation. The charity's annual cost for groceries shot up from $497 to $1,568. In an appeal to the public for help, Eugene Shove, president of the board of directors, said the food prices had escalated so much that even the employed weren't making enough to cover the cost of food.

The deadly flu pandemic arrived in Colorado in the fall of 1918. Harvey Sethman, then a member of the Student Army Training Corps at the University of Colorado at Boulder, told the *Gazette,* "One morning our company lined up for roll call, and one of the fellows who hadn't even seemed sick staggered forward ten or fifteen feet and fell flat on his face. We got an ambulance and took him to the hospital. Two days later he was dead."

On Oct. 4, 1918, Colorado Springs' health officer ordered schools, theaters, moving picture houses, reading rooms and libraries closed. Dr. Gardiner, late to accept the infectious nature of tuberculosis, was in the forefront of the closing order. "I think everything should be closed before the trouble starts, not after it is too late," said Dr. Gardiner, then president of the Pikes Peak chapter of the Red Cross.

Businesses were hemorrhaging money, but no one complained about the closing order except for a woman who called the health department to find out if she could host a Bible class. After being told no, she complained of a card party in progress next door. A health official was dispatched at once to break up the party. "The hostess requested that her guests be allowed to continue the game, provided they should take their chairs and tables out in the yard under the trees. This they were permitted to do," the newspaper reported. Later in the day, another card party was broken up.

Two patients suffering from the flu were ordered out of a Pullman car on a Denver & Rio Grande train and hospitalized. Health officials ordered that the car be taken from the track and sanitized when it reached Pueblo. In Ouray, citizens armed with shotguns departed for a mountain pass to head off people fleeing from flu-ravaged towns. As the pandemic raced south to Mexico, the dead were so plentiful that a shortage of coffins materialized.

The speed with which the flu moved is evident in some of the city's old health and sanitation reports. For example, in September 1918 no flu cases were reported. In October, there were 852 cases and 38 deaths from influenza or influenza-pneumonia. In November, the number of cases had jumped to 1,336 and 56 deaths were reported. By December, the number of cases had declined to 1,122, but the deaths rose to 97. Sadly, one of the victims included Thomas Bernard Carrington, the son of the Rev. Carrington, who had taken to his bed thinking he would get better, but developed double pneumonia and was dead in a week.

News of the flu pandemic pushed some of the horrific war news off the front page. In November of 1918, Armistice was declared. But the raging inflation continued. "During the year just closed the calls on this Association have been the greatest in the history of the organization," the charity's annual report for the year ending Sept. 30, 1919 states. "This was due partly to the influenza epidemic and partly to the increased number of tuberculars in the community. This increase in expenditures was, of course, due to a great extent to the enormous increase in the cost of living. A few years ago it was thought a family of five could live on an income of $15.00 weekly, while now the minimum set by the federal government is $26.00 per week." The charity paid $7,008 for groceries and $1,793 for milk.

Although the number of individuals seen by the organization remained about the same, there was a huge drop in homeless men – from 729 in 1916; to 629 in 1917; to 98 in 1918 and 90 by the end of 1919. The decrease was likely due to the mandatory drafting of soldiers for World War I as well as the fact that the great influx of immigrants from Europe had become a trickle. In another sign of the changing times, the organization now had a Ford automobile and expended $957 for its purchase and for repairs. The visitor, Mrs. Katherine Hart, apparently still used a bicycle and the charity spent $5.25 to repair it.

DEPARTMENT OF

Public Health and Sanitation

Colorado Springs, Colorado

January 1916,

PERRY BOTTS, Commissioner
OMER R. GILLETT, M. D., Health Officer
HENRY L. TESTERMAN, Market Master
J. E. FULLER, Chemist and Bacteriologist

What's Cooking?

In the kitchen of the AspenPointe Café one recent morning, sesame chicken sizzled on a grill. Pots and pans clattered in the dish pit. A catering order was being taken and sandwiches were being wrapped for grab-and-go lunches. The kitchen was a sea of noise, the air warmed and sweetened by the rich odor of cheese-filled pastries. The noon rush hour was only an hour away and the culinary arts trainees were focused on their tasks. Under the collective pressure, their depression and anxieties were cast off momentarily and delicate strands of friendship were forming.

A kitchen is a testing ground, experienced chefs like Mike Cid will say, a hot, stressful, high-paced environment. For AspenPointe, it is also a training ground: for the mentally and physically disabled; for young people who have had scrapes with the law; for former soldiers with post-traumatic stress disorder, and for ordinary job seekers who see the 16-week training program as stepping stone to one day being employed at the five-star Broadmoor Hotel.

"A kitchen is a much harder environment than a regular work place because

there are so many triggers," said Cid, the café's training chef and a graduate of Johnson & Wales University. Cid came from the U.S. Olympic Training Center where he prepared meals for people like Michael Phelps, who has won more Gold Medals than any other athlete. He has a breezy, informal demeanor that puts the trainees at ease even while he's delivering a blunt message: "I tell the students, 'However hard you work here is however hard I will work to get you a job. If you're a top performer and succeeding, I'm going to break my back to get you a really good job.' It's up to them. They control their own destiny."

Maddy Barber, 21, was referred through the Department of Vocational Rehabilitation and hopes to one day open up her own café in California. "I love it here, actually. I'm having a lot of fun," said Barber, who said she has been diagnosed with various learning disabilities and most recently, borderline personality disorder. She also had a job at Souper Salad and tried to nap between shifts. "I have insomnia so I don't sleep much during the night," she said. "Sometimes my day will feel like a dream. It will go by either really fast and I'll have trouble remembering it, or it will go by really slow and I'll be, like, when is this going to end?"

The café is located in the Citizens Service Center at 1675 Garden of the Gods Road. The service center was once part of the Intel campus, which departed the city in 2009. El Paso County purchased the facility and it now houses various county departments and the Department of Motor Vehicles. People waiting to get their license plates can go to the café, buy a scone and a coffee, and wait for their number to show up on a screen. The kitchen is cavernous, the serving stations expansive and the dining area can accommodate more than 350 people. Behind the cafeteria is a meeting room where classes and other functions are held.

The café sells everything from pizza to Thai food to soups and salads. The food is fresh, tasty and artfully arranged. Organic and local foods are purchased and incorporated into dishes whenever possible. Last year the café received several hundred pounds of produce from AspenPointe's community garden on Ruskin Drive. In the 2012 fiscal year, roughly 47,500 customers were served at the Garden of the Gods facility and café went from losing money to making a small profit. AspenPointe operates a second café on Academy Boulevard and a third in Castle Rock.

Crystal Griffin, training program coordinator, said just showing up for work is a challenge for many trainees. "A lot of them haven't worked in a long, long time. They have medical issues. They don't want to get up in the morning. So that's a huge obstacle. Another big obstacle is the awareness of space. This kitchen is public. A lot of them are not used to interacting with other people. They're on display."

The kitchen prepares catered meals for all kinds of events, ranging from business lunches to weddings. The food is reasonably priced and delicious. The breakfast menu includes bagels, pastries, and omelets. Lunch offerings include wraps, fresh soups, and salads. For dinner, customers can order Mile High chicken marsala, Cave of the Winds roast pork, Royal Gorge beef pot roast, Garden of the Gods fajita buffet, Red Rocks potato bar, or General Palmer's build-your-own pasta bar. The kitchen supplies meals for AspenPointe's Lighthouse, the in-patient, high-intensity psychiatric facility on Parkside Drive, and also provides box lunches during new-employee orientations. It also trucks in food during crises like the Waldo Canyon Fire.

The kitchen trains students to be prep cooks, bakers, cashiers and customer

service representatives and has teamed up with Starbucks to offer barista training. "The essence of this kitchen is training," Cid said. "That's the basis for this whole place. We wouldn't be here if it weren't for the students." Students start out in the dish room. "The dish room is another of those triggers. It's hot. It's steamy. It's stressful. If they can handle that, we move them to the next level," he added.

The training program is composed of four tiers. Each tier is four weeks in length and costs $600 or a total of $2,400 for the full session. Tier 1 teaches basic skills, cleanliness and teamwork. Tier 2 focuses on technique. Tier 3 teaches students how to make sauces, sauces and salads. By Tier 4, they are running their own station, which is like a mini-restaurant, and involves prep work, cooking, serving and clean up. Griffin said the organization tries to screen people before they enroll so they will have realistic expectations. "If they can get through Tier One – the grunt work – they're likely to stay." Griffin has no culinary training herself. She was formerly a mediator. "They thought it would be perfect in a kitchen and it really does work. It's a business, as well as a training program, two totally different roles that naturally don't go well together."

When the rush hour was over, Cid and Griffin sat down at a table with the new trainees. Cid reminded the students that they needed to call if they weren't going

to make it to work. "Even if it's an hour or two ahead of time, if you're on the way here and your car breaks down, call me and say, 'Hey, my car broke down. I don't think I'm going to make it in today.' That's totally cool with me. But if your car breaks down and you walk over here and you're two hours late, I'm going to be like, 'I'm sorry.' We've got to be strict."

Griffin cautioned the students that they didn't have to share their background with anybody. "The chefs out here don't have your background. They don't know why you're here. They don't know your history. They don't need to know any of that."

The homework assignment for the new trainees was to go home and think about what a sense of urgency means in a kitchen. "Does a sense of urgency mean I need to move faster? Does a sense of urgency mean I need to think faster? Do I need to plan my steps ahead? Or am I already fast enough?" asked Cid.

Then he switched to the thing that brought them all together: food. He asked them to name their favorite food. One said lasagna; another said stuffed chicken, a third said brownies. "I do love me some brownies. I made turtle brownies the other day with caramels and walnuts. Oh man!" Cid exclaimed.

BERNARD LIVERY.
17

18

When Lilacs Bloomed

In the years following World War I, Colorado Springs was known as the "City of Sunshine" and its major businesses were tourism and sanatoriums. An old woman named Crazy Grace walked the streets dressed as a little girl in curls and ruffles and an old soldier trudged up and down the avenues complaining of his sore feet. The number of automobiles, which stood at roughly 250 in 1909, had increased to more than 5,000 by 1919. Their growing popularity would soon put the city's five livery stables and seven blacksmith shops out of business.

Sunnyrest reaped $381 from the sale of eggs and sold its horse, buggy and wagon for $100. It then purchased an automobile for $403 and spent another $822 to keep it running. In the springtime, when the lilacs bloomed, tuberculosis patients were piled into cars and taken for drives. Winfield Scott Stratton's beautiful trolleys still ran in the summertime and Vaudeville shows cost 17 cents at the Burns Theater. On Armistice Day, a canon sounded at 11 o'clock in the morning marking the end of World War 1. The number of Civil War soldiers marching in the Veteran's Day parade dwindled with each passing year, until, finally, there was none.

General Palmer's world was slipping away. But servants in starched uniforms still went quietly about their business in the old mansions on Wood and Cascade avenues and members of "society" still left embossed calling cards on silver trays.

Facing page: The first automobiles in Colorado Springs. 1901. (Century Chest)

Once or twice a year, Asa Jones and his wife would host a Sunday dinner at their lovely home on Cascade Avenue. After the maid announced dinner, the guests would file in to a dining room where the table was laid with sterling, crystal and fine china. "Mrs. Jones had a buzzer under the carpet at her place, and would press it with her foot when she wished to summon the maid," remembered Mary Beth Stewart Wedberg, who as a young girl accompanied her mother to the gatherings.

Transient men were still sleeping in the basement of City Hall and the charity furnished their meals. In the month of February, the charity spent $2,291. Of that, $435 went for lodging and meals for the homeless. City officials were told that the situation could not continue:

> We regret to have to inform you that it will no longer be possible for this organization to deal with the Homeless Men problem of Colorado Springs and that it will

"I request that said Watt Memorial Fund be used to help and assist poor persons suffering with tuberculosis and particularly the more chronic and advanced cases in the said Watt Memorial Building."

MARJORY PALMER WATT

> be necessary for the City to take over this work as is being done in other cities. During the past few months this association has been confronted with an unusual situation and the calls upon it have been far beyond any expectations. This situation has been due to three causes: local unemployment, influenza and the very large number of homeless men that have come to our city. The last of these, the homeless men, has not been the least of the problems we have had to meet...The load that we are now carrying, due to unemployment and to sickness among the families of our city, will require more funds than are available and we feel all our resources should be conserved for our own people.

At Sunnyrest, Asa Jones remained one of the sanatorium's staunchest supporters, contributing roughly $1,000 a year to its upkeep. Others also contributed generous amounts, including Irving Bonbright, Mr. and Mrs. Clarence Carpenter, George Fowler, Mrs. Hester Giddings, Harry Jackson, Eugene Shove, V.M. Vance and Gov. O. H. Shoup.

In 1919, Sunnyrest raised its fees to $11 a week. Local residents were given preference and out-of-towners were taken when vacancies occurred. The non-residents were required to pay the full cost of their treatment so they "will not be a financial burden to our community." For the year ending Sept. 30, 1919, only 27 of the 102 patients had been residents for two years or more. As before, the majority of patients, or 98 people, were under 40 years of age.

Marjory Palmer and her husband, Dr. Henry Watt. Undated. (CSPM)

For the year ending September 30, 1919, Sunnyrest was able to meet its expenses with roughly $14,000 in contributions and nearly $17,000 from the patients themselves. With the help of $45,000 in donations, the sanatorium constructed a new building that was identical to the first. The donors included B.C. Allen, Marjory Palmer Watt, and Richard Pilkington, a lawyer from St. Helens, England, who gave his gift, "in recognition of the many kindnesses shown to an English family by the people of Colorado."

Marjory was one of General Palmer's three daughters. She married a young English doctor named Henry C. Watt who arrived in the Springs in 1904 for health reasons and moved into Glen Eyrie to take care of her father after he fell from his horse. Both Marjory and her physician husband were reported to have tuberculosis. Gentle and compassionate, often photographed with a dog in her lap, Marjory established a small nutrition camp for children at her home on Culebra Avenue. "Ten undernourished children greatly improved with a special program of the most nourishing food, sun baths, sufficient rest, etc.," writes historian Manley Ormes.

The program was eventually relocated to the Beth-El hospital grounds and renamed the Marjory Palmer-Watt Nutrition Camp School. The children lived at the camp school for up to a year. By 1932, some 450 children "had been restored to health," a fund-raising pamphlet notes. "From cod liver oil at 7:20 in the morning to bed at 7:00 at night, every hour of activity is carefully supervised. The program

Children rest on cots at nutrition camp. 1931. (CSPM)

Asa Jones. (Courtesy Colorado School for Deaf and Blind)

includes school at 8:30, morning lunch at 10, sun baths at 11, rest in the afternoon, recreation from 3:45 to 5:30."

Sunnyrest's new building was used for two years by discharged tubercular soldiers and then reverted to its original class of patients. In 1922, Marjory Palmer Watt donated more than $110,000 in stocks and bonds and cash and her home at 1801 Culebra Avenue to establish the Watt Memorial Fund. Her Culebra Avenue home, one of the most beautiful in the region, was made of white stucco and roofed with the same imported tile used at Glen Eyrie. It had 13 rooms, four baths, sleeping porches, and was "modern throughout, even to oil-burning furnaces," the newspaper reported. Marjory wanted the sanatorium to loosen its restrictions and admit more tuberculars in advanced stages of the disease. In a letter dated Oct. 2, 1922, she wrote, "I request that said Watt Memorial Fund be used to help and assist poor persons suffering with tuberculosis and particularly the more chronic and advanced cases in the said Watt Memorial Building."

By the time Marjory had established the fund, the number of people afflicted with tuberculosis was declining, though drugs capable of eradicating it would not be developed until after World War II. The decline no doubt was brought about better understanding of how the disease was spread and improved hygiene on the part of infected and non-infected alike. Some scholars believe the disease peaked around 1840 and speculate that it was so virulent that it had killed off those who were genetically susceptible. "Around 1900, TB caused nearly 185 deaths per 100,000 people, but this rate had declined to less than 100 deaths per 100,000 people 25 years later," states a report for the City of Colorado Springs. "There certainly were no fewer slums, nor less people residing in them, despite the diligence of the Anti-Tuberculosis League, so it is likely the virulence of the different strains was subsiding, or those of certain gene

A young woman sits on a "Locomobile" in Acacia Park, 1901. (Century Chest)

pools susceptible to the disease had already perished. Regardless, the era of the sanatoriums had also begun to pass at the beginning of the Depression. Great fortunes had been lost and traveling to seek a cure that, once demonstrated, could be replicated anywhere diminished the urge to travel to faraway places to recover one's health."

By 1954, only 12 tubercular patients remained at Sunnyrest. The board of trustees recognized that was "far too small a number to continue to run the sanatorium as a tubercular sanatorium exclusively." Eventually the mission was expanded to include the elderly and others who required nursing care. Emma Diebold, who celebrated her ninety-fourth birthday in Sunnyrest, remembered her grandmother telling her how butter was churned by the movement of the wagons as they rolled toward Colorado and how she learned to make biscuits rise by combining sour cream with Manitou soda spring water. William Bassett, a vinegary man with a sly sense of humor, was a wheat farmer during the Dust Bowl and celebrated his one-hundredth birthday in Sunnyrest. He liked to tell people, "A man can get used to anything, even hanging, if he hangs long enough."

19

A Shy Philanthropist

Even now, seven decades after her death, the strong, upright character of Alice Bemis Taylor is palpable in the few images that remain of her. Often draped in formal dress, a corsage pinned to her shoulder, she is one of Colorado Springs' most well known — and least known — philanthropists. Mrs. Taylor no doubt would have preferred to remain anonymous — the way she conducted much of her charitable giving — but history won't allow it and a few years ago she was inducted into the Colorado Women's Hall of Fame. There, her accomplishments are laid out for all to see, but it is through a visit to the Colorado Springs Historic Day Nursery or the Fine Arts Center that one understands her imagination and her rigor.

So different, the two buildings she constructed, one an English Tudor blend at the corner of Tejon and Rio Grande streets filled with lovely stained glass figures and hand-painted murals, the other a monolithic concrete edifice on the edge of the Colorado College campus brimming with the buoyant energy of life decoding itself through the arts.

Like so many others, the Bemis family came to Colorado Springs in the early 1880s after Mrs. Taylor's mother, Alice Cogswell Bemis, developed a throat ailment. The family initially lived on Weber Street and counted among their neighbors Irving Howbert and author Helen Hunt Jackson. Later they moved to a large spacious home at 506 North Cascade Avenue that is now listed in the National Register.

Mrs. Taylor's parents were New Englanders and philanthropists themselves. Her mother was a descendant of John Cogswell, who departed England in the 1600s with his wife and eight children on board *The Angel Gabriel.* The ship was caught in a terrific gale on Aug. 15, 1625, off the coast of Maine and the family was washed ashore when the vessel broke apart in Boston Harbor. The Cogswells settled in Ipswich, Massachusetts, where they remained for the next 200 years. Cogswell's numerous descendants included Ralph Waldo Emerson and Oliver Wendell Holmes.

Taylor's father, Judson Moss Bemis, was also originally from Massachusetts, though from humbler origins. His family traveled by covered wagon to Buffalo, New York, and then to Illinois where they established a farm. A serious, dark-haired man, he wore a mustache and small beard much like General George Armstrong Custer. By the time he was 12, he was almost doing the labor of a full-grown

man. Through that hard work, he said he learned "the blessedness of drudgery and the value of time and money." With $2,000 and six sewing machines, Bemis founded the J.M. Bemis & Company in St. Louis, Missouri, which originally made textile bags for food products. Today its successor is a global packaging company listed on the New York Stock Exchange.

In 1858, when Bemis established his company, millers were doubtful the machine-made bags would be as strong as hand-sewn ones so he gave his personal guarantee that they would not break. He kept his word and his reputation as an honest businessman grew. During the Civil War, the company produced many different kinds of bags for the Union Army. In 1881, it introduced a cat named "Biddy," a mouser in the St. Louis facility. "In choosing her for the company logo, Judson Moss Bemis wanted to emphasize that in 'letting the cat out of the bag' he had nothing to hide and dealt fairly with his customers," the company's website states. When jute, a strong coarse fabric used in making burlap became popular, the company expanded to India. During the Great Depression, the Bemis company began to sell patterned feed sacks and flour bags. "These bags were printed with decorative patterns and could be used to sew dresses, aprons, pajamas, children's clothes, and other household necessities like draperies, tablecloths, quilts,

Alice Bemis Taylor and daughter. (Colorado Room Information Files, Colorado College Special Collections)

towels, sheets and pillowcases," the company's website adds.

One of the firm's most remarkable achievements was the construction in 1900 of a company town near Jackson, Tennessee, called Bemis. The community featured modest homes, tree-lined streets, schools, shops, churches and a YMCA. "The operators were those known in the south as poor whites," writes a biographer of Alice Cogswell Bemis:

Colorado Springs Day Nursery. 1920s. (Courtesy Early Connections Learning Centers)

> The opening of the mill gave to these people an undreamed of opportunity to earn money. It also offered to them a great privilege and at the same time a possibility of great danger. The privilege was that of being able for the first time in their lives to command money and to use it so that it would make them better and happier; the danger was that they might use it so that moral deterioration would follow. Both these possibilities were foreseen in the first plans for the town, and provision was made for the physical, mental, and spiritual needs of the people that would as far as possible avert danger. A social worker was engaged to live as a friend among the people, and a church, school, and library were provided for them.

Despite her formidable ancestors, the young Alice Bemis enjoyed a typical childhood in Colorado Springs. She went bowling, horseback riding, roller-skating and to dances at the home of General Palmer or his old partner, Dr. William Bell. She also loved to read out loud with family and friends, including May Howbert, the daughter of pioneer Irving Howbert. In 1903, in a quiet ceremony, she married Frederick Morgan Pike Taylor and for the rest of her life was known as "Mrs. F.M. P. Taylor." The couple built a house at 1238 Wood Avenue. There she lived quietly and went about her giving in the anonymous style of General Palmer and her own parents. "Her countless private philanthropies are known only to the fortunate recipients of her kindness," writes Vesta Tutt.

Her father, who died in 1921, left an estate worth $1.5 million and philanthropies valued at $25 million. He gave several buildings to Colorado College, including Bemis Hall, and helped establish the Judson Moss Bemis School of Business with a $100,000 gift in 1914. Her mother donated the lands and funds for a YWCA gymnasium and was one of the founding members of the Day Nursery. When Mrs. Taylor's mother died, she left her daughter $160,000. Using this bequest, Mrs. Taylor built a permanent home for the Day Nursery at the corner of Tejon and Rio Grande.

On Dec. 20, 1923, 50 children were moved into the building, along with six nurses, a cook, and a janitor. Mrs. Taylor spared no expense in building the nursery and its actual cost was around $273,000, said Diane L. Price, president and CEO of Early Connections Learning Centers, formerly Colorado Springs Child Nursery Centers, which now owns and operates the facility. Mrs. Taylor, who had overseen every detail, was so pleased that she gave each man who had worked on the building a $20 gold piece. She was its largest contributor for many years and left money in her will for its upkeep.

Mrs. Taylor was equally involved with the construction of the Colorado Springs Fine Arts Center, which was designed by Santa Fe architect John Gaw Meem and was built at the height of the Great Depression in part to give jobs to the unemployed of Colorado Springs. The home of Spencer Penrose, one of the young 'Socialites' who made a fortune in Cripple Creek, was torn down to make way for the building. Mrs. Taylor was interested in children with emotional and

Small tables and benches were built especially for children. (Courtesy Early Connections Learning Centers)

behavioral problems, too. In 1928, she founded the Bemis-Taylor Child Guidance Clinic, the first psychiatric clinic for children in a city of less than 100,000 and one of the first such clinics for children west of the Mississippi. According to a history by the guidance clinic's longtime secretary, Helen Thurlow, Mrs. Taylor became interested in establishment of such a facility as early as 1923, as the result of a suggestion made to her by Dr. Donald Gregg "in whose sanitarium near Boston she spent some time seeking help for her feelings of depression." Over the next five years, she consulted other physicians and friends about the idea and finally persuaded Dr. Bradford J. Murphey, a Boston psychiatrist affiliated with the Judge Baker Foundation and the New England Home for Little Wanderers, to come to Colorado Springs and open the clinic. Dr. Murphey had turned down the offer once and Mrs. Taylor made a personal trip to Boston to entreat him to come. On Nov. 10, 1927, the *Gazette* broke the news of the new clinic:

> The types of problems to be studied are those in which behavior of the child produces more than ordinary defects in home management, or defects in adjustment to school life, or difficulties in general social adjustment, so that the child becomes a problem in court or that court action is contemplated because of its conduct. With certain exceptions, cases will be studied in the order of acceptance. Exceptions will be made for emergency situations, if these are clearly stated at the time of the application. The waiting list is usually long, so that some time may be expected to elapse between acceptance of the case and its actual study.

The clinic was also located in the Day Nursery in space formerly occupied by the Visiting Nurse Association. It had a board of consultants, consisting of 23 physicians. It also had a 20-member board of advisers, whose members included Justin Hills, longtime director of Associated Charities, and Asa Jones, a longtime board member for both Associated Charities and Sunnyrest Sanatorium. When the clinic's services were expanded to adults in the mid-1960s, the child guidance clinic would be renamed Pikes Peak Mental Health Center and constitutes one of two branches of the modern-day AspenPointe.

A school principal referred the first child to the clinic on Jan. 12, 1928. The following day, two more children were referred by the school district. A week later, a parent referred his first child. In addition to the study of individual children, the clinic also served in a consultative and advisory capacity to other social agencies. Officials in Elbert, Teller, Douglas and Pueblo counties sought assistance from the clinic. Requests also came from adjoining states. From June 1929 to July 1932, it operated a child-placement service. The service was independent of the clinic, had its own board of directors, and the salary and automobile expenses of its sole employee were paid by Mrs. Taylor.

The child guidance clinic movement had its roots in the progressive reforms that were taking place at the beginning of the twentieth century. To many, the child seemed a logical place to begin. In 1908, a Chicago psychiatrist named Dr.

"The clinic is interested in the psychopathic, the delinquent, the recidivist, the psychoneurotic, or the psychotic child, but in the same way that the mental hygienist is interested in the insane, the feeble-minded and the criminal, in the same way that preventative medicine is interested in smallpox or diphtheria."

Dr. Bradford Murphey

William Healy took a tour of American hospitals and clinics throughout the country to find out what kind of psychological work was being done for children. To his surprise, he found nothing at all. Dr. Healy resolved to change that and opened the first child guidance clinic in Chicago. It was called the Juvenile Psychopathic Institute and most of the referrals came from Juvenile Court.

From 1909 to 1915, the Chicago psychopathic institute was the only child guidance clinic in the country and attracted visitors from throughout the United States and Europe. "It served as a nationally known research laboratory and training school for social reformers in the children's field," writes Dr. Bradford Murphey, the psychiatrist-director of the Bemis-Taylor Child Guidance Clinic.

From 1915 to 1921, the fields of child development and child psychiatry grew slowly, largely because of World War I. "In the beginning of the child guidance work a large percent of the children referred to the clinics for study were mentally deficient," Murphey writes. "As the work became better established, however, and more clinics were started, the proportion of children of normal intelligence increased."

Child guidance clinics were established throughout the country. When Smith College in 1918 established a School of Social Work, many graduates found work in the clinics. In fact, writes Dr. Murphey, "This work at Smith College was started because of the great need of trained social workers and was intended to supply such workers especially to child guidance clinics."

After 1921, the child guidance clinics sought to expand their services beyond the juvenile court system to the whole community. To do that, they had to shift their emphasis from the abnormal to the normal child. They began networking with school boards and other social services. "The clinic is interested in the psychopathic, the delinquent, the recidivist, the psychoneurotic, or the psychotic child, but in the same way that the mental hygienist is interested in the insane, the feeble-minded and the criminal, in the same way that preventative medicine is interested in smallpox or diphtheria. The aim of the child guidance clinic is not to cure full-fledged diseases but merely to prevent them," writes Dr. Murphey.

Mrs. Taylor, who by all accounts enjoyed a happy childhood, contributed $15,000 a year to the child guidance clinic for the first 12 years. "She felt that twelve years was a reasonable length of time in which to determine the value of such a service to the community, and that prolonged support by private philanthropy was inadvisable," writes Helen Thurlow.

In 1938, a year before Mrs. Taylor's funding was to expire, Dr. Murphey departed the clinic for a position on the East Coast. A board of directors was formed and in 1938 the clinic was incorporated as a nonprofit and its name changed to the Colorado Springs Child Guidance Clinic. The clinic then entered a period of uncertainty, complicated by the loss of staff due to World War II. Eventually it ceased operations completely and its property was placed in storage. In 1947, the clinic was reopened. Dr. Kenneth Loder, a child and adult psychiatrist from New York, was the new director-psychiatrist. Together with his staff, which consisted of a social worker and a secretary, the clinic moved to the American Red Cross Building at 1600 North Cascade Avenue. Its office consisted of two rooms and a solarium, with the secretary and clinic files located in the lobby. The budget was about $13,000, or $2,000 less than what Mrs. Taylor had contributed. Eighty percent of the funds collectively came from School District Number 11, Colorado College, the City of Colorado Springs and El Paso County. The other 20 percent came from individuals and foundations. The psychiatrist taught a class in "Mental Hygiene" at Colorado College twice a week and conducted a "Mental Hygiene Clinic" for students one-half day per week.

The Day Nursery

The Day Nursery at Tejon and Rio Grande resembles a cottage from a Grimm's fairy tale, its leaded-glass windows, brick pathways and arched doorways hinting at what lies within. Even now, ninety years after its completion, it continues to bewitch visitors. First and foremost, it is a refuge for children and their voices, young and excited, still spill down the stairs and hallways. This is how it should be; the way Alice Bemis Taylor imagined it when she built the Day Nursery in 1923 in the quiet time between two world wars. Everything was made with children in mind, from the child-sized tables and chairs in the dining room to the child-sized library where the bespectacled Harry Potter might feel at home. Even the imported floor tiles are child-sized, like the small round ends of loaves of bread, perfect in their imperfect irregularity, with a turquoise stone every few feet entreating one to step further into this enthralling place.

This is where Mrs. Taylor returned again and again, the place she asked to be driven past before she died. Mrs. Taylor was an extraordinary philanthropist and gave many things to Colorado Springs, but the Day Nursery was said to be her favorite gift. She dedicated it to her mother – Alice Cogswell Bemis – one of the original founders of the Day Nursery. In 1927, four years after the nursery opened, Mrs. Taylor established the Bemis-Taylor Child Guidance Clinic for children with emotional or behavioral problems. It was located on the main floor and was one of the two original branches of what today is AspenPointe.

"Thousands and thousands of children have passed through here and yet look at the condition," says Diane Price, gesturing at the superb craftsmanship on the main floor. "There's a level of respect for the building. An appreciation that resonates with the children and the families," adds Price, who is President and CEO of Early Connections Learning Centers, formerly Colorado Springs Child Nursery Centers, which owns and operates the Day Nursery.

> *"Thousands and thousands of children have passed through here and yet look at the condition. There's a level of respect for the building."*
>
> **Diane Price**

It is on the National Register of Historic Places, but is still very much a living institution. Open from 6:30 a.m. to 6 p.m., it provides early care and education for children primarily between the ages of two and a half and six. The fees are based on a sliding scale and the majority of the children are from working or low–income families.

Every inch of the building seems to have been created to give comfort and happiness to children. That was important because many of the children who historically attended the Day Nursery didn't come from comfortable homes. "In most cases one or both parents are dead, and but for the shelter afforded by the nursery they would be subjected to hardships," a *Gazette* reporter once wrote.

Many of the children boarded at the nursery when it was first established. The mothers might well have been clients of Associated Charities or servants of the well-to-do women who lived on Cascade or Wood avenues. Others were nurses who lived in boarding homes and were employed in the sanatoriums and had to leave their children at the nursery while they worked. "There were men who left their kids here while they looked for wives. Children who were left here during the Great Depression while both parents went away to look for work," said Price. "There were all kinds of reasons children were left here. It was never an orphanage. The parents would always be able to come back and get their children. They were never given up for adoption."

The library is small and cozy, the walls covered with Burl walnut wainscoting and floral bas-reliefs along the ceiling. Tiny side-by-side sinks with individual hooks for washcloths and towels are located in the bathroom. Down the hall is the auditorium, which is a work of art in itself. The flooring is constructed with oak-pegged strips. Decorative chandeliers hang from the ceiling. Along the west wall is a huge fireplace in which several children could stand comfortably. Over the fireplace is a hand-carved wood panel depicting children at play. The room is decorated with lovely pastel murals depicting familiar figures from Mother Goose rhymes. So soft and dreamy are the murals that they seem more like clouds streaming by. They were created and painted by Allen Tupper True, who in recent years has begun to receive some long overdue recognition. True was an illustrator of popular magazines like *Scribner's* and *Colliers Weekly* and gravitated into the creation of larger-than-life murals. He was born in Colorado Springs in 1881, about the time the Bemis family arrived, and his murals hang today on the walls of the Capitol Rotunda, the Brown Palace, the Denver Public Library and other private and public buildings throughout the country.

The dormitories of the Day Nursery were located on the second floor. On the west end was the boys' dormitory and the east side was for girls. On the third floor were a gymnasium and an actual infirmary where operations such as tonsillectomies were done.

Children splash in pool at the Day Nursery. (Courtesy Early Connections Learning Centers)

The idea of a day nursery dates back to France in the early 1800s and a Roman Catholic priest who wanted to establish a home for neglected and abused children. "Baby missions," as they were called, soon spread throughout Europe and the United States. The first Colorado Springs Day Nursery was established in 1897 in a four-room house at 416 E. Boulder Street. During the first year of operation, the directors took turns caring for the children. The nursery quickly outgrew its cottage and moved to 310 S. Wahsatch Avenue where a matron and nurse were employed. Within a year, this house was too small. Through the efforts of Mrs. G. N. Lawrence and Miss Burns, who also served on the board of Associated Charities, a new nursery was constructed for $4,000 at 816 S. Tejon Street. In 1901, after a little boy died of scarlet fever, $1,200 was raised to build a small hospital at the rear of the lot. At the turn of the century, the average number of children cared for day and night was 25. The cost was 10 cents a day per child, or two children for fifteen cents. If they were boarders, the cost was $6 a month for one child, $10 for two children. The money received from parents was not nearly enough to keep the nursery going so the women held lawn parties, fairs, and dinners. The members also contributed $1 a month and many contributed more.

When the Day Nursery at Rio Grande and Tejon opened, a decision was made not to accept children if both parents were alive because that would in effect relieve the parents of their responsibility and break up the home. "The most usual condition in Colorado Springs is where one parent may be very ill with tuberculosis, the other parent must earn the living, and the little child ought not to be left to care for the sick parent," the newspaper wrote in 1924. Nurses and matrons were not allowed to spank the children and food was never denied as a form of punishment. Instead the child might be sent to a room or have a privilege revoked.

Mrs. Taylor, who served as president of the Day Nursery from 1915 to 1922, wanted to do more for children. In a letter she left for the board, she talked about the flu pandemic and how she had wanted to create an umbrella organization with multiple agencies that would support indigent children. "She remarks in the letter that had that wish come true, Colorado Springs would not have lost so many children to influenza," said Price.

20

The Depression

During the Great Depression, food riots broke out in the United States, lines of unemployed men snaked along city blocks, and the number of tramps and hoboes riding the rails increased dramatically. Even women and young girls hit the road. But it wasn't until about two to three years after the Oct. 24, 1929 stock market crash that Associated Charities felt the economic devastation.

As it had done for decades, the charity kept track of home visits; office encounters, telephone conversations, and telegrams and letters written. The category that spiked first was telephone calls, which may have reflected embarrassment on the part of people reaching out for help. In the fiscal year preceding the 1929 crash, there were 4,273 office encounters and 8,669 telephone conversations. In the 1932-1933 fiscal year, office encounters increased to 17,125 and the telephone conversations rose to 15,583. The huge increase continued for the next two years and then began to taper off.

Justin Hills, the charity's longtime agent, expressed frustration with the mounting caseload and diminishing coffers. "This year we know will be the hardest winter we have ever had, and we also know it is mighty hard to raise money for charity. People do not have the money to give," he began an Oct. 9, 1933 letter to E.L. Moseley, the city manager. By then, the charity's annual expenditures were $39,000, with most of its money, or $28,500 coming from the Community Chest. But the Community Chest was struggling and had notified Hills that it planned to reduce its contribution by $5,000. Hills wanted the city to make up the difference. "Knowing how serious the proposition is going to be to take care of the poor this year, we sincerely hope we can get a favorable reply from the City," he wrote. El Paso County, which had frequently partnered with the charity in the past, was watching its dollars, too. To be eligible for county relief, applicants had to sign statements stating they were paupers, he added.

Dorothea Lange's "Migrant Mother," an iconic image from the Great Depression.

By the following year, two federal programs had been created: the Federal Employment Relief Administration and the Federal Transient Bureau, which established 545 camps and shelters throughout the country to aid the homeless and unemployed. These programs took over the bulk of the local charity's casework. In August of 1934, for example, Associated Charities' total caseload was 620. The Federal Employment Relief Administration assumed responsibility for 420 cases and the Federal Transient Bureau took another 140 cases, which left Associated Charities with just 60 cases. They included:

> 1) Unemployable resident people with property or an equity in property but without income.
>
> 2) Supplementary aid to people with inadequate incomes.
>
> 3) People who have resided here one year but less than three years and who, consequently, are not eligible to County aid or to transient aid.
>
> 4) People who had funds in building and loan associations or in the bank that failed and have not yet realized anything and who are unemployable.

A Depression-era soup kitchen.

In 1935, despite the fact that millions of people were still suffering and out of work, the federal government began dismantling its Federal Transient Bureau, thinking people would get jobs through the Works Progress Administration (WPA) or other federal, state and local agencies. But that didn't happen and the homeless population ballooned again. Justin Hills knew from experience many of the homeless would be knocking on the charity's door. In a Sept. 20, 1935, letter to state relief director for the Colorado Emergency Relief Administration, he wrote, "Having had some twenty years experience with transient families in this city I realize the impossibility of this organization escaping responsibility for their care with the Federal office closed. They simply go to the police and the police immediately refer them to us. Also I feel there is a real possibility of some suffering if we do not aid them."

As the old federal programs were ending and new ones, such as Social Security, were being implemented, the poor fell through the cracks. In a paper dated Sept. 8, 1936, the charity wrote, "Some of the unemployed were eligible to the WPA but the WPA did not take on all employable eligibles. This because its quota was filled. Other cases were unemployable but owned property and the County would not assume unless they turned their property over. For the first

*"A great many claimed to be in search of work.
Others were stranded and trying to get to their legal settlement or to relatives.
Of course there were a considerable number who were simply wanderers."*

ASSOCIATED CHARITIES ANNUAL REPORT

five months of operating, the Social Security Office would not accept new applications for Old Age Pensions until the old cases were investigated. Have just started on the new."

In a partial tabulation for 1936, the charity reported that once again misfortunes such as unemployment, under-employment, tuberculosis, other diseases and age-related infirmities were to blame for poverty in families and individuals. What was different during the Great Depression was the number of transients who were accompanied by children. In one year, the charity reported 72 cases and 77 children. "A great many claimed to be in search of work. Others were stranded and trying to get to their legal settlement or to relatives. Of course there were a considerable number who were simply wanderers."

During the Depression, Associated Charities even had its own Works Progress Administration youth project: Teaching girls and young women to sew. The charity supplied the materials and the WPA compensated the 40 young women who were enrolled in the project. They made crib quilts, diapers, vests, sacks, nightgowns, slips, bibs, men's pajamas, dresses, overalls, playsuits and an article of clothing called "outing flannel pajamas."

Hoboes walking the rails during hard times.

Lasting roughly a decade, from 1929 to 1939, the Great Depression was the worst economic calamity in American history. But it did result in the establishment of some social safety nets. No longer would impoverished tuberculars, the aged, or accident-maimed workers be forced to sleep in the basement of City Hall. Nor would they necessarily turn to Associated Charities for food, clothing, or shelter.

With the implementation of the new federal, state and local programs, the charity would find its traditional workload diminishing. Indeed, records show that during the ten-year period of the Great Depression, from 1929 to 1939, the charity's budget reached its highest level – roughly $44,000 – for the fiscal year ending Sept. 30, 1933, and then began to decline. From April 1, 1934 to March 31, 1935, the charity handled 5,004 cases and 15,554 individuals. By contrast, from April 1, 1940, to March 31, 1941, the caseload had dropped to 1,974 cases and 8,194 individuals. The Great Depression changed the landscape for everyone, from countries to individuals to organizations. Associated Charities was more than 50 years old. It had shown itself remarkably capable of adapting to the changing times. More difficulties lay ahead.

21

Uncertainty

The future of Colorado Springs looked bleak in the years immediately before and after World War II. Many houses stood vacant and the bustling downtown where Mrs. Goddard and other socialites exchanged their morning greetings seemed dilapidated and forlorn. The tourism business was in the doldrums and new drugs to combat tuberculosis marked the end of sanatoriums. Without these two major industries, the city's very identity was crumbling.

Hard times were everywhere, from the luxurious Broadmoor Hotel to Colorado College, which was even thinking about closing its doors, writes historian George Fagan. "The future, indeed, looked very bleak for General Palmer's dream city at the foot of Pikes Peak."

Associated Charities was struggling, too. Its traditional 'relief' functions had been taken over by other programs, most notably the federal Social Security Administration, which in 1940 began issuing pension checks. "The development of the Social Security Program," the charity wrote in the forward to its 1943-44 annual report, "has freed the agency to become primarily a service agency." Its relief program in the future would serve as a "supplementary service" to clients not eligible for assistance from the county's Department of Public Welfare, the charity added.

Justin Hills, agent for 28 years, resigned on July 1, 1944, due to ill health. Miss Rose Porter, the agency's executive secretary, replaced him. A college graduate with considerable experience as a social worker, Miss Porter was well qualified for the job, but the wartime shortage of men was probably a factor in her promotion.

The charity's budget declined to levels not seen since 1919. In the 1943-44 fiscal year, total expenditures were $12,451 and income was $15,949. The largest contribution, $3,125, came from the Community Chest followed by $1,571 from the City of Colorado Springs. The charity still had a number of committees and an expansive board of directors that included the wives of Cripple Creek gold kings Charles L. Tutt and A.E. Carlton, as well as May Howbert, the daughter of pioneer Irving Howbert. In its annual report, Associated Charities defined its new mission:

> I. To provide a skilled casework service on problems of family living and individual social adjustment.
>
> II. To promote auspices and resources that contribute to healthy social living in the community, and to combat social conditions that threaten to undermine it.

"During the war period many families have been separated due to military service or defense work. In the post-war period there will be many adjustments to make in the family and much greater emphasis will be needed in family case work."

FAMILY SERVICE BROCHURE

The agency said it no longer intended to take care of transients, except in certain circumstances, and that it would no longer pay the costs for them to be returned to their legal residence. Instead, it would focus on families: "The Associated Charities accepts families for help with problems of family and personal relationships, helps with the achievement of educational objectives; assists the family in parent-child relationships; assists the family in marital adjustments; and assists in family budgeting, vocational planning and with health needs. Financial assistance may or may not be needed as a part of the service to the family."

The charity had an average of 115 cases, with the largest number of referrals from the Department of Public Welfare followed by the American Red Cross. The applicants could be divided into 1) families who needed help in budgeting and household management; 2) families who had special health needs, and 3) families in which "discord" existed between husband and wife or between parent and child.

In its annual report, the charity then went on to describe three representative families. The language, which is markedly different from the days of Miss Schnapp or even Wood Worcester, shows the growing influence of psychiatry, as well as the post-war belief that science could cure almost anything. For the first time, intelligence tests were used as diagnostic tools.

"Mrs. A," who was separated from her husband, had shown an inability to manage her household affairs. The agency helped her draw up a budget and showed her what kind of food to buy. "Mrs. A. is now buying more wisely and the home is being run more smoothly. It is kept clean and the meals provide adequate nutrition. The tests for the children show them to be of normal intelligence."

"Mr. B" had been hospitalized for eight years for an illness. Though the cause of the illness is not specified, the length of his hospitalization suggests tuberculosis. The long hospitalization had created a "dependency" and Mr. B sought shelter of an institution where he could resume his dependent role. "A careful study of his condition reveals that physically and mentally he is able to hold a job. The emotional problem, therefore, must be dealt with." Eventually Mr. B got a job and his confidence increased.

"Case C" involved an unstable woman who was neglectful of her home and dealt unwisely with money. A 15-year-old son had taken care of her for two years and he, too, had begun showing signs of instability. Tests showed that the woman was suffering from Alzheimer's and the organization filed an application to have her admitted to the state mental hospital. Turning its attention to the boy, the agency found him a home with "a motherly person" and helped him find a job earning $17.50 a week. The youth improved markedly, except for his over-reliance on the agency, which he had come to think of as a "parent."

The charity was confident the need for counseling services would grow. "During the war period many families have been separated due to military service or defense work. Mothers have taken employment and special provisions have been made for the care of their children. In the post-war period there will be many adjustments to make in the family and much greater emphasis will be needed in family case work."

22

Maturity Interrupted

In Acacia Park, where the air smelled of frost and grass dying back, men returned from the war played dominoes, chess and checkers under the trees. The muffled voices, the muted click of pieces, soothed the jangled nerves of veterans suffering from post-traumatic stress disorder. Mary Edmonds, who wore a string of pearls around her neck and had an abundance of thick, curly hair, had become the charity's new director and spoke of the difficulties veterans and their families were facing.

"So many of our present case problems are the result of the war. Many boys went directly from High School into some branch of service. Their clothing, food, and spending money were supplied by Uncle Sam, who sent allotment checks to wives of those who married. Some of these wives also had good war jobs, and financial problems were infrequent. When the husbands returned, allotments stopped. Jobs were not so plentiful," she said in an interview with the *Gazette*. She added:

> Actually BEING a husband and father, and meeting the day-to-day responsibilities of married life, involved a major mental adjustment. It had seemed so easy and adequate to know an allotment was being sent home regularly. But the actuality of homemaking was different. They had temporarily shifted their feeling of dependence from their parents to their Uncle Sam. Wives had learned to carry family problems and responsibilities in their absence, and to handle finances for themselves and their children. Resultant bickering and arguments about ways and means are deadly enemies of a happily married life. These young people, whose maturity was interrupted by the most awful war in history, must have help. They don't understand themselves or the predicaments in which they are embroiled.

A widow and the mother of two children, Edmonds had moved to the Springs in 1942 to supervise Red Cross activities at Camp Carson. She had a bachelor's degree and master's degree from Wichita University and had taken some post-graduate courses in social work at the University of Chicago. During her tenure, the charity expanded its programs and deepened its relationship with the Day Nursery, the Child Guidance Clinic and other government entities and nonprofits. Officials at the Day Nursery found her to be a great ally. "The name Mary Edmonds is practically a household word at the Day Nursery," said Mary

"The name Mary Edmonds is practically a household word at the Day Nursery. Whenever difficult family problems come to our attention, which occurrence is not infrequent, it is to Family Service that we turn for counsel and help."

MARY DUNWIDDIE

Dunwiddie, executive secretary. "Whenever difficult family problems come to our attention, which occurrence is not infrequent, it is to Family Service that we turn for counsel and help. Because of this close working relationship with the agency which Mary Edmonds directs, the children of the nursery are enjoying a more complete, more satisfying life than they would otherwise experience."

In May of 1945, the organization had completed its transition into a counseling agency and the board of directors voted to formally change its name to Family Service of Colorado Springs. It was affiliated with a national organization called Family Welfare Association of America. As in the past, it had a large board of directors made up of nearly two dozen people. C.C. Morris was president; Charles Collins, vice president, and Paul Vollmer, treasurer.

Interestingly, the bulk of the people who sought help referred themselves to the agency. Of the 201 families under its care, illness was present in 83 cases; housing was an issue for 138 individuals and 21 women applied for daycare for their children. The influence of the psychoanalysis and Sigmund Freud can be readily seen in the case studies, which abound with references to domineering mothers and dependent and immature children. Take "Johnny A," for example: "It developed in the interviews that the mother had a perfectionist pattern for her son, just as her own mother had for her. She had resented this in her own mother, but was so dominated by her that she attempted to carry out her mother's wishes unconsciously. During the interviews the mother came to realize that she could not be a mature wife and mother so long as her own mother dominated every action of the family."

"Mrs. B" came to the office one day saying that she had tuberculosis and needed to be hospitalized. When the El Paso County Tuberculosis Clinic examined her, she was found to be free of the disease. "I'm sorry, I wanted to go to bed and be taken care of," she said when informed of the results. Her "dependency" problem, a caseworker wrote, dated back to childhood. With the help of a psychiatrist, the woman worked through her issues and secured an office job that paid her $120 a month. "As a result, the client is able to be a useful member of society and to have a healthier relationship to her mother and to other individuals."

By 1950, the baby boom was underway and Colorado Springs was experiencing a housing shortage the likes of which it hadn't seen since the 1870s. The downtown business district was filled with shoppers who prowled the aisles of shoe stores, clothing stores and stationary shops. The city had 122 neighborhood grocery stores. Residents could order by telephone a loaf of Rainbo bread, a package of Lucky Strikes, or a dozen Jonathan apples. The name change from Associated Charities had been "difficult," Edmonds acknowledged in an interview in 1950, but said she believed most residents now understood its changed mission. Inquiries came from:

- The minister. He wishes to refer to the agency one of his members with this problem: Should she ask her daughter and son-in-law to move into her home to live during a long period of illness and unemployment which faces the husband? The minister believes the impersonal approach of the agency worker would be helpful.

- The landlord calls: To refer to the agency his tenant, a conscientious family man who seems to lose one job after another. The landlord thinks maybe the concern over his wife's failing eyesight may be a factor in the tenant's unrest. Can the agency help him?

- The doctor calls: To refer to the agency his patient, a pregnant and unmarried girl who says she wants to keep her baby. The girl's mother is sympathetic with her daughter's desire but does not see how the problem can be met. Would the agency worker talk to his patient about what is possible?

- The lawyer calls: To refer to the agency a woman who came to him reluctantly to discuss divorce. She feels she is a burden to her educated American-born husband because of her foreign speech and habits. The lawyer feels she needs social service.

- The neighbor calls: To ask if the agency can talk to Mrs. A. next door about Homemaker Service. She is going to the hospital for her fourth baby next week. There are no relatives to help her with the care of the children while her husband works. Will the agency's Homemaker be available to help in this instance?

- The businessman calls: To refer to the agency Mrs. C., a good stenographer who is having so much difficulty with family problems that she is being continually called on the telephone and is forgetful on the job. He does not want to become involved in a discussion of personal affairs with her and asks for consultation service.

Men lunching in Acacia Park. (PPLD)

One of the agency's most successful programs was its "Homemaker" service in which a "motherly troubleshooter" was sent into a home where the mother was too ill or harassed to handle her responsibilities. "A Homemaker is a competent woman with some knowledge of home economics, child psychology, nursing, cooking and the art of keeping a family happy and healthy," Edmonds explained.

Family Service continued to work closely with the Child Guidance Clinic, which also expanded its programs in the post-war years. By 1957, the budget for the guidance clinic increased from $13,000 to $31,000. Since children living in the city and county were not charged a fee, the clinic was required to carry on numerous fundraising drives. School District 11, El Paso County, the City of Colorado Springs, and Colorado College remained the major funders.

The referrals included children who showed unreasonable fear or were withdrawn and unhappy; children who exhibited immature behavior or had difficulty learning; children who had habits such as thumb-sucking, bed-wetting, stuttering, or other unusual mannerisms; children who had difficulty forming relationships with adults and peers; children who exhibited unusual sexual activity or indulged in excessive or bizarre fantasies, and children who suffered from bodily disorders that had an underlying emotional component.

One ten-year-old, listening to his parents arguing one night, sensed that divorce was imminent and that he might wind up in an orphanage. "His real life situation was so bad that he took refuge in an imaginary world of his own making filled

A view of Pikes Peak Avenue, 1951.

with elaborate ritualistic detail and compulsive repetitious monotony. His imagination was not the light, delightful fantasy of childhood but represented a deep impoverishment and restriction which narrowed his world rather than enriching it." Another youngster was having trouble in school despite an above-average intelligence. "In the course of treatment it developed that he was very closely identified with a father who felt trapped by his vocational choice. The mother in subtle ways reinforced the father's feeling of inadequacy – feelings which were not justified by objective criteria. When these feelings were discovered, Johnny was freed to attack school work more aggressively without ill-defined fears of retribution."

The guidance clinic continued to reach out to the community, establishing a sheltered workshop for the training of mentally handicapped teenagers and a special class at the YMCA for boys who had "feelings of inferiority about their physical prowess." A remedial tutoring program was started for children whose scholastic problems were thought to be emotional. Frequent consultations with principals and teachers were held. The Juvenile Court, recognizing the need for psychiatric services for children who broke the law, established a relationship with the clinic.

Still, the idea of seeking professional counseling for personal problems carried a stigma and Family Service of Colorado Springs and the Child Guidance Clinic grew slowly. "The spirit of rugged individualism and the belief that families should be able to solve their own problems still prevailed in many minds," one staff member wrote.

The ACCESS Center

Sometimes fresh from a hospitalization or suffering from depression, the clients pass through the doors of the ACCESS Center at 875 W. Moreno Avenue. With the help of counselors, case managers, and medication, the fog lifts and healing begins. In the old days, when the center was called the Kaleidoscope Clubhouse, they might have spent a few months drinking coffee or attending group therapy sessions. And that was about as good as it was going to get. But officials at AspenPointe decided the old model wasn't good enough. A couple of years ago, they repainted, re-plastered, did some remodeling, and then overhauled the mission of the ACCESS Center. (The initials stand for Avenues for Community Placement, Chosen by Clients, to Empower, Build Skills and Self Sufficiency.)

The goal now is to restore people to the world through volunteer opportunities, reintegration into the workforce or a fresh start in college. "Mental health isn't just about working out the demons of the past or the biological underpinnings of your illness. It's about the whole person. All of us, no matter how ill, have a desire to be successful and contribute to society," said Jennifer DeGroff, AspenPointe's director of Outpatient and Integrated Services.

In safe, comfortable classrooms, the visitors can get reacquainted with the poet, the painter, the dancer, the writer silenced years ago. "When we started focusing on what people could do instead of what they couldn't, things started to turn around," said Jennifer Given, a peer specialist who mentors other people. " It's focusing on a future. How do you want to make your life better? It's huge."

Given knows what she's talking about. She spent years drinking and drugging, moving from job to job, and putting up with physical and verbal abuse from her longtime boyfriend. A couple of years ago, she grabbed a razor blade and dug a nine-inch trench up her arm. She was rushed to the emergency room and then taken to AspenPointe's Lighthouse, an acute care facility for people who are homicidal, or suicidal, or suffering from a psychotic break. After she was stabilized, she was referred to the ACCESS Center. She was diagnosed with borderline personality disorder and prescribed medication. In addition to counseling, she began taking leadership and other classes to build her self-confidence and improve her communication skills. She began telling her story and noticed that other people were listening. Six months after she arrived, there was an opening for a peer specialist. She applied and got the job. The first paycheck was wonderful. No direct deposit for her. She wanted to hold the check in her hand. "It was awesome."

There are other success stories. Betsy, a fragile beauty, arrived with her therapist and sat for weeks on a couch, unable to make eye contact with anybody. Slowly, she started to emerge from her shell and began going to classes. One day, something changed. "If you asked her what it was I don't know if she could say what it was," said Julie Reed, manager of the ACCESS Center. "Maybe it was a little bit of everything. If I had to nail it down, it's probably when she began volunteering at Pikes Peak United Way."

Heraldo P., a tall, lithe man who formerly played semi-professional basketball, is studying hard to get his GED. He, too, would like to become a peer specialist some day. He loves music -- the Bobby Blue Band, ZZ Hill, B.B. King – and has worked as a DJ. A couple of years ago, after he broke his leg, he saw an ad on television for AspenPointe's counseling services, and decided to call them. "I was feeling sad a lot. It stopped me from enjoying a lot of things." One day, his therapist suggested he try some classes and he has been taking them ever since. "When I started coming here, I decided I was going to be the best student they ever had." Heraldo has volunteered so many hours that a couple of years ago he earned the "Volunteer of the Year Award." Now in his early sixties, he would like to eventually obtain an associate degree from Pikes Peak Community College. "Everything I've done I've worked hard at," he said.

Oh, and that coffee drinking? It has its place, said Jen DeGroff. People with mental disabilities can be scary to other people and during their informal gatherings they learn how to make small talk, she said. "But it shouldn't take up all of your day," she cautioned.

23

Merger

On Pikes Peak Avenue, Plymouths and Fords and Chevrolets rolled slowly down the street looking for parking spaces. The wide avenue, with its stunning views, was not destined to become the salon-de-reunion that turn-of-the-century town boosters had envisioned. Nor was Colorado Springs destined to become the Switzerland of the West. Instead, the military had become a major economic engine, altering the city's political life and generating new jobs that helped offset the loss from the dwindling tourism business and the closure of sanatoriums.

Peterson Air Force Base had been reactivated. Camp Carson, which had dwindled to a few hundred people after World War II, was growing again. And in 1954, following a grueling campaign, President Dwight Eisenhower had selected Colorado Springs as the site of a new Air Force Academy. More military installations and military-related contractors would follow.

The mansions along Cascade and Wood avenues retained their gentility and the generous spirit manifested by General Palmer and Alice Bemis-Taylor was still very much alive, particularly in the social service organizations that abounded in Colorado Springs. "This town had more social service agencies than any town I had ever been in," remembered former Family Counseling Service board member Joe Pickle, an ordained minister, a Fulbright scholar and longtime faculty member at Colorado College.

A new generation of women had taken up the leadership positions once held by Mrs. Wood and Mrs. Hagerman. Among them was Barbara Yalich, a longtime resident of Colorado Springs and a graduate of Colorado College. When Yalich graduated from college in the early 1950s, there weren't many opportunities for young women. So she poured her energies into the Junior League, eventually becoming regional director and then international director. "The Junior League is a very old woman's organization," she said in an interview in 2012. "Its mission was to train young women to take active roles in the community. It was founded in the 1920s when not many women worked outside the home."

As Yalich traveled the country, she became acquainted with what other Junior League organizations were doing in the arts and in the healthcare industry. She found herself drawn to the plight of the mentally ill. "It was the time of the Vietnam protests and uprisings all over the country. It was also the time of President Kennedy. He began to talk about mental health and mental retardation and we began to learn

"It was the time of the Vietnam protests and uprisings all over the country. It was also the time of President Kennedy. He began to talk about mental health and mental retardation and we began to learn about state hospitals and the horrible mistreatment of the mentally ill."

BARBARA YALICH

about state hospitals and the horrible mistreatment of the mentally ill."

In order to differentiate itself from a military program, Family Service changed its name in 1960 to the Family Counseling Service of Colorado Springs. The average fee per client was $2.39 and the bulk of its income came from the Community Chest. The agency moved from its office on East Boulder Street, where it had been headquartered since the Great Depression, to 1015 North Nevada Ave, to 228 E. Monument Street and finally, in 1965, to a building which formerly housed nurses on the old Cragmor Sanatorium campus.

Between 1965 and 1968, the number of cases rose from 391 to 724 and the number of clinical interviews went from 1,625 to 4,360. Although 30 percent of its clients fell below the poverty line, the other 70 percent were mostly middle class. At every level, debate raged about the future of the family or even if families would have a future. "Where the family will be is in question," wrote Family Counseling's executive director Eugene DeBellis.

In addition to its counseling services, the agency forged new partnerships with other Colorado Springs organizations. It administered and staffed the Big Brothers program; sent two social workers weekly to Harrison School District, and provided diagnostic and evaluation services to Municipal Court. It also provided consultation services to the Department of Vocational Rehabilitation, the YWCA, Headstart, the Colorado Parole Department, the Day Nursery and area clergy. For the first time, group therapy meetings were held. "The secret is in understanding, and getting that emotional learning which enables us to deal happily with ourselves," said DeBellis.

The Child Guidance Clinic, which was also located for a while in the same Cragmor building, grew more quickly than Family Counseling, reversing an historic trend that had existed between the two since the late 1920s. Heading the clinic was Dr. John Mahaffy, the father of three young children, who earned his medical degree from the University of Minnesota. A bearish man with bristling grey hair, Mahaffy had served as a psychiatrist in the Army. He was associated with child guidance clinics in St. Paul, Minnesota, and Evansville, Illinois, before taking over the directorship of the Colorado Springs organization.

"We have troubled children from strict homes, from homes where they are allowed to do exactly as they please, from drinking homes and homes of complete abstainers, from deeply religious families and from families who profess no religion at all," Dr. Mahaffy said in a newspaper interview. Not all children referred to the clinic were accepted, he added. If a problem is chiefly a "disturbed family situation" and not primarily an "emotional or psychiatric problem of the child," then he or she would be referred to other agencies, he said. If accepted for treatment, a study was made, which included interviews with parents and children, as well as diagnostic tests administered by a staff psychologist. "If psychiatric treatment is indicated, that information is given to the parent and parents. Otherwise the case is closed."

In the early years, the Child Guidance Clinic did not charge any fees for its services and continued to be funded through Colorado College, various school districts and other governmental entities, as well as nonprofits and individuals. In 1964, the clinic's board of directors decided to extend services to adults and began casting about for a new name. Should it be the "Pikes Peak Clinic?" the "Pikes Peak Guidance Center?" or the "Colorado Springs Adult and Child Guidance Clinic"? Though the board of directors was worried about the potential negative impact of the words, "mental health," it nevertheless settled upon the Pikes Peak Mental Health Center

The center offered five group therapy sessions for adults, two group therapy sessions for adolescents, and one for boys. In February of 1968, in collaboration with the Colorado State Hospital, the center began offering a one-day-a-week program for former mental patients. The patients began their five-hour gathering with coffee and snacks, then divided into groups, came back together for lunch, and spent the rest of the afternoon in recreational or occupational therapy. The mental health center also began developing a daytime hospitalization program for acutely disturbed and chronically ill patients. The more elaborate program, which would be held three days a week, would offer group and individual psychotherapy, medication management and crisis intervention.

By the spring of 1969, Family Counseling and Pikes Peak Mental Health Center began talking to each other about a possible merger. Yalich, who was then president of the board of the Pikes Peak Mental Health Center, said the Community Research and Planning Council had identified the possible union. "We began to discuss what each of us did and where our money came from," Yalich remembered.

The driving force behind the proposed merger was the monumental legislation signed into law in 1963 by President John F. Kennedy called the Community Mental Health Act. The law increased the pace of deinstitutionalization, a process in which mental patients from large state hospitals were being sent back to their hometowns to be cared for. The emptying of state hospitals actually began in the 1950s and has been attributed to a multitude of factors, including the civil rights movement, popular movies and books, the support of President Kennedy, the development of new psychotropic drugs, and the need by states to reduce costs. "Treating people in the community on an outpatient basis is less costly than housing them," recalled Dr. William Scholton, a former medical director . For patients who had loving families to return to and were able to resume normal lives, it was a positive experience. For others, it was much worse than being warehoused on crowded wards. Some wound up in county-run homes for the poor or nursing homes while others found themselves in jails or prisons or on the streets.

Psychiatrist Leon Eisenberg writes that the number of people in mental hospitals increased dramatically in the first half of the twentieth century, peaking at 550,000 in 1956 and then beginning a slow descent. The patient population at the state mental hospital in Pueblo was roughly 6,000 in the early 1960s and dwindled to less than 500 by 2009. The average patient stay in 1962 in the Pueblo hospital was a shocking 16 years, seven months, and 28 days.

Throughout history, the mentally ill have been demonized and disparaged and their problems attributed to weak or immoral character. In Colorado, in the nineteenth century and early twentieth century, visitors were allowed onto wards at the state hospital in Pueblo to gawk at the patients. Similarly, in Denver, residents could spend a Sunday afternoon viewing patients on the county's crowded insane ward. The disparaging attitude began to change with the release of new books and movies.

In 1908, Clifford Whittingham Beers, a graduate of Yale University and a self-described "neurasthenic," published an extremely influential book called *A Mind that Found Itself*. Beers suffered from a severe bipolar disorder and describes how his fear of contracting epilepsy grew into a full-blown obsession, which led him to jump out his bedroom window. He spent the ensuing months in various mental institutions where he was mistreated and neglected by guards and doctors. When he recovered, he spent the rest of his life advocating for better treatment of the "insane." Beer's autobiographical narrative is tame by today's standards but was revolutionary at the time and "did for the American mental health movement what Thomas Paine's *Common Sense* did for the American Revolution," his publisher wrote.

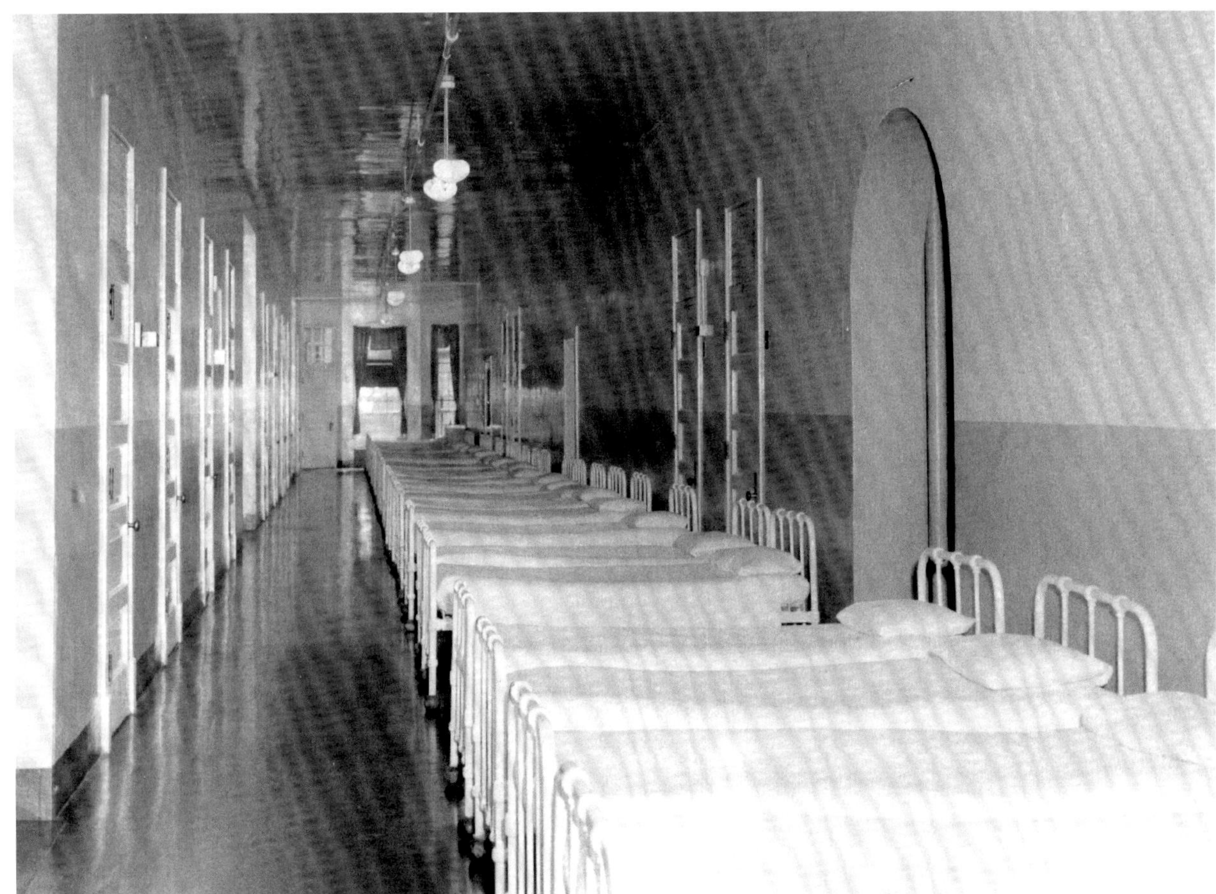

Wards were so crowded at the Colorado State Hospital in Pueblo that officials were forced to put beds in corridors. 1959.
(Courtesy Nell Mitchell/Colorado Mental Health Institute Museum)

The outpouring of sympathy toward the mentally ill increased in 1948 with the debut of a movie called "The Snake Pit," in which Olivia deHavilland plays a young woman who winds up in a mental institution called Juniper Hill. Although her psychiatrist is thoughtful, the matron is abusive and sends her to the "snake pit" where the patients go around mumbling to themselves. In one of the most moving scenes a young woman sings "Going Home," a melody adapted from Dvorak's New World Symphony. Although Olivia deHavilland's character goes home, most of the patients know they will remain at the hospital for the rest of their lives.

Another book that had a powerful effect was Ken Kesey's 1962 novel, *One Flew Over the Cuckoo's Nest.* Considered one of the best novels of the twentieth century and later made into a movie, the novel describes a psychic battle between a controlling Nurse Ratched and a small-town drifter played by Jack Nicholson, who is subdued through repeated electroshock treatments and eventually a lobotomy.

Perhaps the most famous example of a lobotomized patient was Rosemary Kennedy, sister to JFK, who underwent a lobotomy at the age of 23 at the request of her father, Joseph Kennedy. Rosemary was a lovely young woman who apparently suffered some brain damage at birth when she was deprived of oxygen. Her father opted to have her undergo the surgery after she became rebellious and her behavior became erratic. She was given a local anesthetic and then doctors inserted a sharp instrument in her awake brain and began cutting tissue. When her speech became garbled, they withdrew the instrument. She remained institutionalized for the rest of her life.

The legislation signed into law by President Kennedy allocated some $275 million for the establishment of comprehensive community mental health centers nationwide. Lawmakers hoped such centers would prove to be a more medical- and cost-effective way of treating the mentally ill. Centers receiving that designation would be required to offer five major services: 1) In-patient; 2) Out-patient; 3) Partial hospitalization; 4) Emergency services, and 5) Consultation and education. It would take a while to get such centers up and running and some mental patients fell through the cracks. "It was a period of confusion and people being left out, not given the services they needed. They were discharged from the hospital into the community and there were not services in the community for them," remembers Dr. Cynthia Rose, the first female psychiatrist to practice in the Pikes Peak region.

Family Counseling and Pikes Peak Mental Health Center seemed like a logical partnership. The missions were roughly equivalent, the staffs were about the same size (roughly six to seven fulltime employees), and both had a similar mix of psychiatrists, psychologists and social workers. By joining forces, they could cut their costs and eventually reach an even greater number of people. "We got along very well," Yalich added.

There were differences between the two organizations. For one, the Pikes Peak Mental Health Clinic focused on long-term and intense individual therapy with a medicinal component. By contrast, Family Counseling specialized in much shorter interventions dealing with marital discord and parent-child relationships and medicine was not necessarily prescribed. "The difference between the approaches is one only of degree and emphasis rather than of kind," Pickle wrote in a 1969 memo. By then, Pikes Peak Mental Health owned its own building and was located at 1353 Mesita Road, which would soon become 1353 S. Eighth Street. Family Counseling rented space in the Golf Acres Shopping Center at 1422 North Hancock Avenue.

Dr. Cynthia Rose was the first female psychiatrist to practice in the Pikes Peak region.

Blending the staffs and their missions would be the trickiest part. Joel Hefley, a former Colorado Congressman, remembered there being "considerable animosity between the two staffs." When housed in Cragmor, employees used the same front door but rarely interacted with one another and the two directors, Dr. Mahaffy and Eugene DeBellis, were reportedly not on speaking terms.

The two groups sent out more than 150 questionnaires to donors and governmental entities and other community members seeking their input on the proposed merger. They responded favorably. But Dr. Mahaffy, the mental health clinic's longtime director, opposed the deal. In a Sept. 17, 1969, memo he wrote, "I dissent from the decision of the Merger Committee for the following reasons: 1) Never was any sound plan of financing a merged agency presented, 2) The study was too superficial, too hurried and did not involve the staffs of the two agencies from the beginning."

Facing page: A crowded dayroom at the Colorado State Hospital in Pueblo. The eyes were inked out at that time to protect patient privacy. 1959. (Courtesy Nell Mitchell/Colorado Mental Health Institute Museum)

But the board did not share Mahaffy's opposition. "Overall, everyone agreed to it and got behind it," remembered Barbara Yalich. Dr. Mahaffy and Eugene DeBellis departed and the search began for a new executive director. In the interim, 33-year-old Dr. Cynthia Rose was named acting director. A graduate of Boston University's medical school with a pediatric internship from the University of California Hospital in San Francisco, Dr. Rose had been hired at the mental health center by Dr. Mahaffy in 1969. "I was caught in the cross-fire," Dr. Rose recalled in an interview in 2012. "I had just finished my fellowship and wanted to practice child psychiatry and this got thrown into my lap. I figured I was going to have to adapt and find out if there was a place for me."

Once the merger was agreed upon, officials were faced with the dilemma of finding a new name that reflected the combined entity. They settled on a long name that captured both: The Pikes Peak Family Counseling and Mental Health Center. The newly constituted board consisted of 24 people. The merged clinic was now poised to take a giant step into the future.

But one very old problem remained: the homeless. In the years to come, their numbers would include Vietnam veterans discharged from the service with various mental and physical disabilities, a new generation of addicts and alcoholics, and individuals discharged from mental hospitals under the deinstitutionalization movement. In time, men and women carrying backpacks and holding up signs would become visible on virtually every busy street corner in America.

Youth Directions

Not long ago, a teen-ager working at a grocery store helped an older woman take her bags to her car. After the car pulled away, he looked down and saw she had left her purse in the shopping cart. Instead of turning it over to a supervisor, he rummaged through the purse, found some credit cards, and used them to charge some items before going home. He was apprehended and eventually referred to Youth Directions, which is part of AspenPointe Enterprises. A victim offender conference was arranged. The woman, accompanied by her daughter, took a seat on one side of the table and the youthful offender on the other. She was not looking for vengeance, but wanted him to understand the impact of what he had done. She explained that her medications had been in the purse, that she had been forced to pay additional fees as a result of the extra credit-card charges, and that her daughter had taken time off from work trying to help her get her finances straightened out. After hearing the victim's story, the youth began to express genuine remorse for what he had done and seemed to understand how his actions had impacted the victim, family, and the community. He agreed to take some educational and career counseling classes and, at the request of the victim, he volunteered to work at a senior retirement facility. Both sides left feeling transformed.

Thomas Gomez stands in a classroom where GED classes are taught.

Since 2001, when the restorative justice program began under a predecessor called Workout Limited, there have been hundreds of similar transformations. "Although it doesn't always end this way, we occasionally see tough kids who wind up crying. And it's the same with the victims. They come in upset and angry and by the end they're shaking hands with the kid and asking them if they want a mentor," said Adah Rodriguez, former director of Youth Directions at AspenPointe Enterprises

Restorative-based justice has a different paradigm than traditional criminal justice, she said. "In a traditional court system, when a crime is committed three questions are asked: One, who did it? Two, what law was broken? And three, how shall they be punished? With restorative justice, it becomes, Who's responsible? Who was harmed? How can that harm be repaired?" As Rodriguez explains it, the victim has a great deal of input in whatever the offender is required to do and often the measure to repair the harm is offense-specific. "For example, if they stole a bike, it might mean working at a bike shop. If a crime was committed against a senior citizen, it might mean volunteering at a senior citizen center. If property was destroyed, it could possibly mean repairing the damaged property."

Roughly 500 youth annually are referred to the program through the courts, the community or the schools. About 125 victim offender conferences are held each year. The recidivism rate for youth who complete the program is 17 percent compared with more than 30 percent for El Paso County. "Usually it's around 12 percent," said Rodriguez. The youngsters are also taught decision-making skills, communication skills, job-seeking skills, and practical skills, like how to read a bus schedule or look for an apartment. "The ultimate goal is to help these kids become self-sufficient, take accountability for themselves and develop empathy for other people," Rodriguez said.

The restorative justice program is only one facet of the Education and Youth Services program. About 1,500 people also go through the GED preparation and testing program or take advantage of other education and job-training classes. "We spend a lot of time on pre-employment -- helping with job-seeking skills, interviewing, resumé-building, things like that. We also spend a lot of time helping the kids assess their strengths and skills. So, for example, we take them out into the community and put them at Petco or K-Mart and assess those skills and help them find a job that's appropriate for their skills set. If they really want to work in retail, we'll try to find out if retail's a good fit. But maybe they don't do well with customers, so we'll find them a stocking job. We call it career services, but it's really employment because kids are not going to find careers at age sixteen. We try to help them get that entry- level employment and identify some of those career goals. They may want to be a teacher someday. We say, 'Okay. Here's your entry-level job working at McDonald's. Now let's put together a plan to help you get where you need to be next.'"

One young woman who had dropped out of high school was having a hard time making ends meet. She enrolled in the GED program and also signed up for nearly every class AspenPointe offered, including the customer service training program, cashier training and barista training. She wound up with two jobs -- one as a receptionist with AspenPointe and another at Wendy's. But not all teens are ready to take advantage of the classes. "It's really hard to get a 16-year-old to understand why doing this training now will help them in the future. Teenagers just don't think like that. They think in the moment. And we have to constantly remind them, 'Yes, but this class is going to help you get that job.'"

Adah Rodriguez, former director of Youth Directions.

24

Mr. V.

About six months before the merger, Dr. Cynthia Rose flew to San Francisco to attend a conference where she hoped to recruit an executive to lead the new organization. There she ran into an outgoing man named Charles Vorwaller, who was also on a similar recruiting mission for a community mental health program in Sioux City, Iowa. Dr. Rose wasn't interested in moving to Iowa, but she was interested in talking to Vorwaller, who had recently written a paper describing the advantages of mergers like the one being contemplated in Colorado Springs. Then in his mid-thirties, Vorwaller had neatly combed blonde hair and wore the square, heavy eyeglasses that were common in the seventies. "He was very gifted," remembered Barbara Yalich. "He was one of those good-natured, enthusiastic personalities that people couldn't resist going along with."

Dr. Rose and Vorwaller talked at length and then went their separate ways. A couple of days later, when Vorwaller had returned to Iowa, he got a telephone call. Would he be willing come to Colorado Springs to present his views to the entire board? Vorwaller agreed. "They drained my brain," he recalled in an interview in 2012.

Vorwaller was raised on a small farm in the middle of the Salt Lake Valley. When he was seven, his father died and he took over much of the responsibility for running the farm and taking care of the livestock. He was encouraged to become a veterinarian and in 1952, he enrolled in Colorado A&M in Fort Collins. After two years, he was called to serve as a Mormon missionary in Germany where he counseled people who had mental and emotional problems.

Vorwaller discovered that he enjoyed working with people. When he completed his mission, he transferred to the University of Utah where he obtained a bachelor's degree in psychology and sociology and a master's degree with a dual major in administration and psychotherapy. Upon graduation, he entered the Air Force to complete a three-year ROTC commitment and was assigned to be administrative director of a psychiatric clinic at the Forbes Air Force Base Hospital in Topeka, Kansas.

The clinic had close ties with the Menninger Psychiatric Center, which was run by Dr. William and Dr. Karl Menninger. "Dr. Karl," as he was called, was

The AspenPointe playscape, located behind Child and Family Services and the Lighthouse, is used by clients and is also open to the community.

extremely influential in American psychiatry. "He abhorred titles or designations such as psychotics, schizophrenics, neurotics," Vorwaller recalled. "His whole concept was that mental illness was not something that pervades a whole person's existence. Some aspects of their adjustment might be abnormal. But other aspects of their adjustment to life are normal. That's where his unitary concept of mental illness came about."

After finishing his stint in the Air Force, Vorwaller went through the advanced Menninger training program for psychiatric clinical social work. He then became director of psychiatric services for Woodbury County in Sioux City, Iowa. One of his tasks was to bring people back from the state hospital in Cherokee, Iowa. "It was a dumping ground. Out of sight, out of mind. Put them away and forget about it," he said.

Vorwaller and other officials developed an array of services to reintegrate the former patients into the community. That wasn't possible for patients who had been lobotomized or who were taking large doses of Thorazine, a medication that turned their skin purple and led them to be called the "Purple People." The lobotomies in Iowa were done by medical staff who inserted a scalpel-type instrument through the inside corner of an eye into the brain and severed the frontal lobe. After the procedure, the patients were docile and without emotions, but still able to respond to simple commands and take care of themselves. "They had to

Charles Vorwaller, rear, and John Muth, director of the El Paso County Health Department, train for a charity bike-a-thon. July, 1989. (PPLD)

be out of control. Unmanageable. They didn't know what else to do with them. They didn't want to keep them tethered. They didn't want to keep them in chains. So this was thought to be a more humane way," Vorwaller said.

After several additional visits to Colorado Springs, Vorwaller was offered the executive director's job of the merged clinic. He talked it over with his wife, Madeleine, a native of Switzerland, who loved Colorado Springs and its mountains, and he decided to take the position. In the summer of 1970, Vorwaller and his wife and six children packed their bags and began driving west. He was 36 years old and would lead the clinic through one of its greatest expansionary periods. But first, there was the physical and psychological business of actually merging the two agencies.

The combined staff consisted of 22 people and the budget for the coming year was roughly $280,000. The employees crowded into the South Eighth Street location to meet Vorwaller. "Needless to say, my anxiety level was probably higher

"He was a perfect example of Mormon work ethic. He was just a remarkable figure. He gave the example of absolutely always working even as he was a family man with a big family."

Joe Pickle

than anyone else's," he wrote, "but I was very excited to be there."

Vorwaller and his management team established five committees and appointed five chairmen to oversee the development of the major components of a comprehensive community mental health center. He met weekly with board members at the Village Inn. "It was a very creative time. As a board we were responding to everything he was doing," remembered Joe Pickle. "He was a perfect example of Mormon work ethic. He was just a remarkable figure. He gave the example of absolutely always working even as he was a family man with a big family."

Vorwaller made trips to Denver and to Washington, D.C. He also set about getting to know the El Paso County commissioners, the members of the City Council and officials at the United Way. He got the nickname of "Flip-Chart Charlie" because he liked to use charts to describe the clinic's work.

By November 1971, the organization had completed a $1.2 million grant application to the National Institute of Mental Health. It was 412 pages long. Multiple copies were made and enclosed in bright yellow binders. "We hand-carried them to the federal NIMH offices in Denver on November 24, 1971," Vorwaller recalled. A couple of months later, the proposal was approved by the federal agency with a commendation. The staff and board celebrated. But the jubilation turned into discouragement when President Nixon impounded the federal funds for all the clinics nationwide as part of a dispute with Congress over an environmental project that Nixon opposed.

In January 1973, Sandy Arnold, then chairman of the Colorado Legislature's powerful Joint Budget Committee, drove down to Colorado Springs to speak at the organization's annual dinner. The state of Colorado, he hinted, might be willing to pick up most of the funding for the expansion of the mental health center if the center could submit a revised budget request and convince the Legislature to support it. Vorwaller and the staff and the community got busy. A petition supporting the expansion of the clinic received the signatures of more than 5,000 residents. Eventually the Legislature and Gov. Richard Lamm approved the funding. The mental health center thus found itself in an enviable situation; it now had the money to move forward with the creation of a comprehensive facility but wasn't bound by all the federal rules and regulations.

The center also received several other large federal grants. The Law Enforcement Assistance Administration awarded it two multi-year grants totaling in excess of $1 million to establish two programs, one for adults and the other for youths. The National Institute on Alcohol Abuse and Alcoholism also awarded the center a three-year, $1 million grant to establish a broad array of services for alcoholics and their families. The following are some of the activities that were created with the help of federal funds, as well as local and state monies:

1) An after-hours emergency crisis center and adult day treatment program was established at 2828 North Nevada Avenue. Eventually the programs were relocated to 875 West Moreno Avenue, a building purchased by the mental health center after the original owner, Balows Western Wear, went bankrupt. Today the facility is one of AspenPointe's busiest hubs and is called the Adult and Rural campus.

2) Under the guidance of Dr. Cynthia Rose, an 11-bed, acute-care, in-patient psychiatric unit was established on the eleventh floor at Penrose Hospital. The unit had required approval of all the hospital specialties. "One of the more humorous and sad things was that the orthopedists were very concerned that the mental patients would run around and

drop the weights from the patients who were in traction. When we were able to explain the population, they did approve it," she recalled.

3) A 20-bed CARES House established at 525 North Weber Street for individuals with chronic mental impairment who otherwise might have remained at the State Hospital.

4) Using LEAA funds earmarked for the adult program, the center purchased a motel at 3031 West Colorado Avenue known as the Glendale Motel and remodeled it into administrative offices and a residential facility. By 1974, more than 1,600 offenders annually were receiving help, saving the state roughly $1.1 million in incarceration costs. (Eventually this program was spun off and became known as ComCor, Inc., which is still in operation today.)

5) The LEAA-funded youth program, which became known as the Youth Treatment Center, was housed in an older apartment building composed of eight units at 1001 N. Weber Street. The main floor was converted into dormitories and the top floor was remodeled into a large meeting and dining room and kitchen. Later, a stately older home and carriage house located almost directly across the street were acquired and remodeled into a day treatment-school for mentally disturbed youth who could not be maintained in the public school system.

6) A residential alcohol treatment program was established on the lower level of 875 West Moreno. Together with the City of Colorado Springs, the organization also established a 25-bed detox center on East Fountain Boulevard to accommodate referrals and "drop-offs" by law enforcement personnel.

7) Four teams composed of social workers, nurses, psychologists and psychiatrists were created and deployed throughout the community. Team I served the inner city, Team II served the Fountain Valley, Team III served northeast Colorado Springs, and Team IV provided services to Manitou Springs, western and northern El Paso County and Teller and Park counties. Satellite offices for this team were established in Woodland Park and Bailey, Colorado.

As the years passed, the center's income continued to fluctuate, depending on how local, state and federal officials were feeling about mental health and addiction disorders. In the 1976 annual report, Vorwaller described the squabbling between the local and state entities. "Our local funding sources are saying the state should pay more of the Center's costs since we impact directly on state institutions," he wrote. "The state, on the other hand, is expecting the local sources to contribute more since the problems originate locally."

In order to reduce its dependency on traditional funding sources, Vorwaller and the board of directors decided that the mental health center needed some "money trees" to generate additional income. It purchased the 360-unit Altamira apartment complex from the Resolution Trust Corporation for $1.8 million. When it spun off its community corrections program, it sold the property on West Colorado Avenue to a Wendy's franchise, but continued to receive some income as part of the deal. As a consequence, Vorwaller became known as the "Wendy's hamburger guy," despite the fact that neither he nor anyone else in the organization flipped any burgers.

When the center was building the residential treatment facility on Moreno Avenue, it became obvious that it was going to need a kitchen to feed the residents. "Since we had big refrigerators and big stoves, we thought we might as well go further and create meals for staff. Most people who worked in the building would go there and have lunch. We also had groups come to visit," he recalled. That was the genesis for Café Moreno, the precursor to the highly successful AspenPointe Café.

The mental health center also expanded its Budget Counseling activities, which actually had its origins in the old Family Counseling agency. Clients were taught resumé-writing and interviewing skills and the organization helped them

'Where's the popcorn machine? We have to have popcorn for the clients – the aroma of freshly popped popcorn can be so soothing and calming to them."

Charles Vorwaller

restructure their debt. "People would come in. They might have racked up a bill at the utility company or at Penney's or Sears. They couldn't make their payments. So we would negotiate lower payments and teach them budgeting skills and teach them how to be a better employee perhaps to get a raise. We found that was good, but not good enough. So we looked within our own organization for ways we could employ other people," he remembered.

Once patients were stabilized and had their basic needs met, they needed to be taught to become self-sufficient again, to reconnect with the community and find new purpose in their life. A job was one of the best ways of accomplishing that. So, just like the nineteenth-century relief society, the center started helping their former patients find jobs or put them to work in their own businesses. In the mid-1980s, it created a new entity called Aspen Diversified Industries, which one day would lead the organization in a whole new direction. At the Altamira apartment complex, former patients employed by ADI did maintenance, janitorial, yard work and other tasks. Patients were hired at Café Moreno, which had a restaurant in the courthouse, as well as contracts with Phil Long Ford, Cheyenne Mesa and the Farmer's Market. Aspen Diversified Industries also was awarded contracts by the National Institute for the Severely Handicapped and placed people at various federal facilities and military bases. "Instead of being tax consumers, these people were going to be taxpayers," Vorwaller remembered. "That, as a concept, really resonated with politicians."

To accommodate the entrepreneurial ventures and the differing funding streams, writes Vorwaller, "It became crucial to develop a creative corporate structuring model to maintain specific funding streams for specific programs funded only by certain funding sources while at the same time, meeting multiple accountability and reporting requirements." By the mid-1990s, he writes, the center had six separate corporate entities under one umbrella known as Pikes Peak Mental Health Center Systems, Inc. The different entities shared certain departments, like human services and accounting, thereby realizing additional savings, he continues. As traditional funding from government sources dwindled in favor of "capitation" and "managed care," the organization developed programs for clients covered by those contracts, he added.

By 2000, Vorwaller was 66 years old and his hair had whitened. He was ready to turn his attention to new projects. He had made hundreds of flip charts, reviewed thousands of spreadsheets, spent countless days and nights in meetings. He had helped to build the mental health center into an organization of more than 400 employees with a budget of $21 million and a well-endowed Foundation.

The construction of the Lighthouse, a state-of-the-art, 50-bed psychiatric facility, was one of his crowning achievements and he brought to the project the same enthusiasm he had displayed thirty years earlier when he joined the organization. One day, he caught up with Sonia Jackson, then the manager of the Lighthouse.

"Sonia, where's the popcorn machine?" he asked.

"We're in the middle of building a gigantic psychiatric unit and he says, 'Where's the popcorn machine?'" Jackson remembered. "I said, 'I'm sorry Mr. V. I didn't know you wanted to have popcorn.'"

"We have to have popcorn for the clients," Vorwaller responded.

"So he would get into that kind of detail. The client's experience meant everything to him," she said.

Slaying Stigma

The great nineteenth-century Chicago architect Daniel Burnham is quoted as saying, "Make no little plans. They have no magic to stir men's blood and probably will not themselves be realized." Some doubt that Burnham actually uttered those words, but it doesn't really matter to Paul Sexton, a charismatic executive, who has been making big plans – and carrying them out – since he joined AspenPointe eleven years ago.

When the wars in Iraq and Afghanistan were raging, he was tasked to come up with a program to help veterans and led a team that developed the Peer Navigator program, which is basically a buddy system in which an AspenPointe employee, usually former military, helps the vet 'navigate' through the community. It was such a simple, yet innovative and effective program, that the nonprofit was invited to the West Wing of the White House to confer with Matt Flavin, the director of Veterans and Wounded Warrior Policy. They didn't get to meet with President Obama or the First Lady nor did they expect that. But they left behind a handcrafted wooden box that contained a video about the program and Sexton is convinced it will end up in Mr. Obama's presidential library some day.

Deputy CEO Paul Sexton, former board chair Bonnie Martinez, and CEO Morris Roth on a business trip to Washington, D.C.

The Peer Navigator program subsequently gave birth to the Peer-A-Chute program. The idea behind that was startlingly simple, too. Why not take parachutes deployed in battle and destined for the landfill and recycle them into clothing and other articles? Better yet, why not help returning veterans set up their own parachute-sewing businesses in their hometowns with the help of small business loans? The parachute material is silky soft, practically indestructible, and comes in every color imaginable. "And it's got a message around it. These are parachutes that guided our person home and they still have value. Just like a military person's life," said Sexton. "It continues to spread our tax dollars. It's creating new revenue and it's creating hope for the families."

AspenPointe then entered into a partnership with design students at Colorado State University who used the parachute material to design iPad covers, aprons, gowns, backpacks, and coffee-cup insulators. AspenPointe returned to the White House – again – this time to Michelle Obama's suite of offices in the East Wing to meet with a group called Joining Forces. They dropped off more information on the Peer Navigator program and the Peer-A-Chute program, as well as a barbecue apron made from parachute material for President Obama, back packs for the Obama girls with their names emblazoned on them, and a running vest for the family pet that that says 'First Dog." The CSU students are now designing an elegant ballroom gown for Michelle Obama.

"Some people will say, 'You're straying from your core mission by creating these parachute products.' And we're saying, 'No. We're opening up another door that somebody might come through,'" Sexton said. "A person with serious mental illness may never come to us because they're stigmatized by the name, 'mental ill-

Don Nguyen helped develop the Peer-A-Chute program that enables veterans to work out of their homes.

ness.' But if I say, "Would you like to get a job selling parachute products?' they're all over it. They come in and once they get to know us they don't mind going to see our doctors. They trust us."

Sexton thought the Defense Department would be delighted to give them parachutes destined for the landfill, but the DOD's regulations are so arcane that he's learned it's going to take an act of Congress – literally – to obtain them. ("I was naïve enough to believe that if they were headed for a dumpster, we could have them," he said wryly). In the meantime, the organization has been purchasing parachute material at government auctions at very reduced prices and has started buying other textiles, too, including bolts of material that were once destined to be uniforms.

And he has bigger plans. The organization recently purchased a cavernous 30,000-square-foot facility that has been dubbed the Innovation Center. There, AspenPointe will be showcasing its various activities, including the Peer-A-Chute program and their building trades. "We're going to have a full-blown construction laboratory. When I mean full-blown, it will be full-blown. We will have a mock house in it with floors, windows, doors and roofing."

And he's not stopping there. "The things I'm showing you, these things are not impossible." Sexton's real goal is to destigmatize mental illness not just in Colorado Springs but also throughout the world. He likens it to the de-stigmatization of cancer. "Twenty years ago when someone was diagnosed with cancer, it was almost a badge of shame." Mental illness, he said, is the third highest healthcare cost in the United States. "You always hear about cancer. But you never hear about mental health. Why? Because they've done a better job of telling their story. We've got to get out there and tell people our story."

Daniel Burnham helped pioneer the modern skyscraper. In Colorado Springs, AspenPointe is trying to return their clients to the world where they may even achieve greater things. "What I've been telling everybody is, never accept the word, 'no,' and never accept the word, 'can't,'" said Sexton. "Start with a 'yes,' and a 'we can do it.' You may end up getting to a 'no,' but don't limit yourself by not trying. That, to me, is the future of AspenPointe. We'll keep trying new and innovative things. We'll continue to do things people tell us are impossible."

25

Listening Bigger

When Charles Vorwaller announced his retirement, the board of directors was faced with the task of finding a new chief executive officer. They interviewed Morris Roth, a senior vice president who had three children and had lived in the Springs for most of his life. Roth had been with the organization for more than 28 years and could remember the days when budgets were so tight he was asked to hold off cashing his paycheck for a week or so. He was a quiet, thoughtful executive who had the ability to spot talented people, recruit them, and then allow them to use their talent. The board conducted only that one interview. "You're the guy," he was told afterward.

Over the years, Colorado Springs had grown more conservative and some believed – much like the Social Darwinists of an earlier age — that taxpayer money should not be spent on social programs. But Roth continued to advocate for people suffering from serious mental illnesses. Like the people who knocked on the old relief society's doors, they were often jobless or homeless or both. "I think society is no stronger than its weakest link," he said in an interview in 2012. " We have an obligation to assist people and help folks who have had mishaps through no fault of their own."

Over the next decade or so, Roth and his team of dynamic, young managers would take the idea of recovery to the next level. In the process, they would transform the organization. No longer was it enough to sit around a clubhouse and drink coffee. Clubhouses and coffee drinking were fine, but they wanted the clients to reach their potential. The nonprofit and its clients began doing things that at first seemed far removed from the traditional treatment of mental health problems. They hired an artist, a gardener, a cook. They catered lunches, built a community garden, and put on art shows. Soldiers with post-traumatic stress disorder became painters. Schizophrenics found their voices in song and poetry. People with bipolar disorder, who had often worked sporadically or not at all, found jobs. "I've always had a passion that there has to be more for these folks with disabilities. They need work, they need training, they need the kinds of experiences that non-disabled people enjoy," Roth said.

The idea of work is deeply embedded in the organization's history. Mrs. D. Russ Wood and her fellow Victorians often hired people from the relief society themselves or referred them to agencies such as the YMCA. The Rev. Edward

"The core component of our philosophy is that adults with mental illnesses can regain their life purposes, reach their highest potentials and live meaningful and productive lives that take the illness into account, but are not dominated and limited by it."

Morris Roth

Evans-Carrington wanted to start a school that would train poor women in the domestic arts. Wood and Daisy Worcester got men jobs cutting ice on mountain lakes. And during the Great Depression, the charity even launched a small Work Progress Administration project of its own teaching girls and young women to sew.

When Roth assumed the position of president and CEO, he laid out the new direction in the annual report. "The core component of our philosophy is that adults with mental illnesses can regain their life purposes, reach their highest potentials and live meaningful and productive lives that take the illness into account, but are not dominated and limited by it." It would take time for that philosophy to percolate down, but he had patience.

Morris Roth

First, though, Roth had to shepherd the organization through the first decade of the new millennium. It was a decade when two wars began in far-off countries, one of the greatest economic collapses in American history occurred, and Congress passed a complex healthcare reform bill. Throughout the organization's history, it had been confronted with similar challenges but never had they come so closely grouped together. The events would have a profound impact on the nonprofit. While conserving its financial resources, it looked for ways to help returning soldiers and studied the federal healthcare legislation and subsequent developments so it would be positioned to meet the new mandates. Amazingly, the organization not only survived but also thrived, increasing overall revenues to $55 million in 2012, nearly double what they were when Roth took over in July of 2000.

Roth himself has deep roots in Colorado Springs. From his headquarters on Cascade Avenue, he can practically reach out and touch the schools he once attended, including Garfield Elementary and Palmer High School. Upon graduation, he went to the University of Southern Colorado where he obtained his bachelor's degree in sociology. Then he moved to Lincoln, Nebraska, where he earned a master's degree in social work. Along the way, he became acquainted with the cruelties that stressed-out parents can afflict on their children and to this day remembers the serrated stripes on the skin of a little boy who was beaten with a radiator hose and a six-month-old encased in a full-body cast after his father picked him up by the ankles and swung him around.

In 1971, he applied for a job with what was then called Pikes Peak Family Counseling and Mental Health Center. Sixty other people also applied, but Roth got the job. He was lucky, doubly lucky, in fact. He had found his place in the world and he knew it. What he didn't know was that he would remain with the organization for the rest of his career. Colleagues came and went. But Roth found new challenges within the organization itself, counseling clients, supervising other employees and creating new programs. "Sometimes people feel like you have to leave, you have to experience other things, but I didn't feel that way."

In those early days, when a whiff of the Sixties lingered, he wore a corduroy jacket and a mustache. The old annual reports show that everyone who worked at the mental health center – except Charles Vorwaller perhaps — seemed to have had a mustache, a beard, or longish hair. When the teams were deployed through the community, Roth oversaw the team at 441 Manitou Avenue, which was developing outpatient services for the west side of Colorado Springs, as well as Teller and Park counties.

As the years passed, the mental health center's corporate structure grew more complex and more entrepreneurial. Companies were purchased, sold, or spun off. "The question was, 'How can we diversify so that when funding challenges come along they may hurt you but they won't take you down?'" Roth recalled. Part of the answer lay in the purchase of income-producing properties like Altamira Apartments. But this left people confused. Why would a mental health center, they wondered, own an apartment complex? "We are criticized because of this notion that we're straying from our core. Well, we purchased the building so we could provide the core services," Roth explained.

Paul Sexton

By the mid-2000s, the organization had changed its name to Pikes Peak Behavioral Health Group. The components included 1) Pikes Peak Mental Health, which continued to provide core mental health services for adults and children; 2) Connect Care, a managed care company; 3) Aspen Diversified Industries, which had training programs for clients and employed them through various maintenance, furniture assembly and cleaning contracts with local, state and federal entities; 4) Workout, Ltd, a restorative justice program for youth; 5) First Choice, which provided counseling to members of the military and others with commercial insurance; 6) Pikes Peak Foundation for Mental Health, which handled research and grants, educational presentations, and fundraising.

Roth brought in new managers who were brimming with the nineteenth-century reformers' energy yet armed with iPads and the know-how to harness the power of the Internet. Paul Sexton became senior vice president of Aspen Diversified Industries. He doubled its clients and revenue, landed some multi-million dollar contracts, and went on to become deputy chief executive officer. That left the vice president's job at Aspen Diversified Industries open. It was filled by Jonathan Liebert, equally exuberant and entrepreneurial and happy to be following in the footsteps of his father, who worked for Pikes Peak Mental Health for 25 years. Kelly Phillips-Henry, a former psychology instructor at the Air Force Academy and a mother of four, was brought in as a senior vice president and is now chief operating officer. Dr. Fred H. Michel was named the chief medical officer, and Michael Allen was vice president of Health Network & TeleCare.

Other things, large and small, began to change. The guard at the adult mental health facility began wearing civilian clothes. Beautiful artwork by clients began appearing on the walls of hallways. Offices gleamed. Bushes were trimmed. The grass cut. The clients worked alongside the staff, but it was impossible to figure out who was who and that's how the organization wanted it. Clients-turned-employees got no special breaks, no velvet-gloved treatment. They had to punch a clock, meet a deadline and perform like anybody else. Failure meant getting fired and getting fired could be a good thing, said Sexton. "In the old sheltered workshop, we would never consider firing somebody because we would make excuses for their condition. We now say, 'It doesn't matter if you have these issues, just come to work,'" he said. "By doing that, we have moved away from a diagnosis-based methodology to a strength-based methodology. What are you good at? What are your strengths? If you have a strength, we're going to live in that arena because that's how the rest of us live. That's what's different today that wasn't in place twenty years ago."

Despite its long history in Colorado Springs, when the organization did a community survey of 300 people, it found that 75 percent didn't know its various subsidiaries were connected. Equally discouraging, the public didn't know about all the services the organization offered. The nonprofit needed a new name, a name broad enough to encompass all of the diverse activities, from its culinary arts program to its furniture assembly crews to the mental health center where people went for counseling or classes. Hundreds of names were considered and then jettisoned. As Dr. Fred Michel, a psychiatrist and the chief medical officer, puts it, the nonprofit not only has a wide spectrum of services, it has a depth of services that go from in-patient, high-intensity care to outpatient counseling and preventative care. "How do you describe all that we do in one short name?"

Finally, in 2010, the organization settled upon the name 'AspenPointe.' The aspen tree, with its resiliency and remarkable root system, served as a metaphor on several levels. It symbolized the clients and the organization and its roots in Colorado Springs. "Aspens have a very deep-rooted system and while they look beautiful and are spread far apart, the root systems connect and keep the other trees alive. In fact, aspens can't survive on their own. They need to connect to the root system. We believed that was a nice metaphor," said Kelly Phillips-Henry.

Dr. Fred Michel

AspenPointe consolidated seven websites into one coherent and logical site where consumers of its services could easily find just about anything they needed. It also created a centralized call center with one number that clients could call to schedule an appointment or get help. "Our call volume increased from about 1,200 calls per month to eight or nine thousand," said Roxanne Lopez, who oversees the eight-member team. By 2012, the organization felt that the public had a better understanding of who they were and what they did. "The community began to understand that we offered a lot more than mental health services," said Sexton.

Today, the organizational structure basically consists of three major components: AspenPointe Health Services offers the traditional behavioral healthcare services, ranging from wellness programs to in-patient psychiatric facilities. AspenPointe Health Network &TeleCare provides behavioral health managed-care services to providers and telephonic support to people suffering from both physical and mental illness. AspenPointe Enterprises encompasses the GED preparation and testing component, job skills and training programs, art therapy, cafe and culinary arts, the community garden, custodial and construction services and youth programs.

"Our patients come to us with gaps everywhere in their lives," said Dr. Michel. "Having a spectrum of services that can help a person grow in whole ways is the ingenious element of what I think this is about."

Clients, for example, may come into the system needing in-patient or intensive outpatient counseling. Once they're stabilized, the organization can help them get back into the workforce. The reverse is also true. Some clients may take computer classes and realize they need mental health counseling. The Rev. John Stevens, a longtime board member and pastor emeritus of Colorado Springs' First Presbyterian Church, said it was wonderful to be able to refer people to the organization. "It isn't just enough to counsel them. They've got to be able to develop life skills. They've got to be able to function in society," he said. "People who have been in counseling for a year or so and have gotten substantially better need to work to keep from becoming depressed again. When AspenPointe developed this twenty years ago, it was a very unique idea. Up to then, mental health organizations just provided counselors and therapy. Once you got on your feet, you were pretty much on your own."

Since the organization is a nonprofit, any extra money that's made from, say, investments or an apartment complex, is plowed back into one of the entities that's struggling. Last year, AspenPointe received funding to assist 879 people but helped more than 5,000, said Kelly Phillips-Henry. "In this town, there are over 30,000 uninsured people. Because we're the community mental health center, people believe we should be able to serve them all. But those decades are long

"Aspens have a very deep-rooted system and while they look beautiful and are spread far apart, the root systems connect and keep the other trees alive. In fact, aspens can't survive on their own. They need to connect to the root system."

KELLY PHILLIPS-HENRY

gone. So what we try to do is shift resources from our for-profit companies so we can serve more people."

To stretch its dollars, AspenPointe is also rethinking how it delivers its mental healthcare services. Some people may need only medication management or perhaps a short intense round of talk therapy. So now, when patients enter the mental health center, treatment plans are drawn up based on their illnesses and the patients know how long the treatment will last. Years of counseling will likely be a thing of the past. "We can say, 'Hey, you've been in the system 20 years, but your score means you only need this much care.' Our goal, as a system, is to work us out of a job," said Jennifer DeGroff, a tall, willowy psychologist, who directs AspenPointe's outpatient and integrated services. She continues:

> Historically, if you think about mental health, we came out of deinstitutionalization. It used to be if you were crazy you got locked up, lived in that setting your whole life, and then you died. Then the community health center was born and we said, 'We'll have the communities take care of you.' So we are still in this era and we have these folks that feel they need to be here for twenty years because they've got schizophrenia or bipolar disorder. We're trying to reshape the paradigm of our clients and our staff. It doesn't mean you have to be here forever. It means, 'How can we help you today?' 'What's your presenting problem?' And maybe you come back in a year when another problem arises.

DeGroff's office is in the basement of the Adult and Rural campus, the former shopping mall where the $350 Stetson hats were once sold and where the residential alcoholic treatment center was once housed. It is one of AspenPointe's busiest hubs and shares the space with Peak Vista, which offers a range of healthcare services to low-income people. On site is a pharmacy, a lab, large open rooms where group therapy meetings occur, cubicles for one-on-one sessions, classrooms where GED, leadership skills, and art classes are held. Some 4,000 people a year pass through their doors. Most have persistent and serious mental problems and are Medicaid eligible.

AspenPointe is also trying to reduce the stigma around mental illness so the public comes to see that it is no different than any other disease. " Say someone's bipolar and has been on the same medication for three years. Does he or she really need to come to us? Or can they go out into the community?" said DeGroff. "If you think of us like specialty health providers, like endocrinologists, your primary care physician sends you to an endocrinologist to get treatment started and then that endocrinologist sends you back. We want mental healthcare to be thought of in the same way. You come to us for acute exacerbations and then your primary care doctor helps with ongoing problems. We're trying to change the paradigm. Mental illness is no different. It just looks different."

Officials hope the changes will better position the organization to meet the challenges of Obamacare. In the last year or so, the way to the future has become a little clearer, but there are still many unknowns. The organization must continue to provide its core services while looking ahead to what a healthcare delivery system will look like in three, five, or ten years. "It's like dancing on the razor's edge," said Kelly Phillips-Henry, who has been specifically tasked by Morris Roth to develop strategies.

A major thrust of Obamacare is to keep people healthy instead of waiting until they are sick and have to go to the emergency room or require an expensive medical procedure. The wellness movement, as it's called, encourages such things as exercising and eating the right foods and not smoking or drinking to excess. If people live healthier lives, there will be an overall reduction in many diseases, including diabetes, heart disease and cancer. The savings then can be plowed back into preventative programs.

The corporate world already knows the benefits of a healthy workforce and AspenPointe is putting into practice what it's preaching. Through a partnership with the YMCA, it's helping its own employees develop better eating and exercise habits. "We are really stressing wellness as a value. You have to be well to be a model for clients," Roth said.

Phillips-Henry knows that lifestyle changes are hard. She was overweight in high school and made a decision one day to lose the extra pounds. Today she is a slim and elegant woman who has competed in the Ironman Triathlon. "I'm a big believer in the idea that physical and mental wellness happens by the choices we make everyday," she said.

One of the big tasks ahead will be figuring out how to help people make healthy choices. "People in our country say, 'Give me a pill for my diabetes, my high blood pressure, my this or my that instead of saying, 'Should I look at my diet?' 'Should I exercise more?' 'Should I put sunblock on when I go into the sun?' We're doing a lot of sick care in this country." In the future, there will likely be incentives for keeping people healthy. "We have to change the payment structure and the incentive structure," she said.

AspenPointe hopes to develop new partnerships and collaborations in the community. To that end, it has been holding "lunch and learns" with various healthcare providers and the meals have been catered by the AspenPointe Café. Such partnerships could include having a behavioral health specialist on hand to consult with primary care doctors or their patients, said DeGroff. "Depending on how you think about the case, we can help with almost every problem that presents in their office. If the doctors are only listening for the words, 'depression' or 'anxiety,' we can help with ten percent of their patients. But if they're listening for everything else — the socioeconomic factors, the wellness factors — it's 90 to 100 percent. It's training the docs and nurses how to listen bigger."

From back to front, Jonathan Liebert, Dick Sullivan, Michael Allen, Jane Bloise, John McCaa and Kelly Phillips-Henry.

DeGroff said most primary care doctors think they need someone to come in and do therapy. "I try to tell them that's not what you need. What you need is to be able to knock on someone's door four times an hour and get a consultation. It's a more efficient use of a mental health professional's time. We can help with sleep and adherence to medication regimes. That's what we do. So you're going to get more bang for your buck using us that way instead of using us as traditional mental health therapists." The people they have been meeting with have been very receptive, she said. "They want us there yesterday."

Michael Allen, AspenPointe's vice president of Health Network & TeleCare, predicted the eventual merger of behavioral health and physical healthcare. "That's where health reform is going to take us. It's putting the head and body back together. They've been separate for too long."

Epilogue

In the Black Forest, located north of downtown Colorado Springs, the land ripples down from the Front Range of the Rocky Mountains like waves and flattens out onto plains as far as the eye can see. The hills are densely wooded and smell of pine trees. Many residents of Colorado Springs choose to live here because it's close to town and yet offers the delights of country life. Last summer, Black Forest residents could look southwest toward Pikes Peak and see the great plumes of smoke rising from the Waldo Canyon Fire. Little did they know that an even worse catastrophe would befall them almost exactly a year later.

There was much about the two disasters that was sickeningly familiar: The smoke billowing up over the city, the loss of life, the destruction of hundreds of homes, the displacement of thousands of people. Law enforcement officials, firefighters and community leaders knew what to do and reacted quickly.

AspenPointe activated its command center and dispatched crisis counselors to the disaster zone. Some of the counselors were the same people who for the past year had been helping Waldo Canyon Fire victims rebuild their lives. They were all too familiar with the anger and grief caused by such disasters. They met with more than 500 displaced Black Forest families during the crisis. And during an emotional town hall meeting, they circulated through the room and helped to de-escalate tension.

Some of the most effective counseling came from the victims of the Waldo Canyon Fire themselves who put in long hours as volunteers at the Disaster Assistance Center, comforting their distraught neighbors who lived on the other side of the freeway. They also hosted picnics, sent food baskets to evacuees holed up in motels, and did countless other things. In a bittersweet twist of fate, some of the people displaced by the Black Forest Fire found themselves staying at the homes of the Waldo Canyon Fire evacuees they had sheltered the previous summer. "I have been consoling them and now they are consoling me," said one Black Forest resident who had been helping to rewire homes in the Mountain Shadows neighborhood, which had been devastated by the Waldo Canyon Fire.

"These fires have changed us, individually and collectively," said AspenPointe's CEO Morris Roth, who lives in Mountain Shadows and whose own home was damaged during the Waldo Canyon Fire. "Many of our injuries are not visible to the human eye but they will be with us long after new homes, aspens and pine trees have covered over the burn scars. AspenPointe, like the tree for which it is named, will remain resilient and a source of support for this community during these disasters and other challenges that may come our way."

Timeline

July 31, 1871
The first stake driven into ground at the southeast corner of Pikes Peak and Cascade avenues.

1872
Winfield Scott Stratton arrives in Colorado Springs.

Sept. 18, 1873
Panic begins when financial house in New York collapses.

1874
D. Russ Wood building two 'villas' on Weber Street.

Feb. 1, 1875
Colorado Springs Relief Society organized at Colorado College.

1880
El Paso County commissioners purchase a small cottage and three and a half acres of land on the east side of El Paso Street between Boulder and St. Vrain for a county home.

1882
Robert Koch discovers rod-shaped bacterium that causes tuberculosis and warns of its contagious nature.

1884
Relief society reorganized.

Endnotes

Prologue

9 June 26, 2012: *Denver Post* website, June 26, 2012.
9 Hot Shot crews: Letter, Pete Tomitsch, Sept. 23, 2012, Colorado Springs Together website.
9 "whipped away the whole unfinished story": Letter, Gabrielle Huthoefer, Nov. 14, 2012, Colorado Springs Together website.
9 32,000 residents: *Denver Post* website, June 26, 2012.
9 Two people were killed, 346 houses destroyed: *Denver Post* website, Sept. 13, 2012.
9 18,247 acres burned: InciWeb the Incident Information System: Waldo Canyon Fire, Oct. 1, 2012.
9 $350 million: *Gazette* website, July 17, 2012.
9 "The moment the fire": Author interview, Gerald Albrent, Sept. 6, 2012.
9 lines were a mile: AspenPointe website, July 2, 2012.
10 "It was a very humbling: Author interview, Morris Roth, March 1, 2013.
10 Colorado Springs Relief Society: "Relief Society," *Gazette*, Feb. 6, 1875.
10 building on Tejon Street: Ormes, Manley, *The Book of Colorado Springs*, (Colorado Springs: The Dentan Printing Co., 1933), 110.
11 "There are some advantages": Author interview, Morris Roth, May 9, 2012.
11 "They are amazing trees": Author interview, Wayne Shepperd, April 22, 2013.
11 "We look to another 100 years": Author interview, Morris Roth, March 1, 2013.

1 – A Great Migration

13 "all manner of rubbish": All quotes by Mrs. Wood in this chapter come from a paper that she wrote entitled, "A Review of Thirteen Years' Work," which was published in the *Weekly Gazette* on Feb. 4, 1888.
13 "Woodside": Hall, Frank, *History of Colorado, Vol. 3*, (Chicago: The Blakely Printing Company, 1891), 350.
14 Montreal, Canada: Ibid.
14 12 million people: Montgomery, David, "Labor in the Industrial Era," *U.S. Department of Labor Bicentennial History of the American Worker*, (Washington, D.C.: The Department of Labor, 1976), DOL website, 3.
14 "natural law": Palmer, William Jackson, "Westward March of Emigration in the United States," *Legends, Labors & Loves of William Jackson Palmer*, (Colorado Springs: Pikes Peak Library District, 2009), 141.
15 "Consumption made an empire": Anderson, Boswell Preston, letter, Aug. 2, 1901, Colorado Springs Century Chest Collection, Colorado College Special Collections (hereafter Century Chest Collection), Transcription 46.
15 "prudential" committee: "Relief Society," *Gazette*, Feb. 6, 1875.

2 – The World's Sanatorium

16 A few settlers had tried: Howbert, Irving, letter, Aug. 4, 1901, Century Chest Collection, Transcription 75.
16 "Wrapped in blankets": Nicholl, Chris, "William Jackson Palmer: Living While Dying," *Legends, Labors & Love of William Jackson Palmer*, 274.
16 cavalry unit: Sprague, Marshall, *One Hundred Plus, A Centennial Story of Colorado Springs*, (Colorado Springs: Colorado Springs Centennial, Inc., 1971), 1.
16 his own narrow-gauge railroad: Sprague, Marshall. *Newport in the Rockies*, (Athens, Ohio: Swallow Press/Ohio University Press, 1961), 4.
16 The railroad and the coalfields: Andrews, Thomas G., *Killing for Coal*, (Cambridge, Mass.: Harvard University Press, 2008), 35-49.
17 "In the old times": Palmer, William Jackson, "The Westward March of Emigration in the United States," *Legends, Labors & Love of William Jackson Palmer*, 157.
17 10,000 acres: Mayberry, Matt, "General William Jackson Palmer and His Vision for Colorado Springs," Ibid., 190.
17 "Next to General Palmer": "Next to General Palmer, Irving Howbert Could Be Called the Man Who Made Colorado Springs," *Gazette*, May 21, 1967, Biography files, Penrose Library, Pikes Peak Library District.
18 "The ditches meandered": Hall, Frank, *History of Colorado*, Vol. 3, (Chicago: The Blakely Printing Co., 1891), 350.
18 "Do not disturb yourselves": Ibid., 349.
18 "Colonists continue to arrive": "News of the Week," *Out West*, June 13, 1872.
18 "wild and wolly West": Grinnell, Elizabeth Lennox, "Autobiography of Lennox family," Colorado Room Information Files, Colorado College Special Collections.
18 "When we reached": Ibid.
19 "Dead Man's Row": Sprague, Marshall, *Newport in the Rockies*, 59.
19 tree-digging offer: Lennox, William, letter, Aug. 4, 1901, Century Chest Collection, Transcription 61.
19 "handsome Streets and Avenues: "A Year's Work," *Out West*, Aug. 1, 1872.
19 277 lots: "The Fountain Colony," *Out West*, Oct. 17, 1872.
19 "The growth has been steady": "A Year's Work," *Out West*, Aug. 1, 1872.
19 "reservations made for academies": Ibid.
19 "Women were advised": Ellis, Amanda. *The Colorado Springs Story*, (Colorado Springs: Dentan Printing Company, 1954), 23.
19 "For full dress": Ibid., 25.
19 "toilets with ease": *Gazette*, Jan. 11, 1873.
19 Candles and coal oil lamps: Buckman, George Rex, letter, Aug. 3, 1901, Century Chest Collection, Transcription 23.
19 "One of the most potent aids": "The Climate of Colorado," *Out West*, May 16, 1872.
19 "It has been estimated": Ibid.
20 first physician to settle in El Paso County: "Dr. Strickler Passes Away," *Gazette*, Oct. 29, 1908.
20 "Dr. Strickler's surgical skill": Ormes, Manley, *The Book of Colorado Springs*, 277.
20 active in civic life: Ibid.
20 water supply: "Dr. Strickler Passes Away," *Gazette*, Oct. 27, 1908.
20 "The antelope were very plentiful": Anderson, Boswell Preston, letter, Aug. 2, 1901, Century Chest Collection, Transcription, 46.
20 "Drink a lot of whiskey": Ormes, *The Book of Colorado Springs*, 278.
20 Colonel John C. Mosby: Hoff, Bob, "Trooper! Boswell Preston Anderson MD," *Doctors, Disease & Dying in the Pikes Peak Region*, (Colorado Springs: Pikes Peak Library District, 2012), 112.
20 drinking binge: Ibid., 131.
20 Anderson subsequently developed tuberculosis: Ibid., 113.
20 decamped for the Springs: Solly, Samuel Edwin, letter, Aug. 4, 1901, Century Chest Collection, Transcription 70.
20 tall and courtly: Sprague, Marshall, "Healers in Pikes Peak History," *Doctors, Disease & Dying*, 195.
20 Dr. Solly's wife, Elizabeth: City of Colorado Springs, "Historic Preservation Plan," August, 1993.
21 "We are opposed to": "Colorado Grave Yards," *Out West*, June 20, 1872.
21 "Life in our boarding house": Pearson, Albert C., letter, July 31, 1901, Century Chest Collection, Transcription 7
21 "Consumptive patients may look": "The Climate of Colorado," *Out West*, May 16, 1872.
22 "The late war had left": Potter, John, letter, 1901, Century Chest Collection, Transcription 48.
22 "Sickness and old wounds": Dwinnell, Ella, letter, July 28, 1901, Century Chest Collection, Transcription 47.
23 "There was no unfriendliness": Potter, John, letter, 1901, Century Chest Collection, Transcription 48.
23 "Unemployment was endemic: Montgomery, David, "Labor in the Industrial Era," *The American Worker*, DOL website, 5.
23 "Shifting seasonal demands": Ibid.
23 "Each surge in construction": Andrews, Thomas G. *Killing for Coal*, 115.
23 37,000 strikes: Lukas, J. Anthony. *Big Trouble: A Murder in a Small Western Town Sets Off a Struggle for Democracy*, (New York: Simon & Schuster, 1997), 116.

Health Services

24 With roughly 300 employees: All information and quotes come from author interview with Nancy Craney, Aug. 16, 2012, from AspenPointe's Virtual Tour –Health Network, June 7, 2013, and other AspenPointe literature.

Health Network & TeleCare

25 All information and quotes come from author interview with Michael Allen, Aug. 27, 2012 or from AspenPointe's Virtual Tour –Health Network, June 7, 2013.

Enterprises

26 "We call them chronic attenders": Author interview, Jonathan Liebert, May 11, 2012. All interviews from Liebert come from this interview unless otherwise noted.
26 "A social enterprise exists to solve": "Social Enterprise: The Power of Employment," AspenPointe website, Feb. 20, 2012.
27 $20 million: AspenPointe, "End of Year Accomplishments Presentation, FY12," 2.

3 – Catching at Straws

28 "absolute destitution": "Something Needed," *Gazette*, Jan. 11, 1873.
28 "The Landlord of the house": Ibid.

28 "apparently possessed with the insane": Ibid.
28 "We hope that next winter": Ibid.
28 "It will doubtless strike": Ibid.
28 tremendous windstorm: *Gazette*, March 8, 1873.
28 "We urge attention": *Gazette*, May 10, 1873.
29 $300 bankroll: Waters, Frank, *Midas of the Rockies*, (Athens, Ohio: Swallow Press/Ohio University Press, 1937), 60.
29 beating a burro: Ibid., 116.
29 "We should rather like": *Gazette*, Jan. 11, 1873.
29 fierce campaigns: Ormes, *The Book of Colorado Springs*, 291-292
29 "A society of ladies": "A Society of Ladies Will Raise Funds for the Poor," *Weekly Gazette*, Nov. 29, 1873.
29 buckskins and buffalo robes: *Gazette*, Dec. 27, 1873.
29 a good buffalo robe: *Gazette*, Feb. 28, 1874.
29 A Young Men's Christian Association: Ibid.
30 Colorado Springs Relief Society: "Relief Society," *Gazette*, Feb. 6, 1875. There is conflicting information about the actual year that the society was formed. Mrs. Wood on two occasions writes that the relief society was organized in 1874, but the newspaper, as well as local historian Manley Ormes, give the 1875 date. It's possible that the society was *organized* in 1874, but did not hold its first *official* meeting until February of 1875.
30 "In this town": Goddard, Elizabeth Cass, letter, July 27, 1901, Century Chest Collection, Transcription 13.
30 "The blue blood in her veins": Finley, Judith Reid, *Time Capsule 1900, Colorado Springs a Century Ago*, (Colorado Springs: Pastwords Publication, 1998), 37.
30 original relief society: "Relief Society," *Gazette*, Feb. 6, 1875.
30 "Winter pants and coats": Ibid.
30 "Union Thanksgiving Service": "Work Among the Poor," *Weekly Gazette*, Feb. 4, 1888.
31 10 cents: *Gazette*, May 20, 1876.
31 "It is full time for the ladies": *Gazette*, Nov. 4, 1876.
31 "The society is being called upon": "Ladies' Relief Association," *Gazette*, Nov. 11, 1876.
31 Steel forks, hoes, rakes: *Weekly Gazette*, Oct. 26, 1878.
31 "During the four decades": Montgomery, David, "Labor in the Industrial Era," *The American Worker*, DOL website, 4.
32 "viewed in no other light": Andrews, Thomas G., *Killing for Coal*, 85.
32 "At the present time, lots and lands": "Colorado Springs," *Weekly Gazette*, Oct. 27, 1878.
32 Meals were large: Ellis, *The Colorado Springs Story*, 21.
32 "The servant question was a trying one": Solly, Elizabeth, letter, Aug. 1, 1901, Century Chest Collection, Transcription 39.
32 "We say costly": "The Deserving Poor," *Gazette*, Oct. 26, 1878.
32 "The society wants": Ibid.
33 Helping Hand Wood Yard: Invoice, April 21, 1900, Pikes Peak Library District, Carnegie Library, Special Collections, Pikes Peak Family Counseling and Mental Health Center Records, MSS 0178, Box Four, Folder 1. [Hereafter collection referred to as PPFCMHC records].
33 "The tramp is a man": "Legislation Against Tramps," *Gazette*, May 25, 1878.
33 "Part of the extraordinarily hostile": Kusmer, Kenneth L., *Down and Out, On the Road, The Homeless in American History*, (New York: Oxford University Press, 2002), 11.
33 "incorruptible" Matt France: Oldach, Denise R. W., *Here Lies Colorado Springs*, 45.
33 small cottage: Ormes, *The Book of Colorado Springs*, 225-226.

4 – Microbes and Men

34 "illuminating gas": Buckman, George Rex, letter, Aug. 3, 1901, Century Chest Collection, Transcription 23.
34 "From the 1880s to the 1940s": Mayberry, Matt, "On a Cough & a Prayer: The Modern Woodmen Sanatorium & the Tuberculosis Industry in the Pikes Peak Region," *Doctors Disease and Dying*, 245.
34 "If the importance of a disease": http://openx.nobelprize.org/educational/medicine/tuberculosis/readmore.html.
35 "Long before I had": Nicholl, Chris, "Introduction," *Doctor at Timberline, True Tales, Travails, and Triumphs of a Pioneer Colorado Physician*, (Colorado Springs: Pikes Peak Library District, 2008), xiii.
35 "And gradually, by years of practice": Ibid., 5.
36 "was to effect some organization": *Gazette*, Dec. 5, 1884.
36 "In a short, but pointed address": "Work Among the Poor," *Weekly Gazette*, Feb. 4, 1888.
36 "There is at present time": *Gazette*, Sept. 6, 1885.
36 "to aid the poor": Constitution, Women's Aid Society of Colorado Springs, PPFCMHC Records, Box 1, Folder 1.
36 "Members of the Visiting": Ibid.
38 "receive applications from those: Ibid.
38 sewing committee: Ibid.
38 Benjamin Crowell: Howbert, Irving, *Memories of a Lifetime in the Pike's Peak Region*, (Glorieta, NM: The Rio Grande Press, Inc.,1970), 239.
38 "his health had become somewhat": Ibid., 139.
38 silver mine in Leadville: Ibid.
38 taking in $1,237: "Report of Treasurer of Woman's Aid Society," Jan. 25, 1888, PPFCMHC Records, Box 1, Folder 4.
38 "The object of the society then": "Work Among the Poor," *Weekly Gazette*, Feb. 4, 1888.
38 "To this little jug": Ibid.

5 – The Invalid's Wife

39 In 1890: *Gazette*, Feb. 1, 1890.
39 he was a Canadian: Hagerman, Percy, "James John Hagerman: A Sketch of His Life by His Son," 1932, Colorado Room Information Files, Colorado College Special Collections.
39 "That's where you end up": *Colorado Springs Sun*, July 9, 1972.
39 "Agent consulted Mrs. Hagerman": PPFCMHC Records, Box 3, Ledger 1, 91.
39 "unusual amount" of suffering: "Help the Aid Society," *Weekly Gazette*, Feb. 7, 1891.
39 Electric lights: Buckman, George Rex, letter, Aug. 3, 1901, Century Chest Collection, Transcription 23.
39 "gardener's cottage": Sprague, *Newport in the Rockies*, 90.
39 different woods: Fagan, George, "James John Hagerman: Colorado Springs' Titan," 1982, Colorado Room Information Files, Colorado College Special Collections, 3-4.
40 Hagerman had begun his career: Hagerman's early career is taken from Percy Hagerman's paper, which is cited above.
40 "I was a sick man": Ibid., 7.
40 "The town was as dead": Ibid., 8.
40 Shawl and hot pepper: *Colorado Springs Sun*, July 9, 1972.
40 "A rich, ambitious, restless invalid": Fagan, George, "James John Hagerman," 9.
40 "that conformed to the narrow gauge": Sprague, *Newport in the Rockies*, 92.
40 "He cared nothing for society": Hagerman, Percy, "James John Hagerman," 34.
41 "irksome": Ibid.,14.
41 assumed the presidency: Sprague, *Newport in the Rockies*, 91.
41 Jay Gould: Ibid.
41 Sir William Lidderdale: Hagerman, Percy, "James John Hagerman," 16.
41 "passenger cars": *Weekly Gazette*, July 30, 1887.
41 "The Colorado Midland was": Sprague, *Newport in the Rockies*, 94-95.
41 hospital on West Colorado: Ormes, *The Book of Colorado Springs*, 231.
42 "let him and every other investor": Hagerman, Percy, "James John Hagerman," 17.
42 "It was a sensational strike": Ibid., 19.
42 "Colorado Springs people": "Colorado Springs Capitalists Make a Rich Mining Strike," *Weekly Gazette*, Feb. 7, 1891.
42 "The exact amount": *Weekly Gazette*, Feb. 15, 1890.
42 mill workers: Reid, J. Juan, *Colorado College: The First Century, 1874-1974*, (Colorado Springs: Colorado College, 1979), 36.
42 1882 until 1909: "Church Celebrates Fortieth Anniversary," Nov. 1, 1914, Colorado Room Information Files, Colorado College Special Collections, 1.
42 "There was no room large": Ibid., 4.
43 42 families: "Help the Aid Society," *Weekly Gazette*, Feb. 7, 1891
43 "stirring address": "Colorado Springs Aid Society," *Gazette*, Oct. 15, 1891.
43 "This method, having long been thought": Ibid.
43 Louise Schnapp: Ibid.
43 "I think there are none of us": Ibid.
43 whirlwind of activity: Ibid.

War Re-Imagined

45 "I am able": 3rd Annual Spotlight on Hope, Cornerstone Arts Theatre, Colorado College, May 22, 2012.
45 "The mind is so complex": Author interview, Kim Le Nguyen, June 8, 2012. Subsequent quotes from this interview.
45 Cottonwood Center for the Arts: "Art Program Gives Veterans Opportunity for Growth," AspenPointe website, Nov. 29, 2012.

6 – Chronicles of the Poor

53 "They possessed the means to enjoy": Sprague, Marshall, *El Paso Club, A Century of Friendship, 1877-1977*, (Colorado Springs: El Paso Club, 1976), 29.
54 "woman acts at though": PPFCMHC records, Box 3, Ledger 1. All cases in this chapter taken from this ledger book. Oftentimes a family was followed for a long time and subsequent entries are scattered through the book.

Written in the Books

57 gas lights and heated with coal: Buckman, George Rex, letter, Aug. 3, 1901, Century Chest Collection, Transcription 23.
57 "The afternoon being very cold": PPFCMHC records, Box 1, Folder 1, 32.
57 "She is decidedly English": Case Notes, August 30, 1893, PPFCMHC records, Box 2, Folder 6.
57 "Although the furnishing was scant": Ibid.
57 "beastly drunk": PPFCMHC records, Box 3, Ledger 1.
57 train tickets: Case Notes, August 30, 1893, PPFCMHC records, Box 2, Folder 6.

Timeline

1887
Relief society undergoes second reorganization and name changed to the "Women's Aid Society." Constitution drawn up and extensive board of directors elected.

1889
Name changed to Colorado Springs Aid Society.

1890
Mrs. Anna Hagerman becomes president.

July 4, 1891
Winfield Scott Stratton discovers gold on Pikes Peak and Colorado's second gold rush begins.

1893
Federal government repeals Sherman Act, causing the price of silver to plunge and provoking a deep recession.

1894
Cripple Creek labor strike.

1895
Mrs. D. Russ Wood dies.

Jan. 20, 1899
Society reorganized and name changed to Associated Charities. E. Evans-Carrington named manager.

May 2, 1900
"City Hotel" at 10 W. Vermijo Street opens.

1902
Winfield Scott Stratton dies.

1903-1904
Second labor strike.

1907
Another economic panic begins after two men attempt to corner copper market.

March 13, 1909
General Palmer dies.

March 21, 1911
Sunnyrest Sanatorium opens.

1914
World War I starts.

1916
Justin Hills hired to oversee charity.

Oct. 4, 1918
Colorado Springs businesses shut down to prevent spread of Spanish flu.

1919
Only ninety homeless men seek help from charity, which is a huge decline.

1927
Alice Bemis-Taylor establishes Bemis-Taylor Child Guidance Clinic at Day Nursery.

57 "thinning": "Old Records Show Beginning of Organized Relief in Region," *Gazette*, Feb. 24, 1947.
57 Sharon Williams: "Tracing the Family Tree is a Treasure Hunt," *Gazette*, July 12, 1978.
57 "Searching through a mouse-infested closet": Ibid.

7 – The Beauty and Burden of Gold

59 vision in the night: Waters, Frank. *Midas of the Rockies*, 123-124
59 "Too much money": Sprague, *Newport in the Rockies*, 166.
59 $2 million to $120 million: Ibid., 154.
59 Bank deposits: Ibid.
59 Fifty new millionaires: Ibid.
59 "Millionaires' Row": Ibid., 331.
59 "It is the finest house": Lennox, Anna Belle, letter, Aug. 4, 1901, Century Chest Collection, Transcription 61.
60 "During this little expedition": Goddard, Elizabeth, Cass, letter, July 27, 1901, Century Chest Collection, Transcription 13.
60 "Formal dinners are very elegant affairs": Ibid.
60 "Neighbors think him": Ibid., PPFCMHC records, Box 6, Ledger, 298.
61 "Our people are in debt ": Andrews, Thomas, *Killing for Coal*, 176-177.
61 "The geographic distance": Jameson, Elizabeth. *All That Glitters*, (Urbana and Chicago: University of Illinois Press, 1998), 25.
61 "Sullen, malicious, conscienceless": Montgomery, David, "Labor in the Industrial Era," *The American Worker*, DOL website, 6.
63 1,200 deputies: Jameson, Elizabeth, *All That Glitters*, 57.
63 peace settlement: Ibid., 58.
63 "The strike had lasted 130 days": Sprague, Marshall, *Newport of the Rockies*, 155.
63 deficit of about $250: "Aid Society," *Gazette*, Oct. 20, 1895.
63 "In July it was decided": Ibid.
63 the passing of the estimable Mrs. D. Russ Wood: "Mrs. D. Russ Wood Dead," *Gazette*, March 16, 1895.
63 "The society has lost one of its firmest": Ibid.
63 1,500 people: Charles G. Collais, letter, July 31, 1901, Century Chest Collection, Transcription 29.
64 447,000 to 2,072,700: Taft, Philip, "Workers of a New Century," *The American Worker*, DOL website, 1.
64 blacksmiths, tinsmiths, carpenters: Collais, Charles G., letter, July 31, 1901, Century Chest Collection, Transcription 29.
64 pledged $2,500: Ibid.
64 "While there is very little religious sentiment": Ibid.
64 eight-hour day: Ibid.
64 Miners earned $3 a day: Ibid.
64 427 applications: Ledger, PPFCMHC Records, Box 6, 435.
64 "In spite of the avowed objects": Ormes, *The Book of Colorado Springs*, 111.

8 – Are You 'Tubercular?'

67 21 police officers: Robinson, J.R., letter, Aug. 1, 1901, Century Chest Collection, Transcription 3.
67 "the Switzerland that beckons": *Gazette*, Aug. 2, 1905, in City of Colorado Springs, "Evolution of Historic Medians."
67 "That is, you should make it": Ibid.
67 "most desirable" sanatorium: City of Colorado Springs, "Historic Preservation Plan," August, 1993, 22.
67 "Colorado Springs began": Mayberry, Matt, "On a Cough and a Prayer: The Modern Woodmen Sanatorium and the Tuberculosis Industry in the Pikes Peak Region," *Doctors, Disease & Dying*, 250.
67 "plague spot": Gardner, Mark L., *In the Shadow of Pike's Peak*, (Carlsbad, CA: Heritage Media Corp, 1999),102.
67 "The question, 'Are you tubercular?": Ormes, *The Book of Colorado Springs*, 278.
67 There is no more pitiful case: Associated Charities, Sept. 30, 1909, PPFCMHC Records, Box 4, Folder 2, 7.
68 "I then drive about town": Gardiner, Charles Fox, letter, Aug. 3, 1901, Century Chest Collection, Transcription 62.
69 "Thank God we are now beginning" Solly, Samuel Edwin, letter, Aug. 4, 1901, Century Chest Collection, Transcription 70.
69 "The foolish talk of some": Anderson, Boswell Preston, letter, Aug. 2, 1901, Century Chest Collection, Transcription 46.
69 "recovery of earning capacity": Robert Koch, "The Current State of the Struggle against Tuberculosis," Nobel Lecture, Dec. 12, 1905, Nobelprize.org.

9 – The Gordian Knot

70 Born in Wales in 1847: Handwritten Note, Century Chest Collection, Folder Five.
70 shorthand and "type writing": Peirce College website.
70 obituary: "Death Claims Pioneer of Springs," *Gazette*, Jan. 11, 1911.
70 "It was easier for the more fortunate members": Montgomery, David, "Labor in the Industrial Era," *The American Worker*, 5.
71 "The man who consumes": The Associated Charities of Colorado Springs, Report of the First Annual Meeting, Oct. 9, 1899, PPFCMHC Records, Box 4, Folder 2, 19.
71 "One man told me": Ibid., 20.
72 "The first view is that held by [Thomas] Malthus": Ibid., 18.
72 received about $2,191: Ibid., 14.
73 "We need a cottage for women": Ibid., 13.
73 "We have co-operated with the clergy": Ibid., 12.
73 "It is surely wiser to help people": Ibid., 9.
73 "In less than three weeks": Ibid., 9.

The Garden

74 "A lot of kids who": Author interview, Elise Bowan, Aug. 9, 2012.
75 "It can be so healing": Author interview, Adah Rodriguez, Aug. 2, 2012.
75 "The community nearby": Author interview, Dr. Fred Michel, Sept. 8, 2012.

10 – Beggars Begone

76 $1 a year: Associated Charities, Report of the Second Annual Meeting, Oct. 15, 1900, PPFCMHC Records, Box 4, Folder 2,10.
76 "The guest's clothing is treasured": Ibid., 11.
76 purchased for $275: Ibid., 10.
77 "When I was dressed, an axe"; Kusmer, Kenneth L., *Down and Out*, 76-77.
77 "There is now no excuse for street begging": Associated Charities, Report of the Second Annual Meeting, Oct. 15, 1900, PPFCMHC Records, Box 4, Folder 2, 11.
77 "The tramp and beggar were the very negation": Kusmer, Kenneth L. *Down and Out*, 73.
77 $7,223: Associated Charities, Report of the Second Annual Meeting, Oct. 15, 1900, PPFCMHC Records, Box 4, Folder 2, 14.
77 392 requests: Ibid., 8.
77 "To the sick, who have to return": Ibid., 9.
78 "fair profit": Ibid., 11.
78 10,198 meals: Associated Charities, Report of the Third Annual Meeting, Oct. 14, 1901, PPFCMHC Records, Box 4, Folder 2, 6.
78 "pauper spirit": Ibid.
78 "If our city is to be kept free from pauperism": Ibid.
78 "It encourages the lazy": Carrington, Edward Evans, letter, July 29, 1901, Century Chest Collection, Transcription 5.
78 "suggested treatment": Ibid.
78 "Her duty, then": Ibid.
78 "The laundry is to answer": Ibid.
79 "wretched surroundings": Associated Charities, Report of the Third Annual Meeting, Oct. 14, 1901, PPFCMHC Records, Box 4, Folder 2, 7.
79 "She had forfeited control": Ibid.
79 "But he had to labor": Ibid.
79 "I had never heard of her": Ibid., 8.
79 "I will bring you the interest": Ibid., 9.
79 "It used to be the case": Ibid., 14.
79 "So in handling the pauper question": Ibid., 14-15.

11 – The Bobtail and Ragtail of the Earth

80 $925: The Associated Charities of Colorado Springs, First Annual Meeting, Oct. 9, 1899, PPFCMHC Records, Box 4, Folder 2, 22.
80 $1,355: The Associated Charities of Colorado Springs, Second Annual Meeting, Oct. 15, 1900, PPFCMHC Records, Box 4, Folder 2, 15.
80 $1,060: The Associated Charities of Colorado Springs, Third Annual Meeting, Oct. 14, 1901, PPFCMHC Records, Box 4, Folder 2, 13.
80 "clothed and fed as paupers usually are": Waters, *Midas of the Rockies*, 325.
80 "The bobtail and ragtail": Ibid., 279.
80 "To perdition with the poorhouse!": Ibid., 280.
80 " To leave practically his whole fortune": Ibid.
81 "widely from the dreary": Ibid.
81 "no friend" of unions: Jameson, Elizabeth, *All That Glitters*, 201.
81 Stratton's Independence Mine: Ibid., 215.
81 killing thirteen non-union miners: Ibid., 218.
81 "The employers provoked": Ibid., 219.
81 "Rioting, dynamiting": Taft, Philip, "Workers of a New Century," *The American Worker*, DOL website, 4.
81 "coming in contact with the dark side": Associated Charities, Report for Year Ending Sept. 30, 1904, PPFCMHC Records, Box 4, Folder 2, 2.
81 $268.37: Ibid., 7.
83 13,264 meals and 3,869 nights: Ibid.
83 "But for this provision our streets": Ibid., 4.
83 We have this year, through the agency of the wood yard": Ibid.
83 "El Paso County": Ibid., 5.

12 – Death Comes for the General

85 "The year which follows a panic": Associated Charities, Report for Year Ending Sept. 30, 1909, PPFCMHC Records, Box 4, Folder 2, 22.
85 $400: Ibid., 5.
85 $67:Ibid., 15.

85 "General Palmer contributed": Ibid., 5.
85 "There ought to be in this city": Ibid., 27.
86 $100 million and $200 million: Associated Charities, Report for Year Ending Sept. 30, 1909, PPFCMHC Records, Box 4, Folder 2, 25.
86 "Whatever may be the attractions": Ibid.
86 "tramp farms": Kusmer, *Down and Out*, 79-80.
86 "homeless man": Associated Charities, Report for Year Ending Sept. 30, 1909, PPFCMHC Records, Box 4, Folder 2, 25.
86 "One of the evils which organized charity": Ibid., 24.
86 "This gives us redress": Ibid., 25.
86 328 to more than 700: Ibid., The Associated Charities of Colorado Springs, Sept. 30, 1910, PPFCMHC Records, Box 4, Folder 2, 21.
86 1,599: Ibid.
86 "When a group of farmers": Ibid., 6.
87 "It was the awakening of the community": Ibid.
87 "lazy dependence": Ibid., 10.
87 "how the man worked": Ibid.
87 "No group, however, was immune": Kusmer, Kenneth L., *Down and Out*, 121.

Peer Navigators

88 "A vet grabs a vet's hand": Author interview, Paul Sexton, July 6, 2012.
88 $5 million: Author interview, Paul Sexton, March 25, 2013.
88 "People were spitting": Author interview, Rich Lindsey, May 22, 2012. All interviews from Lindsey from this interview.
89 one million claims: *The Economist*, March 23, 2013, 33.
89 "I don't want to be sitting on my porch": Author interview, Paul Sexton, July 6, 2012.

13 – Echoes

90 "Endless duplication of relief": The Associated Charities of Colorado Springs, Sept. 30, 1912, PPFCMHC Records, Box 4, Folder 3, 13.
90 "Such statements as these": Ibid., 9.
90 Wood was born: Fletcher, Russell Holmes, ed., *Who's Who in California, 1942-43*, 232. All biographical information on Daisy and Wood Worcester come from this volume, which is available on Internet.
90 settlement movement: http://ocp.hul.harvard.edu/immigration/settlement.html.
91 "Just sending him home to die": The Associated Charities of Colorado Springs, Report, Sept. 30, 1911, PPFCMHC Records, Box 4, Folder 3, 9-10.
91 "We have no slums, no factories": Ibid., 5.
92 "There were 533": Ibid., 17.
92 "Perhaps by shutting": Ibid., 18.
92 74 had been injured: Ibid., 23.
92 "A big majority of these men: Ibid., 18.
92 "The boy": Ibid., 19.

14 – A Sanatorium of Their Own

93 49.5 percent: "Report of Sunnyrest Sanatorium For the Period Ending March 15, 1913," Colorado Room Information Files, Colorado College Special Collections, 22-25.
93 Red Cross Christmas seals: "A Statement of the Board of Trustees Regarding the Building and Furnishing of The Sunnyrest Sanatorium, Colorado Springs, Colorado," March 1911, Colorado Room Information Files, Colorado College Special Collections, 7.
93 eight dollars a week: Ibid.
93 $1,452: Ibid., 7.
93 Irving P. Bonbright: Ibid., 6.
93 donated $700: Ibid., 10-11
93 $25,000: Ibid., 7.
94 "One of the early problems": "Report of Sunnyrest Sanatorium," March 15, 1913, Colorado Room Information Files, Colorado College Special Collections, 6.
94 Kaiserwerth Deaconesses: Ibid., 5.
94 "These little rooms are deemed": "Colorado Springs Sanatorium for Tuberculosis," Colorado Room Information Files, Colorado College Special Collections, n.d.
95 "The guests found everything": "Over 500 at Opening of New Sanatorium," *Gazette*, March 22, 1911.
95 Graphaphone: "Report of Sunnyrest Sanatorium," March 15, 1913, Colorado Room Information Files, Colorado College Special Collections, 15-16.
95 "pocket electric lights": "A Statement of the Board of Trustees Regarding the Building and Furnishing of The Sunnyrest Sanatorium, Colorado Springs, Colorado," March 1911, Colorado Room Information Files, Colorado College Special Collections, 5.
95 "We should be very glad": Ibid., 6.
95 "We stayed on the sleeping porches": "Sunnyrest Sanatorium-Watt Memorial," March 23, 1986, courtesy Sunny Vista Living Center historic collection.
95 "Being tubercular": Letter, William B. (last name illegible), March 11, 1913, PPFCMHC Records, Box 4, Folder 8.
95 "The experience of the past two years": "Report of Sunnyrest Sanatorium," March 15, 1913, Colorado Room Information Files, Colorado College Special Collections, 7.
95 10 patients were under: Ibid.
95 "There is urgent need": Ibid., 9.
95 "They feared I would contract": "Sunnyrest Sanatorium-Watt Memorial," March 23, 1986, Sunny Vista Living Center historic collection.
96 "I had no strength to walk": Ibid.
96 Asa T. Jones: *The Sun*, July 24, 1972, Biography clippings, Penrose Library, Pikes Peak Library District.
96 board of trustees: Colorado School for Deaf and Blind website.
96 "He would drive us": "Sunnyrest Sanatorium-Watt Memorial," March 23, 1986, Sunny Vista Living Center historic collection.
96 "Sunnyrest was from the first": Ormes, *The Book of Colorado Springs*, 255.

15 – A Winter of Discontent

97 "Probably there has been no time: The Associated Charities of Colorado Springs, Sept. 30, 1912, PPFCMHC Records, Box Four, Folder Three, 5. All subsequent quotes in chapter taken from this annual report.

Sixteenth Case

101 The Associated Charities of Colorado Springs, Sept. 30, 1912, PPFCMHC Records, Box Four, Folder Three.

16 – Desolating Poverty

102 "I believe that": The Associated Charities of Colorado Springs, Report, Sept. 30, 1913, PPFCMHC Records, Box 4, Folder 3, 8.
102 1,467: Ibid., 5.
102 66 widowed women: Ibid., 5.
102 "Their husbands had tired": Ibid.
102 "These are scarcely less pitiable": Ibid.
102 344 homeless men: Ibid, 10.
102 "What a picture these men": Ibid.
103 251 persons: Ibid.
103 "It is not a question": Ibid., 11.
104 1,958 visits: The Associated Charities of Colorado Springs, Sept. 30, 1914, PPFCMHC Records, Box 4, Folder 3, 15.
104 "Poverty exists in Colorado Springs": Ibid., 5.
104 Daisy: Report of the Associated Charities of Colorado Springs, Colorado City, and Manitou, Colorado, Sept. 30, 1915, PPFCMHC Records, Box 4, Folder 3, 10.
104 Worcester School: Fletcher, Russell Holmes. *Who's Who in California*, 1942-43, 232.

17 – The Great War

105 "Large, sunny rooms": R. Laurie Simmons and Thomas H. Simmons, City of Colorado Springs, Department of City Planning, Comprehensive Planning Division, "Boulder Crescent Neighborhood, Colorado Springs, Colorado, Historic Buildings Survey," 2007, 25.
105 2,050: Report of the Associated Charities of Colorado Springs, Colorado City, and Manitou, Colorado, Sept. 30, 1915, PPFCMHC Records, Box 4, Folder 3, 8.
105 432: Ibid.
106 "First, The securing of data": Ibid., 3.
106 "Letters are written": Ibid., 4.
106 $200: Ibid., 7.
106 "The migratory man": Ibid.
107 "practically without beds or bedding": Report of the Associated Charities of Colorado Springs, Colorado City, and Manitou, Colorado, Sept. 30, 1916, PPFCMHC Records, Box 4, Folder 4, 5.
107 "The men, unless sick": Ibid., 4.
107 Justin Hills: "Justin L. Hills, 75, Charities Executive For 28 Years, Dies," *Gazette*, July 1, 1947.
107 $497 to $1,568: Report of the Associated Charities of Colorado Springs, Colorado City, and Manitou, Colorado, Sept. 30, 1917, PPFCMHC Records, Box 4, Folder 4, 9.
107 Harvey Sethman: "State Spanish Flu May Have Started Among Trainees," *Gazette*, Oct. 10, 1976.
107 "I think everything": "Drastic Closing Order Issued to Avert Influenza Epidemic," *Gazette*, Oct. 5, 1918.
107 card party: Ibid.
107 ordered out of a Pullman car: "Epidemic Gaining But Little in City," *Gazette*, Oct. 9, 1918.
107 Ouray: "Shotgun Quarantine in the Ouray District," *Gazette*, Oct. 22, 1918.
108 852 cases, with 38 deaths: Department of Public Health and Sanitation Reports, September through December, 1918, Carnegie Library, Pikes Peak Library District.
108 Thomas Bernard Carrington: "T.B. Carrington is Influenza Victim," *Gazette*, Oct. 21, 1918.
108 "During the year just closed": Report of the Associated Charities of Colorado Springs, Colorado City, and Manitou, Colorado, Sept. 30, 1919, PPFCMHC Records, Box 4, Folder 4, 5.
108 $7008 for groceries: Ibid., 8.
108 huge drop in homeless men: Ibid., 6.
108 Ford automobile and expended $957: Ibid., 8.

Timeline

Oct. 24, 1929
Stock market crashes and Great Depression begins.

1934
Associated Charities' caseload dwindles to 60 cases.

1939
The name of the Bemis-Taylor Child Guidance Clinic changed to the Colorado Springs Child Guidance Clinic.

1942-1947
Child Guidance Clinic ceases operation due to World War II.

1945
Associated Charities changes name to Family Service of Colorado Springs.

1954
President Eisenhower announces new Air Force Academy to be located in Colorado Springs.

1954
Only 12 tuberculosis patients left at Sunnyrest. Trustees vote to expand mission to include elderly and other people who need nursing care.

1956
The number of patients housed in state mental institutions across country peaks at 550,000.

Timeline

1960
Family Service changes name to the Family Counseling Service of Colorado Springs. Fee per client is $2.39.

1962
Average stay in state hospital in Pueblo is 16 years, seven months, and 28 days.

1963
President John F. Kennedy signs into law the Community Mental Health Act, which speeds up deinstitutionalization.

1964
Child Guidance Clinic expands to include adults and named changed to Pikes Peak Mental Health Center.

1969
Merger discussions between Family Counseling and Pikes Peak Mental Health Center.

July 1, 1970
Two agencies merge and become Pikes Peak Family Counseling and Mental Health Center.

July 1, 1970
Charles Vorwaller becomes president and CEO.

What's Cooking?

109 "A kitchen is a much harder environment: Author interview, Mike Cid, Sept. 17, 2012. All subsequent quotes from Cid from this interview.
110 "I love it here": Author interview, Maddy Barber, Sept. 17, 2012.
110 47,500 customers were served: AspenPointe, End-of-Year Accomplishments Presentation, FY12.
110 "A lot of them haven't worked": Author interview, Crystal Griffin, Sept. 17, 2012. All subsequent quotes from Griffin from this interview.

18 – When Lilacs Bloomed

113 Crazy Grace: Wedberg, Mary Beth Stewart, *Remembering Colorado Springs, 1917-1935, Original Poems*, (San Diego, CA, 1989), 20.
113 250 in 1909: City of Colorado Springs, "Historic Medians," nd.
113 five livery stables: Reid, J. Juan, *Growing up in Colorado Springs, The 1920's Remembered*, (Colorado Springs: Century One Press, 1981), 18. The description of Colorado Springs comes from this memoir and Wedberg's memoir.
113 eggs: "Report of Sunnyrest Sanatorium," Sept. 30, 1919, Colorado Room Information Files, Colorado College Special Collections, 11.
113 Vaudeville shows cost 17 cents: Reid, J. Juan. *Growing up in Colorado Springs*, 11.
113 Civil War soldiers: Wedberg, Mary Beth Stewart. *Remembering Colorado Springs*, 16.
113 "Mrs. Jones had a buzzer": Ibid., 36.
113 "We regret to have to inform you": Letter, Associated Charities President to City Council, March 7, 1922, PPFCMHC Records, Box 4, Folder 10.
114 $1,000: "Report of Sunnyrest Sanatorium," Sept. 30, 1919, Colorado Room Information Files, Colorado College Special Collections, 13.
114 will not be a financial burden": Ibid., 5.
114 only 27 had been residents: Ibid., 15.
114 "In recognition of the many kindnesses": Ibid., 9.
114 Henry C. Watt: Sprague, *Newport in the Rockies*, 142.
114 "Ten undernourished children": Ormes, *The Book of Colorado Springs*, 235.
114 450 children: Pamphlet, The Nutrition Camp School, Tim Nicholson Collection, Box 1, Folder (II) C:10, Colorado Springs Pioneers Museum, circa 1932.
114 "From cod liver oil: Ibid.
115 $110,000 in stocks and bonds and cash: Minutes, Sunnyrest Sanatorium Board of Trustees, courtesy Sunny Vista Living Center historic collection, nd.
115 "modern throughout, even to oil-burning furnaces,": "Watts Residence Sold to Lennox," *Gazette*, Sept. 22, 1929.
115 "I request that said Watt": Minutes, Sunnyrest Sanatorium Board of Trustees, courtesy Sunny Vista Living Center historic collection, nd.
115 "Around 1900, TB": City of Colorado Springs, "Historic Preservation Plan," August 1993, 23.
116 "far too small a number": Minutes, Sunnyrest Sanatorium Board of Trustees, Oct. 20, 1954, courtesy Sunny Vista Living Center historic collection.
116 Diebold: Newspaper clipping, courtesy Sunny Vista Living Center historic collection, nd.
116 Bassett: Newspaper clipping, courtesy Sunny Vista Living Center historic collection, nd.

19 – A Shy Philanthropist

117 Ralph Waldo Emerson: *Alice Cogswell Bemis, A Sketch by a Friend*, (Boston, The Merrymount Press, 1920), 5-6.
118 "the blessedness of drudgery": Ibid., 17.
118 "In choosing her": Bemis Company website, 2013.
118 "These bags were printed": Ibid.
119 "The opening of the mill": *Alice Cogswell Bemis, A Sketch by a Friend*, 39.
119 "Her countless private philanthropies": Vesta W. Tutt, "Alice Bemis Taylor," *Extraordinary Women of the Rocky Mountain West*, (Colorado Springs: Pikes Peak Library District, 2010), 107.
119 estate worth $1.5 million: Wills, Julia Ryan, "Alice Bemis Taylor," Colorado Room Information Files, Colorado College Special Collections, 2005, 5.
119 Bemis School of Business: Ibid., 4.
119 50 children: Author interview, Diane L. Price, Feb. 8, 2013.
119 $273,000: Ibid.
119 $20 gold piece: Ibid.
119 in 1928: Thurlow, Helen B., "A History of the Colorado Springs Child Guidance Clinic," August, 1950, PPFCMHC Records, Box 8, Folder 33.
120 "in whose sanitarium near Boston": Ibid.
120 "The types of problems to be studied": Ibid.
120 first child: Thurlow, "A History of the Colorado Springs Child Guidance Clinic."
121 Dr. William Healy: Murphey, Bradford, "The Child Guidance Clinic," PPFCMHC Records, Box 8, Folder 32. History of the movement taken from this paper, which is undated, but originally appeared in the periodical, *The Outlook Journal*.
121 "It served as a nationally known research": Ibid.
121 "In the beginning of the child": Ibid.
121 "This work at Smith": Ibid.
121 "The clinic is interested": Ibid.
121 "She felt that twelve years": Thurlow, Helen B., "A History of the Colorado Springs Child Guidance Clinic, August, 1950, PPFCMHC Records, Box 8, Folder 33.
121 In 1938: Ibid.
121 name changed: "Pikes Peak Mental Health Center," PPFCMHC records, Box 9, Folder 16.
121 Dr. Kenneth Loder: Ibid.
121 American Red Cross building: Ibid.
121 $13,000: Ibid.
121 "Mental Hygiene": "Addendum: History from 1947 to May 1957," PPFCMHC records, Box 9, Folder 16.

The Day Nursery

122 she built the Day Nursery in 1923: Author interview, Diane Price, Feb. 8, 2013.
122 Bemis-Taylor Child Guidance Clinic: "Child Clinic Will Reopen," *Colorado Springs Evening Telegraph*, April 9, 1945, courtesy Historic Day Nursery.
122 "Thousands and thousands of children have passed": Author interview, Diane Price, Feb. 8, 2013.
122 "In most cases one or both parents": "The Colorado Springs Day Nursery," *Gazette*, Jan. 1, 1903.
122 "There were men": Author interview, Diane Price, Feb. 8, 2013.
123 "The idea of a day nursery dates back to France": "The Colorado Springs Day Nursery," *Gazette*, Jan. 1, 1903.
123 four-room house at 416 E. Boulder Street: Letter, Akien, Jessie Adella, 1901, Century Chest Collection, Transcription 68.
123 scarlet fever: Ibid.
123 The cost was 10 cents a day per child: Ibid.
123 the cost was $6 a month for one child: Ibid.
123 a decision was made not to accept children if both parents: "Nursery is Hub of New Community," *Gazette*, March 2, 1924.
123 "The most usual condition": Ibid.
123 "She remarks in the letter": Author interview, Diane Price, Feb. 8, 2013.

20 – The Depression

124 4,273 office encounters: "Services during the Fiscal Year," PPFCMHC Records, Box 4, Folder 6.
124 17,125: Ibid.
124 "This year we know": Letter, Justin Hills to E.L. Moseley, Oct. 9, 1933, Box 4, Folder 11.
124 $39,000: Ibid.
125 caseload was 620: Letter, Justin Hills to E.L. Mosley, Sept. 6, 1934, PPFCMHC Records, Box 4, Folder 11.
125 "Unemployable resident people": Ibid.
125 "Having had some twenty years experience": Letter, Justin Hills to Norma Y. Queen, Sept. 20, 1935, PPFCMHC Records, Box 4, Folder 11.
125 "Some of the unemployed were eligible": Memo, Sept. 8, 1936, PPFCMHC Records, Box 4, Folder 9.
126 "A great many claimed to be in search": Ibid.
126 sew: Ibid.
126 $44,000: Associated Charities, Tabulation, PPFCMHC Records, Box 4, folder 14.
126 5,004 cases and 15,554 individuals: "Services During Fiscal Year," Supplement to 1941-42 budget request to Community Chest, July 11, 1941, PPFCMHC Records, Box 4, Folder 9.
126 1,974 cases and 8,194 individuals: Supplement to 1941-42 budget request to Community Chest, July 11, 1941, PPFCMHC Records, Box 4, Folder 16.

21 – Uncertainty

127 "The future, indeed, looked very bleak" Fagan, George V., *The Air Force Academy: An Illustrated History*, (Boulder: Johnson Books, 1988), 40.
127 "The development of the Social Security Program": The Forty-Fifth Annual Report of The Associated Charities of Colorado Springs, Colo., Oct. 1, 1943 to Sept 30, 1944, PPFCMHC Records, Box 4, Folder 5, 1.
127 $12,451: Ibid., 13.
127 "To provide a skilled case work service": Ibid., 5.
128 "The Associated Charities accepts families for help": Ibid.
128 "Mrs. A. is now buying more wisely": Ibid., 9.
128 A careful study of his condition": Ibid.,10.
128 "Case C": Ibid.
128 "During the war period many families": Ibid., 11.

22 – Maturity Interrupted

129 "So many of our present case problems: "Woman of the Week," *Gazette*, April 29, 1950.
129 "Actually BEING a husband": Ibid.
129 "The name Mary Edmonds": Ibid.
130 change its name: The Associated Charities of Colorado Springs, Colo., a Family Service Society, Oct. 1, 1944 to Sept. 30, 1945, PPFCMHC Records, Box 4, Folder 5, 1.
130 referred themselves: Ibid., 7.
130 It developed in the interviews": Ibid., 11.
130 "I'm sorry": Ibid., 12.

130 122 neighborhood grocery stores: Judith Reid Finley, *Coming of Age in Colorado Springs, 1945-1955*, (Colorado Springs: The Author), 1964,15.
130 "The minister. He wishes to refer": Family Service brochure, Oct. 1, 1948, to Oct. 1, 1949, PPFCMHC Records, Box 5, Folder 2.
131 "A Homemaker is a competent": "Woman of the Week," *Gazette*, April 29, 1950.
131 The referrals: Pamphlet, Colorado Springs Child Guidance Clinic, PPFCMHC Records, Box 8, Folder 32.
131 "His real life situation": Ibid.
132 "In the course of treatment": Ibid.
132 "The spirit of rugged": "Historical Review of Family Counseling Service," PPFCMHC Records, Box 5, Folder 4.

The ACCESS Center

133 "Mental health isn't just about working": Author interview, Jennifer DeGroff, Aug. 20, 2012.
133 "When we started focusing on what": Author interview, Jennifer Given, June 15, 2012.
133 "If you asked her what it was": Author interview, Julie Reed, June 15, 2012.
133 "I was feeling sad a lot": Author interview, Heraldo P., June 15, 2012.

23 – Merger

134 "This town had more social": Author interview, Joe Pickle, July 16, 2012.
134 "The Junior League is": Author interview, Barbara Yalich, June 18, 2012.
134 "It was the time of the Vietnam": Ibid.
135 changed its name: Bosley, Michael, "A Brief History of the Pikes Peak Family Counseling and Mental Health Center," PPFCMHC Records, Box 9, Folder 16, nd.
135 $2.39: Family Counseling Service of Colorado Springs, Annual Report, 1961, PPFCMHC Records, Box 5, Folder 6, 4.
135 office on East Boulder Street: Bosley, Michael, "A Brief History of the Pikes Peak Family Counseling," PPFCMHC Records, Box 9, Folder 16.
135 391 to 724: Family Counseling Service of Colorado Springs, 1968, AspenPointe historical files.
135 Big Brothers program: Ibid.
135 Department of Vocational Rehabilitation: Ibid.
135 "The secret is in understanding": Clipping, PPFCMHC Records, Box 5, Folder 13, circa 1965,
135 "We have troubled children from strict": Newspaper clipping, "Notes from the Woman's Editor," PPFCMHC Records, Box 8, Folder 31.
135 "If psychiatric treatment is indicated": Ibid.
135 new name: Letter, Rose Loring to Mr. Otto, April 12, 1964, PPFCMHC Records Box 8, Folder 30.
135 five group therapy sessions: Pikes Peak Mental Health Center, "A Brief Statement of various programs and staff deployment," circa 1968, AspenPointe historical files.
136 one-day-a-week program: Ibid.
136 "We began to discuss": Author interview, Barbara Yalich, June 18, 2012,
136 "Treating people in the community": Author interview, William Scholton, May 29, 2012.
136 peaking at 550,000: Eisenberg, Leon and Guttmacher, Laurence, "Were We All Asleep at the Switch? A Personal Reminiscence of Pyschiatry from 1940 to 2010," Acta Psychiatrica Scandinavica, Wiley Online Library, 2010, 96.
136 6,000: Mitchell, Nell. *The 13th Street Review, A Pictorial History of the Colorado State Hospital*, (Pueblo, CO: My Friend, The Printer, Inc., 2009), 51.
136 500: Ibid., 103.
136 16 years, seven months, and 28 days: Ibid., 47.
136 a self-described "neurasthenic": Beers, Clifford Whittingham, *A Mind that Found Itself*, (Pittsburgh: The University of Pittsburgh Press, 1907), 10.
136 "did for the American mental health movement": Ibid., back jacket cover.
137 five major services: Gary Holmes to Personnel Committee, "Merging of Family Counseling Service and Pikes Peak Mental Health Center," March 24, 1969, AspenPointe historical files.
137 "It was a period of confusion": Author interview, Cynthia Rose, June 14, 2012.
139 logical partnership: Memo, Gary Holmes to Personnel Committee, "Merging of Family Counseling Service and Pikes Peak Mental Health Center," March 24, 1969, AspenPointe historical files.
139 "We got along": Author interview, Barbara Yalich, June 18, 2012.
139 "The difference between the approaches": Pickle, Joseph, Memorandum to Merger Committee, June 12, 1969.
139 "considerable animosity": Vorwaller, Charles, "Contrasts pre-1970 and post-1970," typescript, AspenPointe historical records.
139 150 questionnaires: Resolution, Family Counseling Service and Pikes Peak Mental Health Center, AspenPointe historical records, circa 1969.
139 "I dissent from": Memo, Dr. John H. Mahaffy, Sept. 17, 1969, in Resolution, Family Counseling Service and Pikes Peak Mental Health Center, AspenPointe historical records.
139 "Overall, everyone": Author interview, Barbara Yalich, June 18, 2012.
139 "I was caught in the cross-fire": Author interview, Dr. Cynthia Rose, June 14, 2012.

Youth Directions

140 "Although it doesn't always end this way": Author interview, Adah Rodriguez, Aug. 2, 2012. All information and quotes taken from this interview or follow-up questions.

24 – Mr. V.

142 "He was very gifted": Author interview, Barbara Yalich, June 18, 2012.
142 "They drained my brain": All quotes from Charles Vorwaller taken from author interviews, May 4 and May 8, 2012, unless otherwise noted. Vorwaller background also taken from interviews and email communication between Vorwaller and author.
145 "It was a very creative": Author interview, Joe Pickle, July 16, 2012.
145 Activities: Compiled from interviews, annual reports, comments from Charles Vorwaller.
145 "One of the more humorous": Author interview, Cynthia Rose, June 14, 2012.
146 1,600 offenders: Pikes Peak Family Counseling and Mental Health Center, 1974 Annual Report, 5.
146 $1.1 million in incarceration: Ibid.
146 "Our local funding sources": "Pikes Peak Family Counseling and Mental Health Center," 1976, AspenPointe historical files.
147 "Sonia, where's the popcorn": Author interview, Sonia Jackson, Aug. 21, 2012.

Slaying Stigma

148 Paul Sexton: Author interview, Paul Sexton, March 25, 2013. All information and quotes in article from this interview.

25 – Listening Bigger

150 Morris Roth: Quotes and background information on Roth taken from author interviews, May 9, 2012, or March 1, 2013.
151 "The core component of our philosophy": Pikes Peak Mental Health, Annual Report, 2000, AspenPointe historical files
151 55 million in 2012: AspenPointe, Annual Report, 2011-2012, 16.
152 "In the old sheltered workshop": Author interview, Paul Sexton, July 6, 2012.
153 "How do you describe": Author interview, Fred Michel, Sept. 8, 2012.
153 "Aspens have a very deep-rooted system": Author interview, Kelly Phillips-Henry, Aug. 31, 2012.
153 "Our call volume": Author interview, Roxanne Lopez, Aug. 3, 2012.
153 "Our patients come to us": Author interview, Fred Michel, Sept. 8, 2012.
153 "It isn't just enough": Author interview, John Stevens, May 7, 2012.
153 879 people: Author interview, Kelly Phillips-Henry, Aug. 31, 2012.
153 "In this town, there are over 30,000: Ibid.
154 "We can say": Author interview, Jennifer DeGroff Aug. 20, 2012.
154 "Historically if you think": Ibid.
154 "Say someone's bipolar": Ibid.
154 "It's like dancing": Author interview, Kelly Phillips-Henry, Aug. 31, 2012.
155 "I'm a big believer": Ibid.
155 "Depending on how you think": Author interview, Jennifer DeGroff, Aug. 20, 2012.
155 "I try to tell them": Ibid.
155 "That's where health reform: Author interview, Michael Allen, Aug. 27, 2012.

Timeline

November 24, 1971
Pikes Peak submits comprehensive mental health center proposal.

2000
Morris Roth becomes president and CEO of Pikes Peak Mental Health Center.

2009
Peer Navigator program begins.

2010
Name changed to AspenPointe.

2010
AspenPointe invited to meet with White House staffers to discuss Peer Navigator program.

Feb. 7, 2012
AspenPointe returns to East Wing of White House to discuss Peer Navigator program and Peer-A-Chute program.

2012
Garden established at 220 Ruskin Drive.

2012
Waldo Canyon Fire.

2013
Black Forest Fire.

August, 2013
Morris Roth retires.

Index

Note: Italicized page numbers indicate photos

Acknowledgments

We are grateful to the patient and professional librarians at the Pikes Peak Library District who helped us with countless tasks related to this book. We also owe a debt of gratitude to Jessy Randall, curator/archivist of Tutt Library Special Collections at Colorado College, and to Coi Drummond-Gehrig of the Denver Public Library. We are also grateful to Diane L. Price and Karen Wiedemann who took us on a tour of the Day Nursery, to the folks at Sunny Vista who allowed us to peruse their historic files, to Nell Mitchell at the Colorado Mental Health Institute Museum, as well as to all the other people who helped us along the way.